SAVITRI

A Legend and a Symbol

SRI AUROBINDO [Pseud]

See Ghose Aurobindo, 1872-1950

SAVITRI

A Legend and a Symbol

PART ONE

(BOOKS I - III)

56-33099

821.91

SRI AUROBINDO ASHRAM
PONDICHERRY

PUBLISHERS:
SRI AUROBINDO ASHRAM
PONDICHERRY

First Complete Edition 1950

SRI AUROBINDO ASHRAM PRESS, PONDICHERRY

PRINTED IN INDIA

400/9/50/2000

PUBLISHERS' NOTE

The first three Books of *Savitri* comprising Part One which is now presented for the first time in a single volume, extensively revised and enlarged by the addition of many new lines, were previously published in 10 fascicles between the years 1946-48.

Books I and III originally appeared serially in the *Sri Aurobindo Mandir Annual* and the quarterly *Advent,* and were simultaneously issued in separate parts. Book I, Canto I was first published in the *Sri Aurobindo Mandir Annual,* August 1946 and was reprinted in an especially limited edition with a portrait frontispiece and three letters of Sri Aurobindo on mystical poetry. This Canto only without the letters and the portrait was reprinted in 1947. Cantos 2 and 3 together appeared in the same Journal in 1947, and Cantos 4 and 5 in *The Advent* for November 1947 and February 1948 respectively.

All the four Cantos of Book III appeared serially in *The Advent,* November 1946 to August 1947.

Book II was published for the first time in book-form in two parts, Part I containing Cantos 1-6 in November 1947 and Part II, Cantos 7-15, in April 1948. Only the first Canto, *The World-Stair*—subsequently reprinted with the First Part—had been published in the *Sri Aurobindo Circle Annual* No. 3, April 1947.

September, 1950

CONTENTS

BOOK ONE

The Book of Beginnings

BOOK TWO

The Book of the Traveller of the Worlds

BOOK THREE

The Book of the Divine Mother

BOOK ONE
The Book of Beginnings

Savitri

Part I –
Book I
The Book of Beginnings

§ 1 § The Symbol Dawn

It was the hour before the Gods awake.
Across the path of the divine Event.
The huge foreboding spirit of Night, alone,
Lay stretched immobile upon Silence' marge.
A mute unconscient sonflore of the Unknown,
Abyss of the unbodied Infinite
Whose fathomless zero occupied the world,
Cradled the cosmic drowse of ignorant Force
In moved creative slumber kindling the suns,
That carries all things in its somnambulist wheel.
Across the vain enormous trance of Space,
Its formless stupor without mind or life,
A shadow spinning through the sullen Vast,
Earth wheeled abandoned in the hollow gulf,
Forgetful of her spirit and her fate.
The impassive skies were neutral, empty, still.
Then a black precurrer yearned towards distant change.
A long lone line of hesitating hue
Like a vague smile tempting a desert heart
Troubled the far rim of life's obscure sleep.
Apparent on some unseen eternal verge
An eye of deity looked through the faint rift,
Calling for the venture of consciousness and joy
Compelled renewed consent to see and feel.
A thought was sown in the unsounded Word,
A sense was born within the darkness' depths,
A memory quivered in the heart of Time,
As of a soul long dead were moved to live;
In the oblivion that succeeds the fall
Blotted the crowded tablets of the past,
And all that was destroyed must be rebuilt
And old endeavour labrized out once more.
At first a hint that hardly dared to be
Amid the night's forlorn indifference,
A slow miraculous gesture's dim appeal,
The insistent thrill of a transfiguring touch
Persuaded the inert black quietude
And beauty and wonder disturbed the fields of God.

A wandering hand of pale enchanted light
That glowed along a fading moment's brink,
Fixed with gold panel and opalescent hinge
A gate of dreams ajar on Mystery's verge.
One lucent corner windowing hidden things
Forced the world's blind immensity to sight.
The brief perpetual sign recurred above.
A glamour from the unreached transcendences
Iridescent with the glory of the Unseen,
A message from the unknown immortal Light
Ablaze upon creation's quivering edge,
Dawn built her aura of magnificent hues
And buried its seed of grandeur in the hours.
An instant's visitor the godhead came.
A crystal shone dazzling earth's forehead curve,
As if the lines of a significant myth
Telling of a greatness of spiritual dawns,
Interpreting a recondite beauty and bliss
In colour's hieroglyphs of mystic sense,
A brilliant code written with the sky for page.

CANTO ONE

THE SYMBOL DAWN

IT was the hour before the Gods awake.
　　Across the path of the divine Event
The huge foreboding mind of Night, alone
In her unlit temple of eternity,
Lay stretched immobile upon Silence' marge.
Almost one felt, opaque, impenetrable,
In the sombre symbol of her eyeless muse
The abysm of the unbodied Infinite;
A fathomless zero occupied the world.
A power of fallen boundless self awake
Between the first and the last Nothingness,
Recalling the tenebrous womb from which it came,
Turned from the insoluble mystery of birth
And the tardy process of mortality
And longed to reach its end in vacant Nought.
As in a dark beginning of all things,
A mute featureless semblance of the Unknown
Repeating for ever the unconscious act,
Prolonging for ever the unseeing will,
Cradled the cosmic drowse of ignorant Force
Whose moved creative slumber kindles the suns
And carries our lives in its somnambulist whirl.
Athwart the vain enormous trance of Space,
Its formless stupor without mind or life,
A shadow spinning through a soulless Void,
Thrown back once more into unthinking dreams,
Earth wheeled abandoned in the hollow gulfs
Forgetful of her spirit and her fate.
The impassive skies were neutral, empty, still.
Then something in the inscrutable darkness stirred;

3

A nameless movement, an unthought Idea
Insistent, dissatisfied, without an aim,
Something that wished but knew not how to be,
Teased the Inconscient to wake Ignorance.
A throe that came and left a quivering trace,
Gave room for an old tired want unfilled,
At peace in its subconscient moonless cave
To raise its head and look for absent light,
Straining closed eyes of vanished memory,
Like one who searches for a bygone self
And only meets the corpse of his desire.
It was as though even in this Nought's profound,
Even in this ultimate dissolution's core
There lurked an unremembering entity,
Survivor of a slain and buried past
Condemned to resume the effort and the pang,
Reviving in another frustrate world.
An unshaped consciousness desired light
And a blank prescience yearned towards distant change.
As if a childlike finger laid on a cheek
Reminded of the endless need in things
The heedless Mother of the universe,
An infant longing clutched the sombre Vast.
Insensibly somewhere a breach began:
A long lone line of hesitating hue
Like a vague smile tempting a desert heart
Troubled the far rim of life's obscure sleep.
Arrived from the other side of boundlessness
An eye of deity pierced through the dumb deeps;
A scout in a reconnaissance from the sun,
It seemed amid a heavy cosmic rest,
The torpor of a sick and weary world,
To seek for a spirit sole and desolate
Too fallen to recollect forgotten bliss.
Intervening in a mindless universe,
Its message crept through the reluctant hush
Calling the adventure of consciousness and joy
And, conquering Nature's disillusioned breast,
Compelled renewed consent to see and feel.
A thought was sown in the unsounded Void,

A sense was born within the darkness' depths,
A memory quivered in the heart of Time
As if a soul long dead were moved to live:
But the oblivion that succeeds the fall,
Had blotted the crowded tablets of the past,
And all that was destroyed must be rebuilt
And old experience laboured out once more.
All can be done if the god-touch is there.
A hope stole in that hardly dared to be
Amid the Night's forlorn indifference.
As if solicited in an alien world
With timid and hazardous instinctive grace,
Orphaned and driven out to seek a home,
An errant marvel with no place to live,
Into a far-off nook of heaven there came
A slow miraculous gesture's dim appeal.
The persistent thrill of a transfiguring touch
Persuaded the inert black quietude
And beauty and wonder disturbed the fields of God.
A wandering hand of pale enchanted light
That glowed along a fading moment's brink,
Fixed with gold panel and opalescent hinge
A gate of dreams ajar on mystery's verge.
One lucent corner windowing hidden things
Forced the world's blind immensity to sight.
The darkness failed and slipped like a falling cloak
From the reclining body of a god.
Then through the pallid rift that seemed at first
Hardly enough for a trickle from the suns,
Outpoured the revelation and the flame.
The brief perpetual sign recurred above.
A glamour from the unreached transcendences
Iridescent with the glory of the Unseen,
A message from the unknown immortal Light
Ablaze upon creation's quivering edge,
Dawn built her aura of magnificent hues
And buried its seed of grandeur in the hours.
An instant's visitor the godhead shone:
On life's thin border awhile the Vision stood
And bent over earth's pondering forehead curve.

Interpreting a recondite beauty and bliss
In colour's hieroglyphs of mystic sense,
It wrote the lines of a significant myth
Telling of a greatness of spiritual dawns,
A brilliant code penned with the sky for page.
Almost that day the epiphany was disclosed
Of which our thoughts and hopes are signal flares;
A lonely splendour from the invisible goal
Almost was flung on the opaque Inane.
Once more a tread perturbed the vacant Vasts;
Infinity's centre, a Face of rapturous calm
Parted the eternal lids that open heaven;
A Form from far beatitudes seemed to near.
Ambassadress twixt eternity and change,
The omniscient Goddess leaned across the breadths
That wrap the fated journeyings of the stars
And saw the spaces ready for her feet.
Once she half looked behind for her veiled sun,
Then, thoughtful, went to her immortal work.
Earth felt the Imperishable's passage close:
The waking ear of Nature heard her steps
And wideness turned to her its limitless eye,
And, scattered on sealed depths, her luminous smile
Kindled to fire the silence of the worlds.
All grew a consecration and a rite.
Air was a vibrant link between earth and heaven;
The wide-winged hymn of a great priestly wind
Arose and failed upon the altar hills;
The high boughs prayed in a revealing sky.
Here where our half-lit ignorance skirts the gulfs
On the dumb bosom of the ambiguous earth,
Here where one knows not even the step in front
And Truth has her throne on the shadowy back of doubt,
On this anguished and precarious field of toil
Outspread beneath some large indifferent gaze,
Impartial witness to our joy and bale,
Our prostrate soil bore the awakening ray.
Here too the vision and prophetic gleam
Lit into miracles common meaningless shapes;
Then the divine afflatus, spent, withdrew,

6

Unwanted, fading from the mortal's range.
A sacred yearning lingered in its trace,
The worship of a Presence and a Power
Too perfect to be held by death-bound hearts,
The prescience of a marvellous birth to come.
Only a little the God-light can stay:
Spiritual beauty illumining human sight
Lines with its passion and mystery Matter's mask
And squanders eternity on a beat of Time.
As when a soul draws near the sill of birth,
Adjoining mortal time to Timelessness,
A spark of deity lost in Matter's crypt
Its lustre vanishes in the inconscient planes,
That transitory glow of magic fire
So now dissolved in bright accustomed air.
The message ceased and waned the messenger.
The single Call, the uncompanioned Power,
Drew back into some far-off secret world
The hue and marvel of the supernal beam:
She looked no more on our mortality.
The excess of beauty natural to God-kind
Could not uphold its claim on time-born eyes;
Too mystic-real for space-tenancy
Her body of glory was expunged from heaven:
The rarity and wonder lived no more.
There was the common light of earthly day.
Affranchised from the respite of fatigue
Once more the rumour of the speed of Life
Pursued the cycles of her blinded quest.
All sprang to their unvarying daily acts;
The thousand peoples of the soil and tree
Obeyed the unforeseeing instant's urge,
And, leader here with his uncertain mind,
Alone who stares at the future's covered face,
Man lifted up the burden of his fate.

And Savitri too awoke among these tribes
That hastened to join the brilliant Summoner's chant
And, lured by the beauty of the apparent ways,
Acclaimed their portion of ephemeral joy.

7

Akin to the eternity whence she came,
No part she took in this small happiness;
A mighty stranger in the human field,
The embodied Guest within made no response.
The call that wakes the leap of human mind,
Its chequered eager motion of pursuit,
Its fluttering-hued illusion of desire,
Visited her heart like a sweet alien note.
Time's message of brief light was not for her.
In her there was the anguish of the gods
Imprisoned in our transient human mould,
The deathless conquered by the death of things.
A vaster Nature's joy had once been hers,
But long could keep not its gold heavenly hue
Or stand upon this brittle earthly base.
A narrow movement on Time's deep abysm,
Life's fragile littleness denied the power,
The proud and conscious wideness and the bliss
She had brought with her into the human form,
The calm delight that weds one soul to all,
The key to the flaming doors of ecstasy.
Earth's grain that needs the sap of pleasure and tears
Rejected the undying rapture's boon:
Offered to the daughter of infinity
Her passion-flower of love and doom she gave.
In vain now seemed the splendid sacrifice.
A prodigal of her rich divinity,
Her self and all she was she had lent to men,
Hoping her greater being to implant
That heaven might native grow on mortal soil.
Hard is it to persuade earth-nature's change;
Mortality bears ill the eternal's touch:
It fears the pure divine intolerance
Of that assault of ether and of fire;
It murmurs at its sorrowless happiness,
Almost with hate repels the light it brings;
It trembles at its naked power of Truth
And the might and sweetness of its absolute Voice.
Inflicting on the heights the abysm's law,
It sullies with its mire heaven's messengers:

Its thorns of fallen nature are the defence
It turns against the saviour hands of Grace;
It meets the sons of God with death and pain.
A glory of lightnings traversing the earth-scene,
Their sun-thoughts fading, darkened by ignorant minds,
Their work betrayed, their good to evil turned,
The cross their payment for the crown they gave,
Only they leave behind a splendid Name.
A fire has come and touched men's hearts and gone;
A few have caught flame and risen to greater life.
Too unlike the world she came to help and save,
Her greatness weighed upon its ignorant breast,
And from its deep chasms welled a dire return,
A portion of its sorrow, struggle, fall.
To live with grief, to confront death on her road,—
The mortal's lot became the Immortal's share.
Thus trapped in the gin of earthly destinies,
Awaiting her ordeal's hour abode,
Outcast from her inborn felicity,
Accepting life's obscure terrestrial robe,
Hiding herself even from those she loved,
The godhead greater by a human fate.
A dark foreknowledge separated her
From all of whom she was the star and stay;
Too great to impart the peril and the pain,
In her torn depths she kept the grief to come.
As one who watching over men left blind
Takes up the load of an unwitting race,
Harbouring a foe whom with her heart she must feed,
Unknown her act, unknown the doom she faced,
Unhelped she must foresee and dread and dare.
The long-foreknown and fatal morn was here
Bringing a noon that seemed like every noon.
For Nature walks upon her mighty way
Unheeding when she breaks a soul, a life;
Leaving her slain behind she travels on:
Man only marks and God's all-seeing eyes.
Even in this moment of her soul's despair,
In its grim rendezvous with death and fear,
No cry broke from her lips, no call for aid;

She told the secret of her woe to none:
Calm was her face and courage kept her mute.
Yet only her outward self suffered and strove;
Even her humanity was half divine:
Her spirit opened to the Spirit in all,
Her nature felt all Nature as its own.
Apart, living within, all lives she bore;
Aloof, she carried in herself the world:
Her dread was one with the great cosmic dread,
Her strength was founded on the cosmic mights;
The universal Mother's love was hers.
Against the evil at life's afflicted roots,
Her own calamity its private sign,
Of her pangs she made a mystic poignant sword.
A solitary mind, a world-wide heart,
To the lone Immortal's unshared work she rose.
At first life grieved not in her burdened breast:
On the lap of earth's original somnolence
Inert, released into forgetfulness
Prone it reposed, unconscious on mind's verge,
Obtuse and tranquil like the stone and star.
In a deep cleft of silence twixt two realms
She lay remote from grief, unsawn by care,
Nothing recalling of the sorrow here.
Then a slow faint remembrance shadowlike moved,
And sighing she laid her hand upon her bosom
And recognised the close and lingering ache,
Deep, quiet, old, made natural to its place,
But knew not why it was there nor whence it came.
The Power that kindles mind was still withdrawn:
Heavy, unwilling were life's servitors
Like workers with no wages of delight;
Sullen, the torch of sense refused to burn;
The unassisted brain found not its past.
Only a vague earth-nature held the frame.
But now she stirred, her life shared the cosmic load.
At the summons of her body's voiceless call
Her strong far-winging spirit travelled back,
Back to the yoke of ignorance and fate,
Back to the labour and stress of mortal days,

Lighting a pathway through strange symbol dreams
Across the ebbing of the seas of sleep.
Her house of Nature felt an unseen sway,
Illumined swiftly were life's darkened rooms,
And memory's casements opened on the hours
And the tired feet of thought approached her doors.
All came back to her: Earth and Love and Doom,
The ancient disputants, encircled her
Like giant figures wrestling in the night:
The godheads from the dim Inconscient born
Awoke to struggle and the pang divine,
And in the shadow of her flaming heart,
At the sombre centre of the dire debate,
A guardian of the unconsoled abyss
Inheriting the long agony of the globe,
A stone-still figure of high and godlike Pain
Stared into space with fixed regardless eyes
That saw grief's timeless depths but not life's goal.
Afflicted by his harsh divinity,
Bound to his throne, he waited unappeased
The daily oblation of her unwept tears.
All the fierce question of man's hours relived.
The sacrifice of suffering and desire
Earth offers to the immortal Ecstasy
Began again beneath the eternal Hand.
Awake she endured the moments' serried march
And looked on this green smiling dangerous world,
And heard the ignorant cry of living things.
Amid the trivial sounds, the unchanging scene
Her soul arose confronting Time and Fate.
Immobile in herself, she gathered force.
This was the day when Satyavan must die.

END OF CANTO ONE

CANTO TWO

THE ISSUE

AWHILE, withdrawn in secret fields of thought,
Her mind moved in a many-imaged past
That lived again and saw its end approach:
Dying, it lived imperishably in her;
Transient and vanishing from transient eyes,
Invisible, a fateful ghost of self,
It bore the future on its phantom breast.
Along the fleeting event's far-backward trail
Regressed the stream of the insistent hours,
And on the bank of the mysterious flood
Peopled with well-loved forms now seen no more
And the subtle images of things that were,
Her witness spirit stood reviewing Time.
All that she once had hoped and dreamed and been,
Flew past her eagle-winged through memory's skies.
As in a many-hued flaming inner dawn,
Her life's broad highways and its sweet bypaths
Lay mapped to her sun-clear recording view,
From the bright country of her childhood's days
And the blue mountains of her soaring youth
And the paradise groves and peacock wings of Love
To joy clutched under the silent shadow of doom
In a last turn where heaven raced with hell.
Twelve passionate months led in a day of fate.
An absolute supernatural darkness falls
On man sometimes when he draws near to God:
An hour comes when fail all Nature's means;
Forced out from the protecting Ignorance
And flung back on his naked primal need,
He at length must cast from him his surface soul

And be the ungarbed entity within:
That hour had fallen now on Savitri.
A point she had reached where life must be in vain
Or, in her unborn element awake,
Her will must cancel her body's destiny.
For only the unborn spirit's timeless power
Can lift the yoke imposed by birth in time.
Only the Self that builds this figure of self
Can rase the fixed interminable line
That joins these changing names, these numberless lives,
These new oblivious personalities
And keeps still lurking in our conscious acts
The trail of old forgotten thoughts and deeds,
Disown the legacy of our buried selves,
The burdensome heirship to our vanished forms
Accepted blindly by the body and soul.
An episode in an unremembered tale,
Its beginning lost, its motive and plot concealed,
A once living story has prepared and made
Our present fate, child of past energies.
The fixity of the cosmic sequences
Fastened with hidden inevitable links
She must disrupt, dislodge by her soul's force
Her past, a block on the immortal's road,
Make a rased ground and shape anew her fate.
A colloquy of the original Gods
Meeting upon the borders of the unknown,
Her soul's debate with embodied Nothingness
Must be wrestled out on a dangerous dim background:
Her being must confront its formless Cause,
Against the universe weigh its single self.
On the bare peak where Self is alone with Nought
And life has no sense and love no place to stand,
She must plead her case upon extinction's verge,
In the world's death-cave uphold life's helpless claim
And vindicate her right to be and love.
Altered must be Nature's harsh economy;
Acquittance she must win from her past's bond,
An old account of suffering exhaust,
Strike out from Time the soul's long compound debt

13

And the heavy servitudes of the Karmic Gods,
The slow revenge of unforgiving Law
And the deep need of universal pain
And hard sacrifice and tragic consequence.
Out of a timeless barrier she must break,
Penetrate with her thinking depths the Void's monstrous hush,
Look into the lonely eyes of immortal Death
And with her nude spirit measure the Infinite's night.
The great and dolorous moment now was close.
A mailed battalion marching to its doom,
The last long days went by with heavy tramp,
Long but too soon to pass, too near the end.
Alone amid the many faces loved,
Aware among unknowing happy hearts,
Her armoured spirit kept watch upon the hours
Listening for a foreseen tremendous step
In the closed beauty of the inhuman wilds.
A combatant in silent dreadful lists,
The world unknowing, for the world she stood:
No helper had she save the Strength within;
There was no witness of terrestrial eyes;
The Gods above and Nature's soul below
Were the spectators of that mighty strife.
Around her were the austere sky-pointing hills,
And the green murmurous broad deep-thoughted woods
Muttered incessantly their muffled spell.
A dense magnificent coloured self-wrapped life
Draped in the leaves' vivid emerald monotone
And set with chequered sunbeams and blithe flowers
Immured her destiny's secluded scene.
There had she grown to the stature of her spirit:
The genius of titanic silences
Steeping her soul in its wide loneliness
Had shown to her her self's bare reality
And mated her with her environment.
Its solitude greatened her human hours
With a background of the eternal and unique.
A force of spare direct necessity
Reduced the heavy framework of man's days
And his overburdening mass of outward needs

To a first thin strip of simple animal wants,
And the mighty wideness of the primitive earth
And the brooding multitude of patient trees
And the musing sapphire leisure of the sky
And the solemn weight of the slowly passing months
Had left in her deep room for thought and God.
There was her drama's radiant prologue lived.
A spot for the eternal's tread on earth
Set in the cloistral yearning of the woods
And watched by the aspiration of the peaks
Appeared through an aureate opening in Time
Where stillness listening felt the unspoken word
And the hours forgot to pass towards grief and change.
Here with the suddenness divine advents have,
Repeating the marvel of the first descent,
Changing to rapture the dull earthly round,
Love came to her hiding the shadow, Death.
Well might he find in her his perfect shrine.
Since first the earth-being's heavenward growth began,
Through all the long ordeal of the race,
Never a rarer creature bore his shaft,
That burning test of the godhead in our parts,
A lightning from the heights on our abyss.
All in her pointed to a nobler kind.
Near to earth's wideness, intimate with heaven,
Exalted and swift her young large-visioned spirit
Voyaging through worlds of splendour and of calm
Overflew the ways of Thought to unborn things.
Ardent was her self-poised unstumbling will;
Her mind, a sea of white sincerity,
Passionate in flow, had not one turbid wave.
As in a mystic and dynamic dance
A priestess of immaculate ecstasies
Inspired and ruled from Truth's revealing vault
Moves in some prophet cavern of the gods,
A heart of silence in the hands of joy
Inhabited with rich creative beats
A body like a parable of dawn
That seemed a niche for veiled divinity
Or golden temple door to things beyond.

Immortal rhythms swayed in her time-born steps;
Her look, her smile awoke celestial sense
Even in earth-stuff, and their intense delight
Poured a supernal beauty on men's lives.
A wide self-giving was her native act;
A magnanimity as of sea or sky
Enveloped with its greatness all that came
And gave a sense as of a greatened world:
Her kindly care was a sweet temperate sun,
Her high passion a blue heaven's equipoise.
As might a soul fly like a hunted bird,
Escaping with tired wings from a world of storms,
And a quiet reach like a remembered breast,
In a haven of safety and splendid soft repose
One could drink life back in streams of honey-fire,
Recover the lost habit of happiness,
Feel her bright nature's glorious ambiance,
And preen joy in her warmth and colour's rule.
A deep of compassion, a hushed sanctuary,
Her inward help unbarred a gate in heaven;
Love in her was wider than the universe,
The whole world could take refuge in her single heart.
The great unsatisfied godhead here could dwell:
Vacant of the dwarf self's imprisoned air
Her mood could harbour his sublimer breath
Spiritual that can make all things divine.
For even her gulfs were secrecies of light.
At once she was the stillness and the word,
A continent of self-diffusing peace,
An ocean of untrembling virgin fire:
The strength, the silence of the gods were hers.
In her he found a vastness like his own,
His high warm subtle ether he refound
And moved in her as in his natural home.
In her he met his own eternity.

Till then no mournful line had barred this ray.
On the frail breast of this precarious earth,
Since her orbed sight in its breath-fastened house,
Opening in sympathy with happier stars

Where life is not exposed to sorrowful change,
Remembered beauty death-claimed lids ignore
And wondered at this world of fragile forms
Carried on canvas-strips of shimmering Time,
The impunity of unborn Mights was hers.
Although she leaned to bear the human load,
Her walk kept still the measure of the gods.
Earth's breath had failed to stain that brilliant glass:
Unsmeared with the dust of our mortal atmosphere
It still reflected heaven's spiritual joy.
Almost they saw who lived within her light
Her playmate in the sempiternal spheres
Descended from its unattainable realms
In her attracting advent's luminous wake,
The white-fire dragon bird of endless bliss
Drifting with burning wings above her days:
Heaven's tranquil shield guarded the missioned child.
A glowing orbit was her early term,
Years like gold raiment of the gods that pass;
Her youth sat throned in calm felicity.
But joy cannot endure until the end:
There is a darkness in terrestrial things
That will not suffer long too glad a note.
On her too closed the inescapable Hand:
The armed Immortal bore the snare of Time.
One dealt with her who meets the burdened great.
Assigner of the ordeal and the path
Who chooses in this holocaust of the soul
Death, fall and sorrow as the spirit's goads,
The dubious godhead with his torch of pain
Lit up the chasm of the unfinished world
And called her to fill with her vast self the abyss.
August and pitiless in his calm outlook,
Heightening the Eternal's dreadful strategy,
He measured the difficulty with the might
And dug more deep the gulf that all must cross.
Assailing her divinest elements,
He made her heart kin to the striving human heart
And forced her strength to its appointed road.
For this she had accepted mortal breath;

17

2

To wrestle with the Shadow she had come
And must confront the riddle of man's birth
And life's brief struggle in dumb Matter's night.
Whether to bear with Ignorance and Death
Or hew the ways of Immortality,
To win or lose the godlike game for man,
Was her soul's issue thrown with Destiny's dice.
But not to submit and suffer was she born;
To lead, to deliver was her glorious part.
Here was no fabric of terrestrial make
Fit for a day's use by busy careless Powers.
An image fluttering on the screen of fate
Half-animated for a passing show,
Or a castaway on the ocean of Desire
Flung to the eddies in a ruthless sport
And tossed along the gulfs of Circumstance,
A creature born to bend beneath the yoke,
A chattel and a plaything of Time's lords,
Or one more pawn who comes destined to be pushed
One slow move forward on a measureless board
In the chess-play of the earth-soul with Doom,—
Such is the human figure drawn by Time.
A conscious frame was here, a self-born Force.
In this enigma of the dusk of God,
This slow and strange uneasy compromise
Of limiting Nature with a limitless Soul,
Where all must move between an ordered Chance
And an uncaring blind Necessity,
Too high the fire spiritual dare not blaze.
If once it met the intense original Flame,
An answering touch might shatter all measures made
And earth sink down with the weight of the Infinite.
A gaol is this immense material world.
Across each road stands armed a stone-eyed law,
At every gate the huge dim sentinels pace.
A grey tribunal of the Ignorance,
An Inquisition of the priests of Night
In judgment sit on the adventurer soul,
And the dual tables and the Karmic norm
Restrain the Titan in us and the God:

Pain with its lash, joy with its silver bribe
Guard the Wheel's circling immobility,
A bond is put on the high climbing mind,
A seal on the too large wide-open heart;
Death stays the journeying discoverer, Life.
Thus is the throne of the Inconscient safe
While the tardy coilings of the aeons pass
And the Animal browses in the sacred fence
And the gold Hawk can cross the skies no more.
But one stood up and lit the limitless flame.
Arraigned by the dark Power that hates all bliss
In the dire court where life must pay for joy,
Sentenced by the mechanic justicer
To the afflicting penalty of man's hopes,
Her head she bowed not to the stark decree
Baring her helpless heart to destiny's stroke.
So bows and must the mind-born will in man
Obedient to the statutes fixed of old,
Admitting without appeal the nether gods.
In her the superhuman cast its seed.
Inapt to fold its mighty wings of dream
Her spirit refused to hug the common soil,
Or, finding all life's golden meanings robbed,
Compound with earth, struck from the starry list,
Or quench with black despair the God-given light.
Accustomed to the eternal and the true,
Her being conscious of its divine founts
Asked not from mortal frailty pain's relief,
Patched not with failure bargain or compromise.
A work she had to do, a word to speak;
Writing the unfinished story of her soul
In thoughts and actions graved in Nature's book,
She accepted not to close the luminous page,
Cancel her commerce with eternity,
Or set a signature of weak assent
To the brute balance of the world's exchange.
A force in her that toiled since earth was made,
Accomplishing in life the great world-plan,
Pursuing after death immortal aims,
Repugned to admit frustration's barren role,

19

Forfeit the meaning of her birth in Time,
Obey the government of the casual fact
Or yield her high destiny up to passing Chance.
In her own self she found her high recourse;
She matched with the iron law her sovereign right:
Her single will opposed the cosmic rule.
To stay the wheels of Doom this greatness rose.
At the Unseen's knock upon the hidden gates
Her strength made greater by the lightning's touch
Awoke from slumber in her heart's recess.
It bore the stroke of That which kills and saves.
Across the awful march no eye can see,
Barring its dreadful route no will can change,
She faced the engines of the universe;
A heart stood in the way of the driving wheels:
Its giant workings paused in front of a mind,
Its stark conventions met the flame of a soul.
A magic leverage suddenly is caught
That moves the veiled Ineffable's timeless will:
A prayer, a master act, a king idea
Can link man's strength to a transcendent Force.
Then miracle is made the common rule,
One mighty deed can change the course of things;
A lonely thought becomes omnipotent.
All now seems Nature's massed machinery;
An endless servitude to material rule
And long determination's rigid chain,
Her firm and changeless habits aping Law,
Her empire of unconscious deft device
Annul the claim of man's free human will.
He too is a machine amid machines;
A piston brain pumps out the shapes of thought,
A beating heart cuts out emotion's modes;
An insentient energy fabricates a soul.
Or the figure of the world reveals the signs
Of a tied Chance repeating her old steps
In circles around Matter's binding-posts.
A random series of inept events
To which reason lends illusive sense, is here,
Or the empiric Life's instinctive search,

Or a vast ignorant mind's colossal work.
But wisdom comes, and vision grows within;
Then Nature's instrument crowns himself her king;
He feels his witnessing self and conscious power;
His soul steps back and sees the Light supreme.
A Godhead stands behind the brute machine.
This truth broke in in a triumph of fire;
A victory was won for God in man,
The deity revealed its hidden face.
The great World-Mother now in her arose:
A living choice reversed fate's cold dead turn,
Affirmed the spirit's tread on Circumstance,
Pressed back the senseless dire revolving Wheel
And stopped the mute march of Necessity.
A flaming warrior from the eternal peaks
Empowered to force the door denied and closed
Smote from Death's visage its dumb absolute
And burst the bounds of consciousness and Time.

END OF CANTO TWO

CANTO THREE

THE YOGA OF THE KING:
THE YOGA OF THE SOUL'S RELEASE

A WORLD'S desire compelled her mortal birth.
    One in the front of the immemorial quest,
Protagonist of the mysterious play
In which the Unknown pursues himself through forms
And limits his eternity by the hours
And the blind Void struggles to live and see,
A thinker and toiler in the ideal's air,
Brought down to earth's dumb need her radiant power.
His was a spirit that stooped from larger spheres
Into our province of ephemeral sight,
A colonist from immortality.
A pointing beam on earth's uncertain roads,
His birth held up a symbol and a sign;
His human self like a translucent cloak
Covered the All-Wise who leads the unseeing world.
Affiliated to cosmic Space and Time
And paying here God's debt to earth and man
A greater sonship was his divine right.
Although consenting to mortal ignorance,
His knowledge shared the Light ineffable.
A strength of the original Permanence
Entangled in the moment and its flow,
He kept the vision of the Vasts behind:
A power was in him from the Unknowable.
An archivist of the symbols of the Beyond,
A treasurer of superhuman dreams,
He bore the stamp of mighty memories
And shed their grandiose ray on human life.
His days were a long growth to the Supreme.

A skyward being nourishing its roots
On sustenance from occult spiritual founts
Climbed through white rays to meet an unseen Sun.
His soul lived as eternity's delegate,
His mind was like a fire assailing heaven,
His will a hunter in the trails of light.
An ocean impulse lifted every breath;
Each action left the footprints of a God,
Each moment was a beat of puissant wings.
The little plot of our mortality
Touched by this tenant from the heights became
A playground of the living Infinite.
This bodily appearance is not all;
The form deceives, the person is a mask;
Hid deep in man celestial powers can dwell.
His fragile ship conveys through the sea of years
An incognito of the Imperishable.
A spirit that is a flame of God abides,
A fiery portion of the Wonderful,
Artist of his own beauty and delight,
Immortal in our mortal poverty.
This sculptor of the forms of the Infinite,
This screened unrecognised Inhabitant,
Initiate of his own veiled mysteries,
Hides in a small dumb seed his cosmic thought.
In the mute strength of the occult Idea
Determining predestined shape and act,
Passenger from life to life, from scale to scale,
Changing his imaged self from form to form,
He regards the icon growing by his gaze
And in the worm foresees the coming god.
At last the traveller in the paths of Time
Arrives on the frontiers of eternity.
In the transient symbol of humanity draped,
He feels his substance of undying self
And loses his kinship to mortality.
A beam of the Eternal smites his heart,
His thought stretches into infinitude:
All in him turns to spirit vastnesses.
His soul breaks out to join the Oversoul,

His life is oceaned by that superlife.
He has drunk from the breasts of the Mother of the worlds;
A topless supernature fills his frame:
She adopts his spirit's everlasting ground
As the security of her changing world
And shapes the figure of her unborn mights.
Immortally she conceives herself in him,
In the creature the unveiled creatrix works:
Her face is seen through his face, her eyes through his eyes;
Her being is his through a vast identity.
Then is revealed in man the overt Divine.
A static Oneness and dynamic Power
Descend in him, the integral Godhead's seals;
His soul and body take that splendid stamp.
A long dim preparation is man's life,
A circle of toil and hope and war and peace
Tracked out by Life on Matter's obscure ground
In his climb to a peak no feet have ever trod,
He seeks through a penumbra shot with flame
A veiled reality half-known, ever missed,
A search for something or someone never found,
Cult of an ideal never made real here,
An endless spiral of ascent and fall
Until at last is reached the giant point
Through which his Glory shines for whom we were made
And we break into the infinity of God.
Across our nature's border line we escape
Into supernature's arc of living light.
This now was witnessed in that son of Force,
In him that high transition laid its base.
Original and supernal Immanence
Of which all Nature's process is the art,
The cosmic Worker set his secret hand
To turn this frail mud-engine to heaven-use.
A Presence wrought behind the ambiguous screen:
It beat his soil to bear a Titan's weight,
Refining half-hewn blocks of natural strength
It built his soul into a statued God.
The Craftsman of the magic stuff of self
Who labours at his high and difficult plan

In the wide workshop of the wonderful world,
Modelled in inward Time his rhythmic parts.
Then came the abrupt transcendent miracle:
The masked immaculate Grandeur could outline,
At travail in the occult womb of life,
His dreamed magnificence of things to be.
A crown of the architecture of the worlds,
A mystery of married Earth and Heaven
Annexed divinity to the mortal scheme.
A Seer was born, a shining Guest of Time.
For him mind's limiting firmament ceased above,
In the griffin forefront of the Night and Day
A gap was rent in the all-concealing vault;
The conscious ends of being went rolling back:
The landmarks of the little person fell,
The island ego joined its continent:
Overpassed was this world of rigid limiting forms:
Life's barriers opened into the Unknown.
Abolished were conception's covenants
And, striking off subjection's rigorous clause
Annulled the soul's treaty with Nature's nescience.
All the grey inhibitions were torn off
And broken the intellect's hard and lustrous lid;
Truth unpartitioned found immense sky-room;
An empyrean vision saw and knew;
The bounded mind became a boundless light,
The finite self mated with Infinity.
His march now soared into an eagle's flight.
Out of apprenticeship to Ignorance
Wisdom upraised him to her master craft
And made him an arch-mason of the soul,
A builder of the Immortal's secret house,
An aspirant to supernal Timelessness:
Freedom and empire called to him from on high;
Above mind's twilight and life's star-led night
There gleamed the dawn of a spiritual day.

   As so he grew into his larger self,
Humanity framed his movements less and less,
A greater being saw a greater world.

A fearless will for knowledge dared to erase
The lines of safety reason draws that bar
Mind's soar, soul's dive into the Infinite.
Even his first steps broke our small earth-bounds
And loitered in a vaster freer air.
In hands sustained by a transfiguring Might
He caught up lightly like a giant's bow
Left slumbering in a sealed and secret cave
The powers that sleep unused in man within.
He made of miracle a normal act
And, turned to a common part of divine works,
Magnificently natural at this height
Efforts that would shatter the strength of mortal hearts,
Pursued in a royalty of mighty ease
Aims too sublime for Nature's daily will:
The gifts of the spirit crowding came to him;
They were his life's pattern and his privilege.
A pure perception lent its lucent joy:
Its intimate vision waited not to think;
It enveloped all Nature in a single glance,
It looked into the very self of things;
Deceived no more by form he saw the soul.
In beings it knew what lurked to them unknown;
It seized the idea in mind, the wish in the heart;
It plucked out from grey folds of secrecy
The motives which from their own sight men hide.
He felt the beating life in other men
Invade him with their happiness and their grief;
Their love, their anger, their unspoken hopes
Entered in currents or in pouring waves
Into the immobile ocean of his calm.
He heard the inspired sound of his own thoughts
Re-echoed in the vault of other minds;
The world's thought-streams travelled into his ken;
His inner self grew near to others' selves
And bore a kinship's weight, a common tie,
Yet stood untouched, king of itself, alone.
A magical accord quickened and attuned
To ethereal symphonies the old earthy strings;
It raised the servitors of mind and life

To be happy partners in the soul's response,
Tissue and nerve were turned to sensitive chords,
Records of lustre and ecstasy; it made
The body's means the spirit's acolytes.
A heavenlier function with a finer mode
Lit with its grace man's outward earthliness;
The soul's experience of its deeper sheaths
No more slept drugged by Matter's dominance.
In the dead wall closing us from wider self,
Into a secrecy of apparent sleep,
The mystic tract beyond our waking thoughts,
A door parted, built in by Matter's force,
Releasing things unseized by earthly sense:
A world unseen, unknown by outward mind
Appeared in the silent spaces of the soul.
He sat in secret chambers looking out
Into the luminous countries of the unborn
Where all things dreamed by the mind are seen and true
And all that the life longs for is drawn close.
He saw the Perfect in their starry homes
Wearing the glory of a deathless form
Lain in the arms of the Eternal's peace,
Rapt in the heart-beats of God-ecstasy.
He lived in the mystic space where thought is born
And will is nursed by an ethereal Power
And fed on the white milk of the Eternal's strengths
Till it grows into the likeness of a god.
In the Witness's occult rooms with mind-built walls
On hidden interiors, lurking passages
Opened the windows of the inner sight.
He owned the house of undivided Time.
Lifting the heavy curtain of the flesh
He stood upon a threshold serpent-watched,
And peered into gleaming endless corridors,
Silent and listening in the silent heart
For the coming of the new and the unknown.
He gazed across the empty stillnesses
And heard the footsteps of the undreamed Idea
In the far avenues of the Beyond.
He heard the secret Voice, the Word that knows,

27

And saw the secret face that is our own.
The inner planes uncovered their crystal doors;
Strange powers and influences touched his life.
A vision came of higher realms than ours,
A consciousness of brighter fields and skies,
Of beings less circumscribed than brief-lived men
And subtler bodies than these passing frames,
Objects too fine for our material grasp,
Acts vibrant with a superhuman light
And movements pushed by a superconscient force,
And joys that never flowed through mortal limbs,
And lovelier scenes than earth's and happier lives.
A consciousness of beauty and of bliss,
A knowledge which became what it perceived,
Replaced the separated sense and heart
And drew all Nature into its embrace.
The mind leaned out to meet the hidden worlds.
Air glowed and teemed with marvellous shapes and hues,
In the nostrils quivered celestial fragrances,
On the tongue lingered the honey of paradise.
A channel of universal harmony,
Hearing was a stream of magic audience,
A bed for occult sounds earth cannot hear.
Out of a covert tract of slumber self
The voice came of a truth submerged, unknown
That flows beneath the cosmic surfaces
Only mid an omniscient silence heard,
Held by intuitive heart and secret sense.
It caught the burden of secrecies sealed and dumb,
It voiced the unfulfilled demand of earth
And the song of promise of unrealised heavens
And all that hides in an omnipotent Sleep.
In the unceasing drama carried by Time
On its long listening flood that bears the world's
Insoluble doubt on a pilgrimage without goal,
A laughter of sleepless pleasure foamed and spumed
And murmurings of desire that cannot die:
A cry came of the world's delight to be,
The grandeur and greatness of its will to live,
Recall of the soul's adventure into space,

A traveller through the magic centuries
And being's labour in Matter's universe,
Its search for the mystic meaning of its birth
And joy of high spiritual response
Its throb of satisfaction and content,
In all the sweetness of the gifts of life,
Its large breath and pulse and thrill of hope and fear,
Its taste of pangs and tears and ecstasy,
Its rapture's poignant beat of sudden bliss,
The sob of its passion and unending pain.
The murmur and whisper of the unheard sounds
Which crowd around our hearts but find no window
To enter, swelled into a canticle
Of all that suffers to be still unknown
And all that labours vainly to be born
And all the sweetness none will ever taste
And all the beauty that will never be.
Inaudible to our deaf mortal ears
The wide world-rhythms wove their stupendous chant
To which life strives to fit our rhyme-beats here,
Melting our limits in the illimitable,
Tuning the finite to infinity.
A low muttering rose from the subconscient caves,
The stammer of the primal ignorance;
Answer to that inarticulate questioning,
There stooped with lightning neck and thunder's wings
A radiant hymn to the Inexpressible
And the anthem of the superconscient light.
All was revealed there none can here express;
Vision and dream were fables spoken by truth
Or symbols more veridical than fact,
Or were truths enforced by supernatural seals.
Immortal eyes approached and looked in his,
And beings of many kingdoms neared and spoke:
The ever-living whom we name as dead
Could leave their glory beyond death and birth
To utter the wisdom which exceeds all phrase:
The kings of evil and the kings of good,
Appellants at the reason's judgment seat,
Proclaimed the gospel of their opposites,

And all believed themselves spokesmen of God:
The gods of light and titans of the dark
Battled for his soul as for a costly prize.
In every hour loosed from the quiver of Time
There rose a song of new discovery,
A bow-twang's hum of young experiment.
Each day was a spiritual romance,
As if he was born into a bright new world;
Adventure leaped an unexpected friend,
And danger brought a keen sweet tang of joy:
Each happening was a deep experience.
There were high encounters, epic colloquies,
And counsels came couched in celestial speech,
And honeyed pleadings breathed from occult lips
To help the heart to yield to rapture's call,
And sweet temptations stole from beauty's realms
And sudden ecstasies from a world of bliss.
It was a reign of wonder and delight;
All now his bright clairaudience could receive,
A contact thrilled of mighty unknown things.
Awakened to new unearthly closenesses,
The touch replied to subtle infinities,
And with a silver cry of opening gates
Sight's lightnings leaped into the invisible.
Ever his consciousness and vision grew;
They took an ampler sweep, a loftier flight;
He passed the border marked for Matter's rule
And passed the zone where thought replaces life.
Out of this world of signs suddenly he came
Into a silent self where world was not
And looked beyond into a nameless vast.
These symbol figures lost their right to live,
All tokens dropped our sense can recognise;
There the heart beat no more at body's touch,
There the eyes gazed no more on beauty's shape.
In rare and lucent intervals of hush
Into a signless region he could soar
Packed with the deep contents of formlessness
Where world was into a single being rapt
And all was known by the light of identity

And spirit was its own self-evidence.
The Supreme's gaze looked out through human eyes
And saw all things and creatures as itself
And knew all thought and word as its own voice.
There unity is too close for search and clasp
And love is a yearning of the One for the One,
And beauty is a sweet difference of the Same
And oneness is the soul of multitude.
There all the truths unite in a single truth,
And all ideas rejoin Reality.
There knowing herself by her own termless self,
Wisdom supernal, wordless, absolute
Sat uncompanioned in the eternal Calm,
All-seeing, motionless, sovereign and alone.
There knowledge needs not words to embody Idea;
Idea seeking a house in boundlessness,
Weary of its homeless immortality,
Asks not in thought's carved brilliant cell to rest
Whose single window's clipped outlook on things
Sees only a little arc of God's vast sky.
The boundless with the boundless there consorts;
While there, one can be wider than the world;
While there, one is one's own infinity.
His centre was no more in earthly mind,
A power of seeing silence filled his limbs:
Caught by a voiceless white epiphany
Into a vision that surpasses forms,
Into a living that surpasses life,
He neared the still consciousness sustaining all.
The voice that only by speech can move the mind
Became a silent knowledge in the soul;
The strength that only in action feels its truth
Was lodged now in a mute omnipotent peace.
A leisure in the labour of the worlds,
A pause in the joy and anguish of the search
Restored the stress of Nature to God's calm.
A vast unanimity ended life's debate.
The war of thoughts that fathers the universe,
The clash of forces struggling to prevail
In the tremendous shock that lights a star

As in the building of a grain of dust,
The grooves that turn their dumb ellipse in space
Ploughed by the seeking of the world's desire,
The long regurgitations in Time's flood,
The torment edging the dire force of lust
That wakes kinetic in earth's dullard slime
And carves a personality out of mud,
The sorrow by which Nature's hunger is fed,
The oestrus which creates with fire of pain,
The fate that punishes virtue with defeat,
The tragedy that destroys long happiness,
The weeping of Love, the quarrel of the Gods,
Ceased in a truth which lives in its own light.
His soul stood free, a witness and a king.
Absorbed no more in the moment-ridden flux
Where mind incessantly drifts as on a raft
Hurried from phenomenon to phenomenon,
He abode at rest in indivisible Time.
As if a story long written but acted now,
In his present he held his future and his past,
Felt in the seconds the uncounted years
And saw the hours like dots upon a page.
An aspect of the unknown Reality
Altered the meaning of the cosmic scene.
This huge material universe became
A small result of a stupendous force:
Overtaking the moment the eternal Ray
Illumined that which never yet was made.
Thought lay down in a mighty voicelessness;
The toiling thinker widened and grew still,
Wisdom transcendent touched his quivering heart:
His soul could sail beyond thought's luminous bar;
Mind screened no more the shoreless infinite.
Across a void retreating sky he glimpsed
Through a last glimmer and drift of vanishing stars
The superconscient realms of motionless peace
Where judgment ceases and the word is mute
And the Unconceived lies pathless and alone.
There came not form or any mounting voice;
There only were Silence and the Absolute.

Out of that stillness mind new-born arose
And woke to truths once inexpressible,
And forms appeared, dumbly significant,
A seeing thought, a self-revealing voice.
He knew the source from which his spirit came:
Movement was married to the immobile Vast;
He plunged his roots into the Infinite,
He based his life upon Eternity.

    Only a while at first these heavenlier states,
These large wide-poised upliftings could endure.
The high and luminous tension breaks too soon,
The body's stone stillness and the life's hushed trance,
The breathless might and calm of silent mind;
Or slowly they fail as sets a golden day.
The restless nether members tire of peace;
A nostalgia of old little works and joys,
A need to call back small familiar selves,
To tread the accustomed and inferior way,
The need to rest in a natural poise of fall,
As a child who learns to walk can walk not long,
Replace the titan will for ever to climb,
On the heart's altar dim the sacred fire.
An old pull of subconscious cords renews;
It draws the unwilling spirit from the heights,
Or a dull gravitation drags us down
To the blind driven inertia of our base.
This too the supreme Diplomat can use,
He makes our fall a means for greater rise.
For into the ignorant nature's gusty field,
Into the half-ordered chaos of mortal life
The formless Power, the Self of eternal light
Follow in the shadow of the spirit's descent;
The twin duality for ever one
Chooses its home mid the tumults of the sense.
He comes unseen into our darker parts
And, curtained by the darkness, does his work,
A subtle and all-knowing guest and guide,
Till they too feel the need and will to change.
All here must learn to obey a higher law,

3

Our body's cells must hold the Immortal's flame.
Else would the spirit reach alone its source
Leaving a half-saved world to its dubious fate.
Nature would ever labour unredeemed;
Our earth would ever spin unhelped in space,
And this immense creation's purpose fail
Till at last the frustrate universe sank undone.
Even his godlike strength to rise must fall:
His greater consciousness withdrew behind;
Dim and eclipsed, his human outside strove
To feel again the old sublimities,
Bring the high saving touch, the ethereal flame,
Call back to its dire need the divine Force.
Always the power poured back like sudden rain,
Or slowly in his breast a presence grew
It clambered back to some remembered height
Or soared above the peak from which it fell.
Each time he rose there was a larger poise,
A dwelling on a higher spirit plane;
The Light remained in him a longer space.
In this oscillation between earth and heaven,
In this ineffable communion's climb
There grew in him as grows a waxing moon
The glory of the integer of his soul.
A union of the Real with the unique,
A gaze of the Alone from every face,
The Presence of the Eternal in the hours
Widening the mortal mind's half-look on things,
Bridging the gap between man's force and Fate
Made whole the fragment-being we are here.
At last was won a firm spiritual poise,
A constant lodging in the Eternal's realm,
A safety in the Silence and the Ray,
A settlement in the Immutable.
His heights of being lived in the still Self;
His mind could rest on a supernal ground
And look down on the magic and the play
Where the God-child lies on the lap of Night and Dawn
And the Everlasting puts on Time's disguise.
To the still heights and to the troubled depths

His equal spirit gave its vast assent:
A poised serenity of tranquil strength,
A wide unshaken look on Time's unrest
Faced all experience with unaltered peace.
Indifferent to the sorrow and delight,
Untempted by the marvel and the call,
Immobile it beheld the flux of things,
Calm and apart supported all that is:
His spirit's stillness helped the toiling world.
Inspired by silence and the closed eyes' sight
His force could work with a new luminous art
On the crude material from which all is made
And the refusal of Inertia's mass
And the grey front of the world's Ignorance
And nescient Matter and the huge error of life.
As a sculptor chisels a deity out of stone
He slowly chipped off the dark envelope,
Line of defence of Nature's ignorance,
The illusion and mystery of the Inconscient
In whose black pall the Eternal wraps his head
That he may act unknown in cosmic Time.
A splendour of self-creation from the peaks,
A transfiguration in the mystic depths,
A happier cosmic working could begin
And fashion the world-shape in him anew,
God found in Nature, Nature fulfilled in God.
Already in him was seen that task of Power:
Life made its home on the high tops of self;
His soul, mind, heart became a single sun;
Only life's lower reaches remained dim.
But there too, in the uncertain shadow of life,
There was a labour and a fiery breath;
The ambiguous cowled celestial puissance worked
Watched by the inner Witness's moveless peace.
Even on the struggling Nature left below
Strong periods of illumination came:
Lightnings of glory after glory burned,
Experience was a tale of blaze and fire,
Air rippled round the argosies of the Gods,
Strange riches sailed to him from the Unseen;

Splendours of insight filled the blank of thought,
Knowledge spoke to the inconscient stillnesses,
Rivers poured down of bliss and luminous force,
Visits of beauty, storm-sweeps of delight
Rained from the all-powerful Mystery above.
Thence stooped the eagles of Omniscience.
A dense veil was rent, a mighty whisper heard;
Repeated in the privacy of his soul,
A wisdom-cry from rapt transcendences
Sang on the mountains of an unseen world;
The voices that an inner listening hears
Conveyed to him their prophet utterances,
And flame-wrapt outbursts of the immortal Word
And flashes of an occult revealing Light
Approached him from the unreachable secrecy.
An inspired Knowledge sat enthroned within
Whose seconds illumined more than reason's years:
An ictus of revealing lustre fell
As if a pointing accent upon Truth,
And like a sky-flare showing all the ground
A swift intuitive discernment shone.
One glance could separate the true and false,
Or raise its rapid torch-fire in the dark
To check the claimants crowding through mind's gates
Covered by the forged signatures of the gods,
Detect the magic bride in her disguise
Or scan the apparent face of thought and life.

Oft inspiration with her lightning feet,
A sudden messenger from the all-seeing tops,
Traversed the soundless corridors of his mind
Bringing her rhythmic sense of hidden things.
A music spoke transcending mortal speech.
As if from a golden phial of the All-Bliss,
A joy of light, a joy of sudden sight,
A rapture of the thrilled undying Word
Poured into his heart as into an empty cup,
A repetition of God's first delight
Creating in a young and virgin Time.
In a brief moment caught, a little space,

All-Knowledge packed into great wordless thoughts
Lodged in the expectant stillness of his depths
A crystal of the ultimate Absolute,
A portion of the inexpressible Truth
Revealed by silence to the silent soul.
The intense creatrix in his stillness wrought;
Her power fallen speechless grew more intimate;
She looked upon the seen and the unforeseen,
Unguessed domains she made her native field.
All-vision gathered into a single ray,
As when the eyes stare at an invisible point
Till through the intensity of one luminous spot
An apocalypse of a world of images
Enters into the kingdom of the seer.
A great nude arm of splendour suddenly rose;
It rent the gauze opaque of Nescience:
Her lifted finger's keen unthinkable tip
Bared with a stab of flame the closed Beyond.
An eye awake in voiceless heights of trance,
A mind plucking at the unimaginable,
Overleaping with a sole and perilous bound
The high black wall hiding superconscience,
She broke in with inspired speech for scythe
And plundered the Unknowable's vast estate.
A gleaner of infinitesimal grains of Truth,
A sheaf-binder of infinite experience,
She pierced the guarded mysteries of World-Force
And her magic methods wrapt in a thousand veils;
Or she gathered the lost secrets dropped by Time
In the dust and crannies of his mounting route
Mid old forsaken dreams of hastening Mind
And buried remnants of forgotten space.
A traveller between summit and abyss
She joined the distant ends, the viewless deeps,
Or streaked along the roads of Heaven and Hell
Pursuing all knowledge like a questing hound.
A reporter and scribe of hidden wisdom talk,
Her shining minutes of celestial speech,
Passed through the masked office of the occult mind,
Transmitting gave to prophet and to seer

The inspired body of the mystic Truth.
A recorder of the inquiry of the gods,
Spokesman of the silent seeings of the Supreme,
She brought immortal words to mortal men.
Above the reason's brilliant slender curve,
Released like radiant air dimming a moon,
Broad spaces of a vision without line
Or limit swam into his spirit's ken.
Oceans of being met his voyaging soul
Calling to infinite discovery;
Timeless domains of joy and absolute power
Stretched out surrounded by the eternal hush;
The ways that lead to endless happiness
Ran like dream-smiles through meditating vasts:
Disclosed stood up in a gold moment's blaze
White sun-steppes in the pathless Infinite.
Along a naked curve in bourneless Self
The points that run through the closed heart of things
Shadowed the indeterminable line
That carries the Everlasting through the years.
The magician order of the cosmic Mind
Coercing the freedom of infinity
With the stark array of Nature's symbol facts
And life's incessant signals of event,
Transmuted chance recurrences into laws,
A chaos of signs into a universe.
Out of the rich wonders and the intricate whorls
Of the spirit's dance with Matter as its mask
The balance of the world's design grew clear,
Its symmetry of self-arranged effects
Managed in the deep perspectives of the soul,
And the realism of its illusive art,
Its logic of infinite intelligence,
Its magic of a changing eternity.
A glimpse was caught of things for ever unknown
The letters stood out of the unmoving Word.
In the immutable nameless Origin
Was seen emerging as from fathomless seas
The trail of the Ideas that made the world,
And, sown in the black earth of Nature's trance,

The seed of the Spirit's blind and huge desire
From which the tree of cosmos was conceived
And spread its magic arms through a dream of space.
Immense realities took on a shape:
There looked out from the shadow of the Unknown
The bodiless Namelessness that saw God born
And tries to gain from the mortal's mind and soul
A deathless body and a divine name.
The immobile lips, the great surreal wings,
The visage masked by superconscient Sleep,
The eyes with their closed lids that see all things,
Appeared of the Architect who builds in trance.
The original Desire born in the Void
Peered out; he saw the hope that never sleeps,
The feet that run behind a fleeting fate,
The ineffable meaning of the endless dream.
As if a torch held by a power of God,
The radiant world of the everlasting Truth
Glimmered like a faint star bordering the night
Above the golden Overmind's shimmering ridge.
Even were caught as through a cunning veil
The smile of love that sanctions the long game,
The calm indulgence and maternal breasts
Of Wisdom suckling the child-laughter of Chance,
Silence the nurse of the Almighty's power,
The omniscient hush, womb of the immortal Word,
And of the Timeless the still brooding face,
And the creative eye of Eternity.
The inspiring goddess entered a mortal's breast,
Made there her study of divining thought
And sanctuary of prophetic speech
And sat upon the tripod seat of mind:
All was made wide above, all lit below.
In darkness' core she dug out wells of light,
On the undiscovered depths imposed a form,
Lent a vibrant cry to the unuttered vasts,
And through great shoreless, voiceless, starless breadths
Bore earthward fragments of revealing thought
Hewn from the silence of the Ineffable.
A voice in the heart uttered the unspoken Name,

A dream of seeking thought wandering through space
Entered the invisible and forbidden house:
The treasure was found of a supernal Day.
In the deep subconscient glowed her jewel-lamp;
Lifted, it showed the riches of the Cave
Where, by the miser traffickers of sense
Unused, guarded beneath Night's dragon paws,
In folds of velvet darkness draped they sleep
Whose priceless value could have saved the world.
A darkness carrying morning in its breast
Looked for the eternal wide returning gleam,
Waiting the advent of a larger ray
And rescue of the lost herds of the Sun.
In a splendid extravagance of the waste of God
Dropped carelessly in creation's spendthrift work,
Left in the chantiers of the bottomless world
And stolen by the robbers of the Deep,
The golden shekels of the Eternal lie,
Hoarded from touch and view and thought's desire,
Locked in blind antres of the ignorant flood
Lest men should find them and be even as Gods.
A vision lightened on the viewless heights,
A wisdom illumined from the voiceless depths:
A deeper interpretation greatened Truth,
A grand reversal of the Night and Day;
All the world's values changed heightening life's aim;
A wiser word, a larger thought came in
Than what the slow labour of human mind can bring,
A secret sense awoke that could perceive
A Presence and a Greatness everywhere.
The universe was not now this senseless whirl
Borne round inert on an immense machine;
It cast away its grandiose lifeless front,
A mechanism no more or work of Chance,
But a living movement of the body of God.
A spirit hid in forces and in forms
Was the spectator of the mobile scene:
The beauty and the ceaseless miracle
Let in a glow of the Unmanifest:
The formless Everlasting moved in it

Seeking its own perfect form in souls and things.
Life kept no more a dull and meaningless shape.
In the struggle and upheaval of the world
He saw the labour of a godhead's birth:
A secret knowledge masked as Ignorance;
Fate covered with unseen necessity
The game of chance of an omnipotent Will.
A glory and a rapture and a charm,
The All-Blissful sat unknown within the heart;
Earth's pains were the ransom of its prisoned delight.
A glad communion tinged the passing hours;
The days were travellers on a destined road,
The nights companions of his musing spirit.
A heavenly impetus quickened all his breast;
The trudge of time changed to a splendid march;
The divine Dwarf towered to unconquered worlds,
Earth grew too narrow for his victory.
Once only registering the heavy tread
Of a blind Power on human littleness,
Life now became a sure approach to God,
Existence a divine experiment
And cosmos the soul's opportunity.
The world was a conception and a birth
Of Spirit in Matter into living forms,
And Nature bore the Immortal in her womb,
That she might climb through him to eternal life.
His being lay down in bright immobile peace
And bathed in wells of pure spiritual light;
It wandered in wide fields of wisdom-self
Lit by the rays of an everlasting sun.
Even his body's subtle self within
Could raise the earthly parts towards higher things
And feel on it the breath of heavenlier air.
Already it journeyed towards divinity:
Upbuoyed upon winged winds of rapid joy,
Upheld to a Light it could not always hold,
It left mind's distance from the Truth supreme
And lost life's incapacity for bliss.
All now suppressed in us began to emerge.

Thus came his soul's release from Ignorance,
His mind and body's first spiritual change.
A wide God-knowledge poured down from above,
A new world-knowledge broadened from within:
His daily thoughts looked up to the True and One,
His commonest doings welled from an inner Light.
Awakened to the lines that Nature hides,
Attuned to her movements that exceed our ken,
He grew one with a covert universe.
His grasp surprised her mightiest energies' springs;
He spoke with the unknown Guardians of the worlds,
Forms he descried our mortal eyes see not.
His wide eyes bodied viewless entities,
He saw the cosmic forces at their work
And felt the occult impulse behind man's will.
Time's secrets were to him an oft-read book;
The records of the future and the past
Outlined their excerpts on the etheric page.
One and harmonious by the Maker's skill,
The human in him paced with the divine.
His acts betrayed not the interior flame.
This forged the greatness of his front to earth.
A genius heightened in his body's cells
That knew the meaning of his fate-hedged works
Akin to the march of unaccomplished Powers
Beyond life's arc in spirit's immensities.
Apart he lived in his mind's solitude,
A demigod shaping the lives of men:
One soul's ambition lifted up the race;
A Power worked, but none knew whence it came.
The universal strengths were linked with his;
Feeling earth's smallness with their boundless breadths,
He drew the energies that transmute an age.
Immeasurable by the common look,
He made great dreams a mould for coming things
And cast his deeds like bronze to front the years.
His walk through Time outstripped the human stride.
Lonely his days and splendid like the sun's.

END OF CANTO THREE

CANTO FOUR

THE SECRET KNOWLEDGE

ON a height he stood that looked towards greater heights.
    Our early approaches to the Infinite
Are sunrise splendours on a marvellous verge
While lingers yet unseen the glorious sun.
What now we see is a shadow of what must come.
The earth's uplook to a remote unknown
Is a preface only of the epic climb
Of human soul from its flat earthly state
To the discovery of a greater self
And the far gleam of an eternal Light.
This world is a beginning and a base
Where Life and Mind erect their structured dreams;
An unborn Power must build reality.
A deathbound littleness is not all we are:
Immortal our forgotten vastnesses
Await discovery in our summit selves;
Unmeasured breadths and depths of being are ours.
Akin to the ineffable secrecy,
Mystic, eternal in unrealised Time,
Neighbours of Heaven are Nature's altitudes.
To these high-peaked dominions sealed to our search
Too far from surface Nature's postal routes,
Too lofty for our mortal lives to breathe,
Deep in us a forgotten kinship points
And a faint voice of ecstasy and prayer
Calls to those lucent lost immensities.
Even when we fail to look into our souls
Or lie embedded in earthly consciousness,
Still have we parts that grow towards the Light,
Yet are there luminous tracts and heavens serene

And Eldoradoes of splendour and ecstasy
And temples to the Godhead none can see.
A shapeless memory lingers in us still
And sometimes, when our sight is turned within,
Earth's ignorant veil is lifted from our eyes;
There is a short miraculous escape.
This narrow fringe of clamped experience
We leave behind meted to us as life,
Our little walks, our insufficient reach.
Our souls can visit in great lonely hours
Still regions of imperishable Light,
All-seeing eagle-peaks of silent Power
And moon-flame oceans of swift fathomless Bliss
And calm immensities of spirit Space.
In the unfolding process of the Self
Sometimes the inexpressible Mystery
Elects a human vessel of descent.
A breath comes down from a supernal air,
A presence is borne, a guiding Light awakes,
A stillness falls upon the instruments:
Fixed sometimes like a marble monument,
Stone-calm, the body is a pedestal
Supporting a figure of eternal Peace.
Or a revealing Force sweeps blazing in;
Out of some vast superior continent
Knowledge breaks through trailing its radiant seas,
And Nature trembles with the power, the flame.
A greater Personality sometimes
Possesses us which yet we know is ours:
Or we adore the Master of our souls.
Then the small bodily ego thins and falls;
No more insisting on its separate self,
Losing the punctilio of its separate birth,
It leaves us one with Nature and with God.
In moments when the inner lamps are lit
And the life's cherished guests are left outside,
Our spirit sits alone and speaks to its gulfs.
A wider consciousness opens then its doors;
Invading from spiritual silences
A ray of the timeless Glory stoops awhile

To commune with our seized illumined clay
And leaves its huge white stamp upon our lives.
In the oblivious field of mortal mind,
Revealed to the closed prophet eyes of trance
Or in some deep internal solitude
Witnessed by a strange immaterial sense,
The signals of eternity appear.
The truth mind could not know unveils its face,
We hear what mortal ears have never heard,
We feel what earthly sense has never felt,
We love what common hearts repel and dread;
Our minds hush to a bright Omniscient;
A Voice calls from the chambers of the soul;
We meet the ecstasy of the Godhead's touch
In golden privacies of immortal fire.
These signs are native to a larger self
That lives within us by ourselves unseen;
Only sometimes a holier influence comes,
A tide of mightier surgings bears our lives
And a diviner Presence moves the soul.
Or through the earthly coverings something breaks,
A grace and beauty of spiritual light,
The murmuring tongue of a celestial fire.
Ourself and a high stranger whom we feel,
It is and acts unseen as if it were not;
It follows the line of sempiternal birth,
Yet seems to perish with its mortal frame.
Assured of the Apocalypse to be,
It reckons not the moments and the hours;
Great, patient, calm it sees the centuries pass,
Awaiting the slow miracle of our change
In the sure deliberate process of world-force
And the long march of all-revealing Time.
It is the origin and the master-clue,
A Silence overhead, an inner Voice,
A living image seated in the heart,
An unwalled wideness and a fathomless point,
The truth of all these cryptic shows in space,
The Real towards which our strivings move,
The secret grandiose meaning of our lives.

A treasure of honey in the combs of God,
A Splendour burning in a tenebrous cloak,
It is our glory of the flame of God,
Our golden fountain of the world's delight,
An immortality cowled in the cape of death,
The shape of our unborn divinity.
It guards for us our fate in depths within
Where sleeps the eternal seed of transient things.
Always we bear in us a magic key
Concealed in life's hermetic envelope.
A burning witness in the sanctuary
Regards through Time and the blind walls of Form;
A timeless Light is in his hidden eyes;
He sees the secret things no words can speak
And knows the goal of the unconscious world
And the heart of the mystery of the journeying years.

But all is screened, subliminal, mystical;
It needs the intuitive heart, the inward turn,
It needs the power of a spiritual gaze.
Else to our waking mind's small moment look
A goalless voyage seems our dubious course
Some Chance has settled or hazarded some Will,
Or a Necessity without aim or cause
Unwillingly compelled to emerge and be.
In this dense field where nothing is plain or sure,
Our very being seems to us questionable,
Our life a vague experiment, the soul
A flickering light in a strange ignorant world,
The earth a brute mechanic accident,
A net of death in which by chance we live.
All we have learned appears a doubtful guess,
The achievement done a passage or a phase
Whose further end is hidden from our sight,
A chance happening or a fortuitous fate.
Out of the unknown we move to the unknown.
Ever surround our brief existence here
Grey shadows of unanswered questionings;
The dark Inconscient's signless mysteries
Stand up unsolved behind Fate's starting line;

46

An aspiration in the Night's profound,
Seed of a perishing body and half-lit mind,
Uplifts its lonely tongue of conscious fire
Towards an undying Light for ever lost.
Only it hears, sole echo of its call,
The dim reply in man's unknowing heart
And meets, not understanding why it came
Or for what reason is the suffering here,
God's sanction to the paradox of life
And the riddle of the Immortal's birth in Time.
Along a path of aeons serpentine
In the coiled blackness of her nescient course
The Earth-Goddess toils across the sands of Time.
A Being is in her whom she hopes to know,
A Word speaks to her heart she cannot hear,
A Fate compels whose form she cannot see.
In her unconscious orbit through the Void
Out of her mindless depths she strives to rise,
A perilous life her gain, a struggling joy;
A Thought that can conceive but hardly knows
Arises slowly in her and creates
The idea, the speech that labels more than it lights;
A trembling gladness that is less than bliss
Invades from all this beauty that must die.
Alarmed by the sorrow dragging at her feet
And conscious of the high things not yet won,
Ever she nurses in her sleepless breast
An inward urge that takes from her rest and peace.
Ignorant and weary and invincible
She seeks through the soul's war and quivering pain
The pure perfection her marred nature needs,
A breath of Godhead on her stone and mire.
A faith she craves that can survive defeat,
The sureness of a love that knows not death,
The radiance of a truth for ever sure.
A light grows in her, she assumes a voice,
Her state she learns to read and the act she has done,
But the one needed truth eludes her grasp,
Herself and all of which she is the sign.
An inarticulate whisper drives her steps

47

Of which she feels the force but not the sense;
A few rare intimations come as guides,
Immense divining flashes cleave her brain,
And sometimes in her hours of dream and muse
The truth that she has missed looks out on her
As if far off and yet within her soul.
A change comes near that flees from her surmise
And, ever postponed, compels attempt and hope,
Yet seems too great for mortal hope to dare.
A vision meets her of supernal Powers
That draw her as if mighty kinsmen lost
Approaching with estranged great luminous gaze.
Then is she moved to all that she is not
And stretches arms to what was never hers.
Outstretching arms to the unconscious Void,
Passionate she prays to invisible forms of Gods
Soliciting from dumb Fate and toiling Time
What most she needs, what most exceeds her scope,
A Mind unvisited by illusion's gleams,
A Will expressive of soul's deity,
A Strength not forced to stumble by its speed,
A Joy that drags not sorrow as its shade.
For these she yearns and feels them destined hers:
Heaven's privilege she claims as her own right.
Just is her claim the all-witnessing Gods approve,
Clear in a greater light than reason owns:
Our intuitions are its title-deeds;
Our souls accept what our blind thoughts refuse.
Earth's winged chimeras are Truth's steeds in Heaven,
The impossible God's sign of things to be.
But few can look beyond the present state
Or overleap this matted hedge of sense.
All that transpires on earth and all beyond
Are parts of an illimitable plan
The One keeps in his heart and knows alone.
Our outward happenings have their seed within,
And even this random Fate that imitates Chance,
This mass of unintelligible results,
Are the dumb graph of truths that work unseen:
The laws of the Unknown create the known.

The events that shape the appearance of our lives
Are a cipher of subliminal quiverings
Which rarely we surprise or vaguely feel,
Are an outcome of suppressed realities
That hardly rise into material day:
They are born from the spirit's sun of hidden powers
Digging a tunnel through emergency.
But who shall pierce into the cryptic gulf
And learn what deep necessity of the soul
Determined casual deed and consequence?
Absorbed in a routine of daily acts,
Our eyes are fixed on an external scene;
We hear the crash of the wheels of Circumstance
And wonder at the hidden cause of things.
Yet a foreseeing Knowledge might be ours,
If we could take our spirit's stand within,
If we could hear the muffled daemon voice.
Too seldom is the shadow of what must come
Cast in an instant on the secret sense
Which feels the shock of the invisible,
And seldom in the few who answer give
The mighty process of the cosmic Will
Communicates its image to our sight,
Identifying the world's mind with ours.
Our range is fixed within the crowded arc
Of what we observe and touch and thought can guess
And rarely dawns the light of the Unknown
Waking in us the prophet and the seer.
The outward and the immediate are our field,
The dead past is our background and support;
Mind keeps the soul prisoner, we are slaves to our acts;
We cannot free our gaze to reach wisdom's sun.
Inheritor of the brief animal mind,
Man, still a child in Nature's mighty hands,
In the succession of the moments lives;
To a changing present is his narrow right;
His memory stares back at a phantom past,
The future flees before him as he moves;
He sees imagined garments, not a face.
Armed with a limited precarious strength,

He saves his fruits of work from adverse chance.
A struggling ignorance is his wisdom's mate.
He waits to see the consequence of his acts,
He waits to weigh the certitude of his thoughts,
He knows not what he shall achieve or when;
He knows not whether at last he shall survive,
Or end like the mastodon and the sloth
And perish from the earth where he was king.
He is ignorant of the meaning of his life,
He is ignorant of his high and splendid fate.
Only the Immortals on their deathless heights
Dwelling beyond the walls of Time and Space,
Masters of living, free from the bonds of Thought,
Who are overseers of Fate and Chance and Will
And experts of the theorem of world-need,
Can see the Idea, the Might that change Time's course,
Come maned with light from undiscovered worlds,
Hear, while the world toils on with its deep blind heart,
The galloping hooves of the unforeseen event,
Bearing the superhuman rider, near
And, impassive to earth's din and startled cry,
Return to the silence of the hills of God;
As lightning leaps, as thunder sweeps, they pass
And leave their mark on the trampled breast of Life.
Above the world the world-creators stand,
In the phenomenon see its mystic source.
These heed not the deceiving outward play,
They turn not to the moment's busy tramp,
But listen with the still patience of the Unborn
For the slow footsteps of far Destiny
Approaching through huge distances of Time,
Unmarked by the eye that sees effect and cause,
Unheard mid the clamour of the human plane.
Attentive to an unseen Truth they seize
A sound as of invisible augur wings,
Voices of an unplumbed significance,
Mutterings that brood in the core of Matter's sleep.
In the heart's profound audition they can catch
The murmurs lost by life's uncaring ear,
A prophet-speech in thought's omniscient trance.

Above the illusion of the hopes that pass,
Behind the appearance and the overt act,
Behind the clock-work chance and vague surmise,
Amid the wrestle of force, the trampling feet,
Across the triumph, fighting and despair,
They watch the Bliss for which earth's heart has cried,
On the long road which cannot see its end
Winding undetected through the sceptic days
And to meet it guide the unheedful moving world.
Thus will the masked Transcendent mount his throne.
When darkness deepens strangling the earth's breast
And man's corporeal mind is the only lamp,
As a thief's in the night shall be the covert tread
Of one who steps unseen into his house.
A Voice ill-heard shall speak, the soul obey,
A power into mind's inner chamber steal,
A charm and sweetness open life's closed doors
And beauty conquer the resisting world,
The truth-light capture Nature by surprise,
A stealth of God compel the heart to bliss
And earth grow unexpectedly divine.
In Matter shall be lit the spirit's glow,
In body and body kindled the sacred birth;
Night shall awake to the anthem of the stars,
The days become a happy pilgrim march,
Our will a force of the Eternal's power,
And thought the rays of a spiritual sun.
A few shall see what none yet understands;
God shall grow up while the wise men talk and sleep;
For man shall not know the coming till its hour
And belief shall be not till the work is done.

   A consciousness that knows not its own truth,
A vagrant hunter of misleading dawns,
Between the being's dark and luminous ends
Moves here in a half-light that seems the whole:
An interregnum in Reality
Cuts off the integral Thought, the total Power;
It circles or stands in a vague interspace,
Doubtful of its beginning and its close,

Or runs upon a road that has no end;
Far from the original Dusk, the final Flame
In some huge void Inconscience it lives,
Like a thought persisting in a wide emptiness.
As if an unintelligible phrase
Suggested a million renderings to the Mind,
It lends a purport to the random world.
A conjecture leaning upon doubtful proofs,
A message misunderstood, a thought confused
Missing its aim is all that it can speak
Or a fragment of the universal word.
It leaves two giant letters void of sense
While without sanction turns the middle sign
Carrying an enigmatic universe,
As if a present without future or past
Repeating the same revolution's whirl
Turned on its axis in its own Inane.
Thus is the meaning of creation veiled;
For without context reads the cosmic page:
Its signs stare at us like an unknown script,
As if appeared screened by a foreign tongue
Or code of splendour signs without a key
A portion of a parable sublime.
It wears to the perishable creature's eyes
The grandeur of a useless miracle;
Wasting itself that it may last awhile,
A river that can never find its sea,
It runs through life and death on an edge of Time;
A fire in the Night is its mighty action's blaze.
This is our deepest need to join once more
What now is parted, opposite and twain,
Remote in sovereign spheres that never meet
Or fronting like far poles of Night and Day.
We must fill the immense lacuna we have made,
Re-wed the closed finite's lonely consonant
With the open vowels of Infinity,
A hyphen must connect Matter and Mind,
The narrow isthmus of the ascending soul:
We must renew the secret bond in things,
Our hearts recall the lost divine Idea,

Reconstitute the perfect word, unite
The Alpha and the Omega in one sound;
Then shall the Spirit and Nature be at one.
Two are the ends of the mysterious plan.
In the wide signless ether of the Self,
In the unchanging Silence white and nude,
Aloof, resplendent like gold dazzling suns
Veiled by the Ray no mortal eye can bear,
The Spirit's free and absolute potencies
Burn in the solitude of the thoughts of God.
A rapture and a radiance and a hush
Delivered from the approach of wounded hearts,
Denied to the Idea that looks at grief,
Remote from the Force that cries out in its pain,
In his inalienable bliss they live.
Immaculate in self-knowledge and self-power,
Calm they repose on the eternal Will.
Only his law they count and him obey;
They have no goal to reach, no aim to serve.
Implacable in their timeless purity,
All barter or bribe of worship they refuse;
Unmoved by cry of revolt and ignorant prayer
They reckon not our virtue and our sin,
They bend not to the voices that implore,
They hold no traffic with error and its reign:
They are guardians of the silence of the Truth,
They are keepers of the immutable decree.
A deep surrender is their source of might,
A still identity their way to know,
Motionless is their action like a sleep.
At peace, regarding the trouble beneath the stars,
Deathless, watching the works of Death and Chance,
Immobile, seeing the millenniums pass,
Untouched while the long map of Fate unrolls,
They look on our struggle with impartial eyes,
And yet without them cosmos could not be.
Impervious to desire and doom and hope,
Their station of inviolable might
Moveless upholds the world's enormous task,
Its ignorance is by their knowledge lit,

Its yearning lasts by their indifference.
As the height draws the low ever to climb,
As the breadths draw the small to adventure vast,
Their aloofness drives man to surpass himself.
Our passion heaves to wed the eternal calm,
Our dwarf-search mind to meet the Omniscient's force.
Acquiescing in the wisdom that made hell
And the harsh utility of death and tears,
Acquiescing in the gradual steps of Time,
Careless they seem of the grief that stings the world's heart,
Careless of the pain that rends its body and life;
Above joy and sorrow is that grandeur's walk:
They have no portion in the good that dies,
Mute, pure, they share not in the evil done;
Else might their strength be marred and could not save.
Alive to the truth that dwells in God's extremes,
Awake to a motion of all-seeing Force,
The slow venture of the long ambiguous years
And the unexpected good from woeful deeds,
The immortal sees not as we vainly see.
He looks on hidden aspects and screened powers,
He knows the law and natural line of things.
Undriven by a brief life's will to act,
Unharassed by the spur of pity and fear,
He makes no haste to untie the cosmic knot
Or the world's torn jarring heart to reconcile.
In Time he waits for the Eternal's hour.
Yet a spiritual secret aid is there;
While a tardy Evolution's coils wind on
And Nature hews her way through adamant
A divine intervention thrones above.
Alive in a dead rotating universe
We whirl not here upon a casual globe
Abandoned to a task beyond our force;
Even through the tangled anarchy called Fate
And through the bitterness of death and fall
An outstretched Hand is felt upon our lives.
It is near us in unnumbered bodies and births;
In its unshaken grasp it keeps for us safe
The one inevitable supreme result

No will can take away and no doom change,
The crown of conscious Immortality,
The godhead promised to our struggling souls
When first man's heart dared death and suffered life.
One who has shaped this world is ever its lord:
Our errors are his steps upon the way;
He works through the fierce vicissitudes of our lives,
He works through the hard breath of battle and toil,
He works through our sins and sorrows and our tears,
His knowledge overrules our nescience;
Whatever the appearance we must bear,
Whatever our strong ills and present fate,
When nothing we can see but drift and bale,
A mighty Guidance leads us still through all.
After we have served this great divided world
God's bliss and oneness are our inborn right.
A date is fixed in the calendar of the Unknown,
An anniversary of the Birth sublime:
Our soul shall justify its chequered walk,
All will come near that now is naught or far.
These calm and distant Mights shall act at last.
Immovably ready for their destined task,
The ever-wise compassionate Brilliances
Await the sound of the Incarnate's voice
To leap and bridge the chasms of Ignorance
And heal the hollow yearning gulfs of Life
And fill the abyss that is the universe.
Here meanwhile at the Spirit's opposite pole
In the mystery of the deeps that God has built
For his abode below the Thinker's sight,
In this compromise of a stark absolute Truth
With the Light that dwells near the dark end of things,
In this tragi-comedy of divine disguise,
This long far seeking for joy ever near,
In the grandiose dream of which the world is made,
In this gold dome on a black dragon base,
The conscious Force that acts in Nature's breast,
A dark-robed labourer in the cosmic scheme
Carrying clay images of unborn gods,
Executrix of the inevitable Idea

Hampered, enveloped by the hoops of Fate,
Patient trustee of slow eternal Time,
Absolves from hour to hour her secret charge.
All she foresees in masked imperative depths;
The dumb intention of the unconscious gulfs
Answers to a will that sees upon the heights,
And the evolving Word's first syllable
Ponderous, brute-sensed, contains its luminous close,
Privy to a summit victory's vast descent
And the portent of the soul's immense uprise.

    All here where each thing seems its lonely self
Are figures of the sole transcendent One:
Only by him they are, his breath is their life;
An unseen Presence moulds the oblivious clay.
A playmate in the mighty Mother's game,
One came upon the dubious whirling globe
To hide from her pursuit in force and form.
A secret spirit in the Inconscient's sleep,
A shapeless Energy, a voiceless Word,
He was here before the elements could emerge,
Before there was light of mind or life could breathe.
Accomplice of her cosmic huge pretence,
His semblances he turns to real shapes
And makes the symbol equal with the truth:
He gives to his timeless thoughts a form in Time.
He is the substance, he the self of things;
She has forged from him her works of skill and might:
She wraps him in the magic of her moods
And makes of his myriad truths her countless dreams.
The Master of being has come close to her,
An immortal child born in the fugitive years.
In objects wrought, in the persons she conceives,
Dreaming she chases her idea of him,
And catches here a look and there a gest:
Ever he repeats in them his ceaseless births.
He is the Maker and the world he made,
He is the vision and he is the seer;
He is himself the actor and the act,
He is himself the knower and the known,

He is himself the dreamer and the dream.
There are Two who are One and play in many worlds;
In Knowledge and Ignorance they have spoken and met
And light and darkness are their eyes' interchange.
Our pleasure and pain are their wrestle and embrace,
Our deeds, our hopes are intimate to their tale;
They are married secretly in our thought and life.
The universe is an endless masquerade:
For nothing here is utterly what it seems,
It is a dream-fact vision of a truth
Which but for the dream would not be wholly true,
A phenomenon stands out significant
Against dim backgrounds of eternity;
We accept its face and pass by all it means;
A part is seen, we take it for the whole.
Thus have they made their play with us for roles:
Author and actor with himself as scene,
He moves there as the Soul, as Nature she.
Here on the earth where we must fill our parts,
We know not how shall run the drama's course;
Our uttered sentences veil in their thought.
Her mighty plan she holds back from our sight:
She has concealed her glory and her bliss
And disguised the Love and Wisdom in her heart.
Of all the marvel and beauty that are hers
Only a darkened little we can feel.
He too wears a diminished Godhead here,
He has forsaken his omnipotence,
His calm he has foregone and infinity.
He knows her only, he has forgotten himself;
To her he abandons all to make her great.
He hopes in her to find himself anew,
Incarnate, wedding his infinity's peace
To her creative passion's ecstasy.
Although possessor of the earth and heavens,
He leaves to her the cosmic management
And watches all, the Witness of her scene.
A supernumerary on her stage,
He speaks no words or hides behind the wings.
He takes birth in her world, waits on her will,

57

Divines her enigmatic gesture's sense,
The fluctuating chance turns of her mood,
Works out her meanings she seems not to know
And serves her secret purpose in long Time.
As one too great for him he worships her;
He adores her as his regent of desire,
He yields to her as the mover of his will,
He burns the incense of his nights and days
Offering his life, a splendour of sacrifice.
A rapt solicitor for her love and grace,
His bliss in her to him is his whole world:
He grows through her in all his being's powers;
He reads by her God's hidden aim in things.
Or, a courtier in her countless retinue,
Content to be with her and feel her near
He makes the most of the little that she gives
And all she does drapes with his own delight.
A glance can make his whole day wonderful,
A word from her lips with happiness wings the hours.
He leans on her for all he does and is:
He builds on her largesses his proud fortunate days
And trails his peacock-plumaged joy of life
And suns in the glory of her passing smile.
In a thousand ways he serves her royal needs;
He makes the hours pivot around her will,
Makes all reflect her whims; all is their play:
This whole wide world is only he and she.

   This is the knot that ties together the stars:
The Two who are one are the secret of all power,
The Two who are one are the might and right in things.
His soul, silent, supports the world and her,
His acts are her commandment's registers.
Happy, inert he lies beneath her feet:
His breast he offers for her cosmic dance
Of which our lives are the quivering theatre,
And none could bear but for his strength within,
Yet none would leave because of his delight.
His works, his thoughts have been devised by her,
His being is a mirror vast of hers:

Active, inspired by her he speaks and moves;
His deeds obey her heart's unspoken demands:
Passive, he bears the impacts of the world
As if her touches shaping his soul and life:
His journey through the days is her sun-march;
He runs upon her roads; hers is his course.
A witness and student of her joy and dole,
A partner in her evil and her good,
He has consented to her passionate ways,
He is driven by her sweet and dreadful force.
His sanctioning name initials all her works;
His silence is his signature to her deeds;
In the execution of her drama's scheme,
In her fancies of the moment and its mood,
In the march of this obvious ordinary world
Where all is deep and strange to the eyes that see
And Nature's common forms are marvel-wefts,
She through his witness sight and motion of might
Unrolls the material of her cosmic Act,
Her happenings that exalt and smite the soul,
Her force that moves, her powers that save and slay,
Her Word that in the silence speaks to our hearts,
Her silence that transcends the summit Word,
Her heights and depths to which our spirit moves,
Her events that weave the texture of our lives
And all by which we find or lose ourselves,
Things sweet and bitter, magnificent and mean,
Things terrible and beautiful and divine.
Her empire in the cosmos she has built,
He is governed by her subtle and mighty laws.
His consciousness is a babe upon her knees,
Her endless space is the playground of his thoughts,
His being a field of her vast experiment;
She binds to knowledge of the shapes of Time
And the creative error of limiting mind
And chance that wears the rigid face of fate
And her sport of death and pain and Nescience,
His changed and struggling immortality.
His soul is a subtle atom in a mass,
His substance a material for her works.

His spirit survives amid the death of things,
He climbs to eternity through being's gaps,
He is carried by her from Night to deathless Light.
This grand surrender is his free-will's gift,
His pure transcendent force submits to hers.
In the mystery of her cosmic ignorance,
In the insoluble riddle of her play,
A creature made of perishable stuff,
In the pattern she has set for him he moves,
He thinks with her thoughts, with her trouble his bosom heaves;
He seems the thing that she would have him seem,
He is whatever her artist will can make.
Although she drives him on her fancy's roads,
At play with him as with her child or slave,
To freedom and the Eternal's mastery
And immortality's stand above the world,
She moves her seeming puppet of an hour.
Even in his mortal session in body's house
An aimless traveller between birth and death,
Ephemeral dreaming of immortality,
To reign she spurs him. He takes up her powers;
He has harnessed her to the yoke of her own law.
His face of human thought puts on a crown.
Held in her leash, bound to her veiled caprice,
He studies her ways if so he may prevail
Even for an hour and she work out his will;
He makes of her his moment passion's serf:
To obey she feigns, she follows her creature's lead:
For him she was made, lives only for his use.
But conquering her, then is he most her slave;
He is her dependent, all his means are hers;
Nothing without her he can, she rules him still.
At last he wakes to a memory of Self:
He sees within the face of deity,
The Godhead breaks out through the human mould:
Her highest heights she unmasks and is his mate.
Till then he is a plaything in her game;
Her seeming regent, yet her fancy's toy,
A living robot moved by her energy's springs,
He acts as in the movements of a dream,

An automaton stepping in the grooves of Fate,
He stumbles on driven by her whip of Force:
His thought labours, a bullock in Time's fields;
His will he thinks his own, is shaped in her forge.
Obedient to World-Nature's dumb control,
Driven by his own formidable Power,
His chosen partner in a titan game
Her will he has made the master of his fate,
Her whim the dispenser of his pleasure and pain;
He has sold himself into her regal power
For any blow or boon that she may choose:
Even in what is suffering to our sense,
He feels the sweetness of her mastering touch,
In all experience meets her blissful hands;
On his heart he bears the happiness of her tread
And the surprise of her arrival's joy
In each event and every moment's chance.
All she can do is marvellous in his sight:
He revels in her, a swimmer in her sea,
A tireless amateur of her world-delight,
He rejoices in her every thought and act
And gives consent to all that she can wish;
Whatever she desires he wills to be:
The Spirit, the innumerable One
He has left behind his lone eternity,
He is an endless birth in endless Time,
Her finite's multitude in an infinite space.

 The master of existence lurks in us
And plays at hide and seek with his own Force;
In Nature's instrument loiters secret God.
The Immanent lives in man as in his house;
He has made the universe his pastime's field,
A vast gymnasium of his works of might.
All-knowing he accepts our darkened state,
Divine, wears shapes of animal or man;
Eternal, he assents to Fate and Time,
Immortal, dallies with mortality.
The All-Conscious ventured into Ignorance,
The All-Blissful bore to be insensible.

Incarnate in a world of strife and pain,
He puts on joy and sorrow like a robe
And drinks experience like a strengthening wine.
He whose transcendence rules the pregnant Vasts,
Prescient now dwells in our subliminal depths,
A luminous individual Power, alone.
  The Absolute, the Perfect, the Alone
Has called out of the Silence his mute Force
Where she lay in the featureless and formless hush
Guarding from Time by her immobile sleep
The ineffable puissance of his solitude.
The Absolute, the Perfect, the Alone
Has entered with his silence into space:
He has fashioned these countless persons of one self;
He lives in all, who lived in his Vast alone;
Space is himself and Time is only he.
The Absolute, the Perfect, the Immune,
One who is in us as our secret self,
Our mask of imperfection has assumed,
He has made this tenement of flesh his own,
His image in the human measure cast
That to his divine measure we might rise;
Then in a figure of divinity
The Maker shall recast us and impose
A plan of godhead on the mortal's mould
Lifting our finite minds to his infinite,
Touching the moment with eternity.
This transfiguration is earth's due to heaven:
A mutual debt binds man to the Supreme:
His nature we must put on as he put ours;
We are sons of God and must be even as he:
His human portion, we must grow divine.
Our life is a paradox with God for key.

  But meanwhile all is a shadow cast by a dream
And to the musing and immobile Spirit
Life and himself don the aspect of a myth,
The burden of a long unmeaning tale.
For the key is hid and by the Inconscient kept;
The secret God beneath the threshold dwells.

In a body obscuring the immortal Spirit
A nameless Resident vesting unseen powers,
With Matter's shapes and motives beyond thought
And the hazard of an unguessed consequence,
An omnipotent indiscernible Influence,
He sits, unfelt by the form in which he lives
And veils his knowledge by the groping mind.
A wanderer in a world his thoughts have made,
He turns in a chiaroscuro of error and truth
To find a wisdom that on high is his.
As one forgetting he searches for himself;
As if he had lost an inner light he seeks:
As a sojourner lingering amid alien scenes
He journeys to a home he knows no more.
His own self's truth he seeks who is the Truth;
He is the Player who became the play,
He is the Thinker who became the thought;
He is the many who was the silent One.
In the symbol figures of the cosmic Force
And in her living and inanimate signs
And in her complex tracery of events
He explores the ceaseless miracle of himself,
Till the thousandfold enigma has been solved
In the single light of an all-witnessing Soul.
    This was his compact with his mighty mate,
For love of her and joined to her for ever
To follow the course of Time's eternity,
Amid magic dramas of her sudden moods
And the surprises of her masked Idea
And the vicissitudes of her vast caprice.
Two seem his goals, yet ever are they one
And gaze at each other over bourneless Time;
Spirit and Matter are their end and source.
A seeker of hidden meanings in life's forms,
Of the great Mother's wide uncharted will
And the rude enigma of her terrestrial ways
He is the explorer and the mariner
On a secret inner ocean without bourne:
He is the adventurer and cosmologist
Of a magic earth's obscure geography.

In her material order's fixed design
Where all seems sure and even when changed, the same,
Even though the end is left for ever unknown
And ever unstable is life's shifting flow,
His paths are found for him by silent fate;
As stations in the ages' weltering flood
Firm lands appear that tempt and stay awhile,
Then new horizons lure the mind's advance.
There comes no close to the finite's boundlessness,
There is no last certitude in which thought can pause
And no terminus of the soul's experience.
A limit, a farness never wholly reached,
An unattained perfection calls to him
From distant boundaries in the Unseen:
A long beginning only has been made.

This is the sailor on the flow of Time,
This is World-Matter's slow discoverer,
Who, launched into this small corporeal birth,
Has learnt his craft in tiny bays of self,
But dares at last unplumbed infinitudes,
A voyager upon eternity's seas.
In his world-adventure's crude initial start
Behold him ignorant of his godhead's force,
Timid initiate of its vast design.
An expert captain of a fragile craft,
A trafficker in small impermanent wares,
At first he hugs the shore and shuns the breadths,
Dares not to affront the far-off perilous main.
He in a petty coastal traffic plies,
His pay doled out from port to neighbour port,
Content with his safe round's unchanging course,
He hazards not the new and the unseen.
But now he hears the sound of larger seas.
A widening world calls him to distant scenes
And journeyings in a larger vision's arc
And peoples unknown and still unvisited shores.
On a commissioned keel his merchant hull
Serves the world's commerce in the riches of Time
Severing the foam of a great land-locked sea

To reach unknown harbour lights in distant climes
And open markets for life's opulent arts,
Rich bales, carved statuettes, hued canvases,
And jewelled toys brought for an infant's play
And perishable products of hard toil
And transient splendours won and lost by the days.
Or passing through a gate of pillar-rocks,
Venturing not yet to cross oceans unnamed
And journey into a dream of distances
He travels close to unfamiliar coasts
And finds new haven in storm-troubled isles,
Or, guided by a sure compass in his thought,
He plunges through a bright haze that hides the stars,
Steering on the trade-routes of Ignorance.
His prow pushes towards undiscovered shores,
He chances on unimagined continents:
A seeker of the islands of the Blest,
He leaves the last lands, crosses the ultimate seas,
He turns to eternal things his symbol quest;
Life changes for him its time-constructed scenes,
Its images veiling infinity.
Earth's borders recede and the terrestrial air
Hangs round him no longer its translucent veil.
He has crossed the limit of mortal thought and hope,
He has reached the world's end and stares beyond;
The eyes of mortal body plunge their gaze
Into Eyes that look upon eternity.
A greater world Time's traveller must explore.
At last he hears a chanting on the heights
And the far speaks and the unknown grows near:
He crosses the boundaries of the unseen
And passes over the edge of mortal sight
To a new vision of himself and things.
He is a spirit in an unfinished world
That knows him not and cannot know itself:
The surface symbol of his goalless quest
Takes deeper meanings to his inner view;
His is a search of darkness for the light,
Of mortal life for immortality.
In the vessel of an earthly embodiment

5

Over the narrow rails of limiting sense
He looks out on the magic waves of Time
Where mind like a moon illumines the world's dark.
There is limned ever retreating from the eyes,
As if in a tenuous misty dream-light drawn,
The outline of a dim mysterious shore.
A sailor on the Inconscient's fathomless sea,
He voyages through a starry world of thought
On Matter's deck to a spiritual sun.
Across the noise and multitudinous cry,
Across the rapt unknowable silences,
Through a strange mid-world under supernal skies,
Beyond earth's longitudes and latitudes,
His goal is fixed outside all present maps.
But none learns whither through the unknown he sails
Or what secret mission the great Mother gave.
In the hidden strength of her omnipotent Will,
Driven by her breath across life's tossing deep,
Through the thunder's roar and through the windless hush,
Through fog and mist where nothing more is seen,
He carries her sealed orders in his breast.
Late will he know, opening the mystic script,
Whether to a blank port in the Unseen
He goes, or armed with her fiat, to discover
A new mind and body in the city of God
And enshrine the Immortal in his glory's house
And make the finite one with Infinity.
Across the salt waste of the endless years
Her ocean winds impel his errant boat,
The cosmic waters plashing as he goes,
A rumour around him and danger and a call.
Always he follows in her force's wake.
He sails through life and death and other life,
He travels on through waking and through sleep.
A power is on him from her occult force
That ties him to his own creation's fate,
And never can the mighty traveller rest
And never can the mystic voyage cease,
Till the nescient dusk is lifted from man's soul
And the morns of God have overtaken his night.

As long as Nature lasts, he too is there;
For this is sure that he and she are one.
Even when he sleeps, he keeps her on his breast:
Whoever leaves her, he will not depart
To repose without her in the Unknowable.
There is a truth to know, a work to do;
Her play is real; a Mystery he fulfils:
There is a plan in the Mother's deep world-whim,
A purpose in her vast and random game.
This ever she meant since the first dawn of life,
This constant will she covered with her sport,
To evoke a person in the impersonal Void,
With the Truth-Light strike earth's massive roots of trance,
Wake a dumb self in the inconscient depths
And raise a lost power from its python sleep
That the eyes of the Timeless might look out from Time
And the world manifest the unveiled Divine.
For this he left his white infinity
And laid on the Spirit the burden of the flesh,
That Godhead's seed might flower in mindless Space.

END OF CANTO FOUR

CANTO FIVE

THE YOGA OF THE KING:
THE YOGA OF THE SPIRIT'S FREEDOM
AND GREATNESS

THIS knowledge first he had of time-born men.
   Admitted through a curtain of bright mind
That hangs between our thought and absolute sight,
He found the occult cave, the mystic door
Near to the well of vision in the soul,
And entered where the Wings of Glory brood
In the sunlit space where all is for ever known.
Indifferent to doubt and to belief,
Avid of the naked real's single shock
He shore the cord of mind that ties the earth-heart
And cast away the yoke of Matter's law.
The body's rules bound not the spirit's powers:
When life had stopped its beats, death broke not in;
He dared to live when breath and thought were still.
Thus could he step into that magic place
Which few can even glimpse with hurried glance
Lifted for a moment from mind's laboured works
And the poverty of Nature's earthly sight.
All that the Gods have learned is there self-known.
There in a hidden chamber closed and mute
Are kept the record graphs of the cosmic scribe,
And there the tables of the sacred Law,
There is the Book of Being's index page,
The text and glossary of the Vedic truth
Are there; the rhythms and metres of the stars
Significant of the movements of our fate:
The symbol powers of number and of form,
And the secret code of the history of the world
And Nature's correspondence with the soul

Are written in the mystic heart of life.
In the glow of the Spirit's room of memories
He could recover the luminous marginal notes
Dotting with light the crabbed ambiguous scroll,
Rescue the preamble and the saving clause
Of the dark Agreement by which all is ruled
That rises from material Nature's sleep
To clothe the Everlasting in new shapes.
He could re-read now and interpret new
Its strange symbol letters, scattered abstruse signs,
Resolve its oracle and its paradox,
Its riddling phrases and its blindfold terms,
The deep oxymoron of its truth's repliques,
And recognise as a just necessity
Its hard conditions for the mighty work,—
Nature's impossible Herculean toil
Only her warlock wisecraft could enforce,
Its law of opposition of the Gods,
Its list of inseparable contraries.
The dumb great Mother in her cosmic trance
Exploiting for creation's joy and pain
Infinity's sanction to the birth of form,
Accepts indomitably to execute
The will to know in an inconscient world,
The will to live under a reign of death,
The thirst for rapture in a heart of flesh,
And works out through the appearance of a soul
By a miraculous birth in plasm and gas
The mystery of God's covenant with the Night.
Once more was heard in the still cosmic Mind
The Eternal's promise to his labouring Force
Inducing the world-passion to begin,
The cry of birth into mortality
And the opening verse of the tragedy of Time.
Out of the depths the world's buried secret rose;
He read the original ukase kept back
In the locked archives of the spirit's crypt,
And saw the signature and fiery seal
Of Wisdom on the dim Power's hooded work
Who builds in Ignorance the steps of Light.

A sleeping deity opened deathless eyes:
He saw the unshaped thought in soulless forms,
Knew Matter pregnant with spiritual sense,
Mind dare the study of the Unknowable,
Life its gestation of the Golden Child.
In the light flooding thought's blank vacancy,
Interpreting the universe by soul signs
He read from within the text of the without:
The riddle grew plain and lost its catch obscure.
A larger lustre lit the mighty page.
A purpose mingled with the whims of Time,
A meaning met the stumbling pace of Chance
And Fate revealed a chain of seeing will;
A conscious wideness filled the old dumb Space.
In the Void he saw throned the Omniscience supreme.

A Will, a hope immense now seized his heart,
And to discern the superhuman's form
He raised his eyes to unseen spiritual heights,
Aspiring to bring down a greater world.
The glory he had glimpsed must be his home.
A brighter heavenlier sun must soon illume
This dusk room with its dark internal stair,
The infant soul in its small nursery school
Mid objects meant for a lesson hardly learned
Outgrow its early grammar of intellect
And its imitation of Earth-Nature's art,
Its earthly dialect to God-language change,
In living symbols study Reality
And learn the logic of the Infinite.
The Ideal must be Nature's common truth,
The body illumined with the indwelling God,
The heart and mind feel one with all that is,
A conscious soul live in a conscious world.
As through a mist a sovereign peak is seen,
The greatness of the eternal Spirit appeared,
Exiled in a fragmented universe
Amid half-semblances of divine things.
These now could serve no more his regal turn:
The Immortal's pride refused the doom to live

A miser of the scanty bargain made
Between our littleness and bounded hopes
And the compassionate Infinitudes.
His height repelled the lowness of earth's state:
A wideness discontented with its frame
Resiled from poor assent to Nature's terms,
The harsh contract spurned and the diminished lease.
Only beginnings are accomplished here;
Our base's Matter seems alone complete,
An absolute machine without a soul.
Or all seems a misfit of half ideas,
Or we saddle with the vice of earthly form
A hurried imperfect glimpse of heavenly things,
Guesses and travesties of celestial types.
Here chaos sorts itself into a world,
A brief formation drifting in the void:
Apings of knowledge, unfinished arcs of power,
Flamings of beauty into earthly shapes,
Love's broken reflexes of unity
Swim, fragment mirrorings of a floating sun.
A packed assemblage of crude tentative lives
Are pieced into a tessellated whole.
There is no perfect answer to our hopes;
There are blind voiceless doors that have no key;
Thought climbs in vain and brings a borrowed light,
Cheated by counterfeits sold to us in life's mart,
Our hearts clutch at a forfeited heavenly bliss.
There is provender for the mind's satiety,
There are thrills of the flesh, but not the soul's desire.
Here even the highest rapture Time can give
Is a mimicry of ungrasped beatitudes,
A mutilated statue of ecstasy,
A wounded happiness that cannot live,
A brief felicity of mind or sense
Thrown by the World-Power to her body-slave,
Or a simulacrum of enforced delight
In the seraglios of Ignorance.
For all we have acquired soon loses worth,
An old disvalued credit in Time's bank,
Imperfection's cheque drawn on the Inconscient.

71

An inconsequence dogs every effort made,
And chaos waits on every cosmos formed:
In each success a seed of failure lurks.
He saw the doubtfulness of all things here,
The incertitude of man's proud confident thought,
The transience of the achievements of his force.
A thinking being in an unthinking world,
An island in the sea of the Unknown,
He is a smallness trying to be great,
An animal with some instincts of a god,
His life a story too common to be told,
His deeds a number summing up to nought,
His consciousness a torch lit to be quenched,
His hope a star above a cradle and grave.
And yet a greater destiny may be his,
For the eternal Spirit is his truth.
He can re-create himself and all around
And fashion new the world in which he lives:
He, ignorant, is the Knower beyond Time,
He is the Self above Nature, above Fate.

His soul retired from all that he had done.
Hushed was the futile din of human toil,
Forsaken wheeled the circle of the days;
In distance sank the crowded tramp of life.
The Silence was his sole companion left.
Impassive he lived immune from earthly hopes,
A figure in the ineffable Witness' shrine
Pacing the vast cathedral of his thoughts
Under its arches dim with infinity
And heavenward brooding of invisible wings.
A call was on him from intangible heights;
Indifferent to the little outpost Mind,
He dwelt in the wideness of the Eternal's reign.
His being now exceeded thinkable Space,
His boundless thought was neighbour to cosmic sight:
A universal light was in his eyes,
A golden influx flowed through heart and brain;
A force came down into his mortal limbs,
A current from eternal seas of Bliss;

He felt the invasion and the nameless joy.
Aware of his occult omnipotent Source,
Allured by the omniscient Ecstasy,
A living centre of the Illimitable
Widened to equate with the world's circumference,
He turned to his immense spiritual fate.
Abandoned on a canvas of torn air,
A picture lost in far and fading streaks,
The earth-nature's summits sank below his feet:
He climbed to meet the infinite more above.
The Immobile's ocean-silence saw him pass,
An arrow leaping through eternity
Suddenly shot from the tense bow of Time,
A ray returning to its parent sun.
Opponent of that glory of escape,
The black Inconscient swung its dragon tail
Lashing a slumberous Infinite by its force
Into the deep obscurities of form:
Death lay beneath him like a gate of sleep.
One-pointed to the immaculate Delight,
Questing for God as for a splendid prey,
He mounted burning like a cone of fire.
To a few is given that godlike rare release.
One among many thousands never touched,
Engrossed in the external world's design,
Is chosen by a secret witness Eye
And driven by a pointing hand of Light
Across his soul's unmapped immensitudes.
A pilgrim of the everlasting Truth,
Our measures cannot hold his measureless mind;
He has turned from the voices of the narrow realm
And left the little lane of human Time.
In the hushed precincts of a vaster plan
He treads the vestibules of the Unseen,
Or listens following a bodiless Guide
To a lonely cry in boundless vacancy.
All the deep cosmic murmur falling still,
He lives in the hush before the world was born,
His soul left naked to the timeless One.
Far from compulsion of created things

Thought and its shadowy idols disappear,
The moulds of form and person are undone.
The ineffable Wideness knows him for its own.
A lone forerunner of the Godward earth,
Among the symbols of yet unshaped things
Watched by closed eyes, mute faces of the Unborn,
He journeys to meet the Incommunicable,
Hearing the echo of his single steps
In the eternal courts of Solitude.
A nameless Marvel fills the motionless hours.
His spirit mingles with Eternity's heart
And bears the silence of the Infinite.

In a divine retreat from mortal thought,
In a prodigious gesture of soul-sight,
His being towered into pathless heights,
Naked of its vesture of humanity.
As thus it rose, to meet him bare and pure
A strong Descent leaped down. A Might, a Flame,
A Beauty half-visible with deathless eyes,
A violent Ecstasy, a Sweetness dire,
Enveloped him with its stupendous limbs
And penetrated nerve and heart and brain
That thrilled and fainted with the epiphany:
His nature shuddered in the Unknown's grasp.
In a moment shorter than Death, longer than Time,
By a power more ruthless than Love, happier than Heaven,
Taken sovereignly into eternal arms,
Haled and coerced by a stark absolute bliss,
In a whirlwind circuit of delight and force
Hurried into unimaginable depths,
Upborne into immeasurable heights,
It was torn out from its mortality
And underwent a new and bourneless change.
An Omniscient knowing without sight or thought,
An indecipherable Omnipotence,
A mystic Form that could contain the worlds,
Yet make one human breast its passionate shrine,
Drew him out of his seeking loneliness
Into the magnitudes of God's embrace.

As when a timeless Eye annuls the hours
Abolishing the agent and the act,
So now his spirit shone out wide, blank, pure:
His wakened mind became an empty slate
On which the Universal and Sole could write.
All that represses our fallen consciousness
Was taken from him like a forgotten load:
A fire that seemed the body of a god
Consumed the limiting figures of the past
And made large room for a new self to live.
Eternity's contact broke the moulds of sense.
A greater force than the earthly held his limbs,
Huge workings bared his undiscovered sheaths,
Strange energies wrought and screened tremendous hands,
Unwound the triple cord of mind and freed
The heavenly wideness of a Godhead's gaze.
As through a dress the wearer's shape is seen,
There reached through forms to the hidden absolute
A cosmic feeling and transcendent sight.
Increased and heightened were the instruments.
Illusion lost her aggrandising lens;
As from her failing hand the measures fell,
Atomic looked the things that loomed so large.
The little ego's ring could join no more;
In the enormous spaces of the self
The body now seemed only a wandering shell,
His mind the many-frescoed outer court
Of an imperishable Inhabitant:
His spirit breathed a superhuman air.
The imprisoned deity rent its magic fence
As with a sound of thunder and of seas,
Vast barriers crashed around the huge escape.
Immutably coeval with the world,
Circle and end of every hope and toil
Inexorably drawn round thought and act,
The fixed immovable peripheries
Effaced themselves beneath the Incarnate's tread.
The dire velamen and the bottomless crypt
Between which life and thought for ever move,
Forbidden still to cross the dim dread bounds,

The guardian darknesses mute and formidable,
Empowered to circumscribe the wingless spirit
In the boundaries of Mind and Ignorance,
Protecting no more a dual eternity
Vanished rescinding their enormous role:
Once figure of creation's vain ellipse,
The expanding zero lost its giant curve.
The old adamantine vetoes stood no more:
Overpowered were earth and Nature's obsolete rule;
The python coils of the restricting Law
Could not restrain the swift arisen God:
Abolished were the scripts of destiny.
There was no small death-hunted creature more,
No fragile form of being to preserve
From an all-swallowing Immensity.
The great hammer-beats of a pent-up world-heart
Burst open the narrow dams that keep us safe
Against the forces of the universe.
The soul and cosmos faced as equal powers.
A boundless being in a measureless Time
Invaded Nature with the infinite;
He saw unpathed, unwalled his titan scope.

    All was uncovered to his sealless eye.
A secret Nature stripped of her defence,
Once in a dreaded half-light formidable,
Overtaken in her mighty privacy
Lay bare to the burning splendour of his will.
In shadowy chambers lit by a strange sun
And opening hardly to hid mystic keys
Her perilous arcanes and hooded Powers
Confessed the advent of a mastering Mind
And bore the compulsion of a time-born gaze.
Incalculable in their wizard modes,
Immediate and invincible in the act,
Her secret strengths native to greater worlds
Lifted above our needy limited scope,
The occult privilege of demigods
And the sure power-pattern of her cryptic signs,
Her diagrams of geometric force,

Her potencies of marvel-fraught design
Courted employment by an earth-nursed might.
A conscious Nature's quick machinery
Armed with a latent splendour of miracle
The prophet-passion of a seeing Mind,
And the lightning bareness of a free soul-force.
All once impossible deemed could now become
A natural limb of possibility,
A new domain of normalcy supreme.
An almighty occultist erects in space
This seeming outward world which tricks the sense;
He weaves his hidden threads of consciousness,
He builds bodies for his shapeless energy;
Out of the unformed and vacant Vast he has made
His sorcery of solid images,
His magic of formative number and design,
The fixed irrational links none can annul,
This criss-cross tangle of invisible laws;
His infallible rules, his covered processes,
Achieve unerringly an inexplicable
Creation where our error carves dead frames
Of knowledge for a living ignorance.
In her mystery's moods divorced from the Maker's laws
She too as sovereignly creates her field,
Her will shaping the undetermined vasts,
Making a finite of infinity;
She too can make an order of her caprice,
As if her rash superb wagered to outvie
The veiled Creator's cosmic secrecies.
The rapid footsteps of her phantasy,
Amid whose falls wonders like flowers rise,
Are surer than reason, defter than device
And swifter than Imagination's wings.
All she new-fashions by the thought and word
Compels all substance by her wand of Mind.
Mind is a mediator divinity:
Its powers can undo all Nature's work:
Mind can suspend or change earth's concrete law.
Affranchised from earth-habit's drowsy seal
The leaden grip of Matter it can break;

Indifferent to the angry stare of Death,
It can immortalise a moment's work:
A simple fiat of its thinking force,
The casual pressure of its slight assent
Can liberate the Energy dumb and pent
Within its chambers of mysterious trance:
It makes the body's sleep a puissant arm,
Holds still the breath, the beatings of the heart,
While the unseen is found, the impossible done,
Communicates without means the unspoken thought;
It moves events by its bare silent will,
Acts at a distance without hands or feet.
This giant Ignorance, this dwarfish Life
It can illumine with a prophet sight,
Invoke the bacchic rapture, the Fury's goad,
In our body arouse the demon or the god,
Call in the Omniscient and Omnipotent,
Awake a forgotten Almightiness within.
In its own plane a shining emperor,
Even in this rigid realm, Mind can be king:
The logic of its demigod Idea,
In the leap of a transitional moment brings
Surprises of creation never achieved
Even by Matter's strange unconscious skill.
All's miracle here and can by miracle change.
This is that secret Nature's edge of might.
On the margin of great immaterial planes,
In kingdoms of an untrammelled glory of force,
Where Mind is master of the life and form
And soul fulfils its thoughts by its own power,
She meditates upon mighty words and looks
On the unseen links that join the parted spheres.
Thence to the initiate who observes her laws
She brings the light of her mysterious realms:
Here where he stands, his feet on a prostrate world,
His mind no more cast into Matter's mould,
Over their bounds in spurts of splendid strength
She carries their magician processes
And the formulas of their stupendous speech,
Till heaven and hell become purveyors to earth

And the universe the slave of mortal will.
A mediatrix with veiled and nameless gods
Whose alien will touches our human life,
Imitating the World-Magician's ways
She invents for her self-bound free will its grooves
And feigns for magic's freaks a binding cause.
All worlds she makes the partners of her deeds,
Accomplices of her mighty violence,
Her daring leaps into the impossible:
From every source she has taken her cunning means,
She draws from the free-love marriage of the planes
Elements for her creation's tour-de-force:
A wonder-weft of knowledge incalculable,
A compendium of divine invention's feats
She has combined to make the unreal true
Or liberate suppressed reality:
In her unhedged Circean wonderland
Pell-mell she shepherds her occult mightinesses;
Her mnemonics of the craft of the Infinite,
Jets of the screened subliminal's caprice,
Tags of the gramarye of Inconscience,
Freedom of a sovereign Truth without a law,
Thoughts that were born in the immortals' world,
Oracles that break out from behind the shrine,
Warnings from the daemonic inner voice
And peeps and lightning-leaps of prophecy
And intimations to the inner ear,
Abrupt interventions stark and absolute
And the superconscient's unaccountable acts,
Have woven her balanced web of miracles
And the weird technique of her tremendous art.
This bizarre kingdom passed into his charge.
As one resisting more the more she loves,
Her great possessions and her power and law
She gave, compelled, with a reluctant joy;
Herself she gave for rapture and for use.
Absolved from aberrations in deep ways,
The ends she recovered for which she was made:
She turned against the evil she had helped
Her engined wrath, her invisible means to slay;

Her dangerous moods and arbitrary force
She surrendered to the service of the soul
And the control of a spiritual will.
A greater despot tamed her despotism.
Assailed, surprised in the fortress of her self,
Conquered by her own unexpected King,
Fulfilled and ransomed by her servitude,
She yielded in a vanquished ecstasy,
Her sealed hieratic wisdom forced from her,
Fragments of the mystery of omnipotence.

A border sovereign is the occult Force.
A threshold guardian of the earth-scene's Beyond,
She has canalised the outbreaks of the Gods
And cut through vistas of intuitive sight
A long road of shimmering discoveries.
The worlds of a marvellous Unknown were near,
Behind her an ineffable Presence stood:
Her reign received their mystic influences,
Their lion-forces crouched beneath her feet;
The future sleeps unknown behind their doors.
Abysms infernal gaped round the soul's steps
And called to its mounting vision peaks divine:
An endless climb and adventure of the Idea
There tirelessly tempted the explorer mind.
And countless voices visited the charmed ear;
A million figures passed and were seen no more.
This was a forefront of God's thousandfold house,
Beginnings of the half-screened Invisible.
A magic porch of entry glimmering
Quivered in a penumbra of screened Light,
A court of the mystical traffic of the worlds,
A balcony and miraculous façade.
Above her lightened high immensities;
All the unknown looked out from boundlessness:
It lodged upon an edge of hourless Time,
Gazing out of some everlasting Now,
Its shadows gleaming with the birth of gods,
Its bodies signalling the Bodiless,
Its foreheads glowing with the Oversoul,

Its forms projected from the Unknowable,
Its eyes dreaming of the Ineffable,
Its faces staring into eternity.
Life in him learned its huge subconscient rear;
The little fronts unlocked to the unseen Vasts:
Her gulfs stood nude, her far transcendences
Flamed in transparencies of crowded light.

    A giant order was discovered here
Of which the tassel and extended fringe
Are the scant stuff of our material lives.
This overt universe whose figures hide
The secrets merged in superconscient light,
Wrote clear the letters of its glowing code:
A map of subtle signs surpassing thought
Was hung upon a wall of inmost mind.
Illumining the world's concrete images
Into significant symbols by its gloss,
It offered to the intuitive exegete
Its reflex of the eternal Mystery.
Ascending and descending twixt life's poles
The serried kingdoms of the graded Law
Plunged from the Everlasting into Time,
Then glad of a glory of multitudinous mind
And rich with life's adventure and delight
And packed with the beauty of Matter's shapes and hues
Climbed back from Time into undying Self,
Up a golden ladder carrying the Soul,
Tying with diamond threads the Spirit's extremes.
In this drop from consciousness to consciousness
Each leaned on the occult Inconscient's power,
The fountain of its needed Ignorance,
Archmason of the limits by which it lives.
In this soar from consciousness to consciousness
Each lifted tops to That from which it came,
Origin of all that it had ever been
And home of all that it could still become.
An organ scale of the Eternal's acts,
Mounting to their climax in an endless Calm,
Paces of the many-visaged Wonderful,

Predestined stadia of the evolving Way,
Measures of the stature of the growing soul,
They interpreted existence to itself
And, mediating twixt the heights and deeps,
United the veiled married opposites
And linked creation to the Ineffable.
A last high world was seen where all worlds meet;
In its summit gleam where Night is not nor Sleep,
The light began of the Trinity supreme.
All there discovered what it seeks for here.
It freed the finite into boundlessness
And rose into its own eternities.
The Inconscient found its heart of consciousness,
The idea and feeling groping in Ignorance
At last clutched passionately the body of Truth,
The music born in Matter's silences
Plucked nude out of the Ineffable's fathomlessness
The meaning it had held but could not voice;
The perfect rhythm now only sometimes dreamed
An answer brought to the torn earth's hungry need
Rending the night that had concealed the Unknown,
Giving to her her lost forgotten soul.
A grand solution closed the long impasse
In which the heights of mortal effort end.
A reconciling Wisdom looked on life;
It took the striving undertones of mind
And took the confused refrain of human hopes
And made of them a sweet and happy call:
It lifted from an underground of pain
The inarticulate murmur of our lives
And found for it a sense illimitable.
A mighty oneness its perpetual theme,
It caught the soul's faint scattered utterances,
Read hardly twixt our lines of rigid thought
Or mid this drowse and coma on Matter's breast
Heard like disjointed mutterings in sleep;
It grouped the golden links that they had lost
And showed to them their divine unity,
Saving from the error of divided self
The deep spiritual cry in all that is.

All the great Words that toiled to express the One
Were lifted into an absoluteness of light,
An ever-burning Revelation's fire
And the immortality of the eternal Voice.
There was no quarrel more of truth with truth;
The endless chapter of their differences
Retold in light by an omniscient Scribe,
Travelled through difference towards unity,
Mind's winding search lost every tinge of doubt
Led to its end by an all-seeing speech
That garbed the initial and original thought
With the finality of an ultimate phrase:
United were Time's creative mood and tense
To the style and syntax of Identity.
A paean swelled from the lost musing deeps;
An anthem pealed to the triune ecstasies,
A cry of the moments to the Immortal's bliss.
As if the strophes of a cosmic ode,
A hierarchy of climbing harmonies
Peopled with voices and with visages
Aspired in a crescendo of the Gods
From Matter's abysses to the Spirit's peaks.
Above were the Immortal's changeless seats,
White chambers of dalliance with Eternity
And the stupendous gates of the Alone.
Across the unfolding of the seas of self
Appeared the deathless countries of the One.
A many-miracled consciousness unrolled
Vast aim and process and unfettered norms,
A larger Nature's great familiar roads.
Affranchised from the net of earthly sense
Calm continents of potency were glimpsed;
Homelands of beauty shut to human eyes,
Half-seen at first through wonder's gleaming lids,
Surprised the vision with felicity;
Sunbelts of knowledge, moonbelts of delight
Stretched out in an ecstasy of widenesses
Beyond our indigent corporeal range.
There he could enter, there awhile abide.
A voyager upon uncharted routes

Fronting the viewless danger of the Unknown,
Adventuring across enormous realms,
He broke into another Space and Time.

END OF CANTO FIVE

END OF BOOK ONE

BOOK TWO

The Book of the Traveller of the Worlds

CANTO ONE

THE WORLD-STAIR

A LONE he moved watched by the infinity
  Around him and the Unknowable above.
All could be seen that shuns the mortal eye,
All could be known the mind has never grasped;
All could be done no mortal will can dare.
A limitless movement filled a limitless peace.
In a profound existence beyond earth's
Parent or kin to our ideas and dreams
Where Space is a vast experiment of the soul,
In a deep oneness of all things that are,
The universe of the Unknown arose.
A self-creation without end or pause
Revealed the grandeurs of the Infinite:
It flung into the hazards of its play
A million moods, a myriad energies,
The world-shapes that are fancies of its Truth
And the formulas of the freedom of its Force.
It poured into the Ever-stable's flux
A bacchic rapture and revel of Ideas,
A passion and motion of everlastingness.
There rose unborn into the Unchanging's surge
Thoughts that abide in their deathless consequence,
Words that immortal last though fallen mute,
Acts that brought out from Silence its dumb sense,
Lines that convey the inexpressible.
The Eternal's stillness saw in unmoved joy
His universal Power at work display
In plots of pain and dramas of delight
The wonder and beauty of her will to be.
All, even pain, was the soul's pleasure here;

87

Here all experience was a single plan,
The thousandfold expression of the One.
All came at once into his single view;
Nothing escaped his vast intuitive sight,
Nothing drew near he could not feel as kin:
He was one spirit with that immensity.
Images in a supernal consciousness
Embodying the Unborn who never dies,
The structured visions of the cosmic Self
Alive with the touch of being's eternity
Looked at him like form-bound spiritual thoughts
Figuring the movements of the Ineffable.
Aspects of being donned world-outline; forms
That open moving doors on things divine,
Became familiar to his hourly sight;
The symbols of the Spirit's reality,
The living bodies of the Bodiless
Grew near to him, his daily associates.
The exhaustless seeings of the unsleeping Mind,
Letterings of its contact with the invisible,
Surrounded him with countless pointing signs;
The voices of a thousand realms of Life
Missioned to him her mighty messages.
The heaven-hints that invade our earthly lives,
The dire imaginations dreamed by Hell,
Which if enacted and experienced here
Our dulled capacity soon would cease to feel
Or our mortal frailty could not long endure,
Were set in their sublime proportions there.
There lived out in their self-born atmosphere,
They resumed their topless pitch and native power;
Their fortifying stress upon the soul
Bit deep into the ground of consciousness
The passion and purity of their extremes,
The absoluteness of their single cry
And the sovereign sweetness or violent poetry
Of their beautiful or terrible delight.
All thought can know or widest sight perceive
And all that thought and sight can never know,
All things occult and rare, remote and strange

Were near to heart's contact, felt by spirit-sense.
Asking for entry at his nature's gates
They crowded the widened spaces of his mind,
His self-discovery's flaming witnesses,
Offering their marvel and their multitude.
These now became new portions of himself,
The figures of his spirit's greater life,
The moving scenery of his large time-walk
Or the embroidered tissue of his sense:
These took the place of intimate human things
And moved as close companions of his thoughts,
Or were his soul's natural environment.
Tireless the heart's adventure of delight,
Endless the kingdoms of the Spirit's bliss,
Unnumbered tones struck from one harmony's strings;
Each to its wide-winged universal poise,
Its fathomless feeling of the All in one,
Brought notes of some perfection yet unseen,
Its single retreat into Truth's secrecies,
Its happy sidelight on the Infinite.
All was found there the Unique had dreamed and made
Tinging with ceaseless rapture and surprise
And an opulent beauty of passionate difference
The recurring beat that moments God in Time.
Only was missing the sole timeless Word
That carries eternity in its lonely sound,
The Idea self-luminous key to all ideas,
The integer of the Spirit's perfect sum
That equates the unequal All to the equal One,
The single sign interpreting every sign,
The absolute index to the Absolute.

There walled apart by its own innerness
In a mystical barrage of dynamic light
He saw a lone immense high-curved world-pile
Erect like a mountain chariot of the Gods
Motionless under an inscrutable sky.
As if from Matter's plinth and viewless base
To a top as viewless, a carved sea of worlds
Climbing with foam-maned waves to the Supreme

Ascended towards breadths immeasurable;
It hoped to soar into the Ineffable's reign:
A hundred levels raised it to the Unknown.
So it towered up to heights intangible
And disappeared in the hushed conscious Vast
As climbs a storeyed temple-tower to heaven
Built by the aspiring soul of man to live
Near to his dream of the Invisible.
Infinity calls to it as it dreams and climbs;
Its spire touches the apex of the world;
Mounting into great voiceless stillnesses
It marries the earth to screened eternities.
Amid the many systems of the One
Made by an interpreting creative joy
Alone it points us to our journey back
Out of our long self-loss in Nature's deeps;
Planted on earth it holds in it all realms:
It is a brief compendium of the Vast.
This was the single stair to being's goal.
A summary of the stages of the spirit,
Its copy of the cosmic hierarchies
Refashioned in our secret air of self
A subtle pattern of the universe.
It is within, below, without, above.
Acting upon this visible Nature's scheme
It wakens our earth-matter's heavy doze
To think and feel and to react to joy;
It models in us our diviner parts,
Lifts mortal mind into a greater air,
Makes yearn this life of flesh to intangible aims,
Links the body's death with immortality's call:
Out of the swoon of the Inconscience
It labours towards a superconscient Light.
If earth were all and this were not in her,
Thought could not be nor life-delight's response:
Only material forms could then be her guests
Driven by an inanimate world-force.
Earth by this golden superfluity
Bore thinking man and more than man shall bear;
This higher scheme of being is our cause

And holds the key to our ascending fate;
It calls out of our dense mortality
The conscious spirit nursed in Matter's house.
The living symbol of these conscious planes,
Its influences and godheads of the unseen,
Its unthought logic of Reality's acts
Arisen from the unspoken truth in things,
Have fixed our inner life's slow-scaled degrees.
Its steps are paces of the soul's return
From the deep adventure of material birth,
A ladder of delivering ascent
And rungs that Nature climbs to deity.
Once in the vigil of a deathless gaze
These grades had marked her giant downward plunge,
The wide and prone leap of a godhead's fall.
Our life is a holocaust of the Supreme.
The great World-Mother by her sacrifice
Has made her soul the body of our state;
Accepting sorrow and unconsciousness
Divinity's lapse from its own splendours wove
The many-patterned ground of all we are.
An idol of self is our mortality.
Our earth is a fragment and a residue;
Her power is packed with the stuff of greater worlds
And steeped in their colour-lustres dimmed by her drowse;
An atavism of higher births is hers,
Her sleep is stirred by their buried memories
Recalling the lost spheres from which they fell.
Unsatisfied forces in her bosom move;
They are partners of her greater growing fate
And her return to immortality;
They consent to share her doom of birth and death;
They kindle partial gleams of the All and drive
Her blind laborious spirit to compose
A meagre image of the mighty Whole.
The calm and luminous Intimacy within
Approves her work and guides the unseeing Power.
His vast design accepts a puny start.
An attempt, a drawing half-done is the world's life;
Its lines doubt their concealed significance,

Its curves join not their high-intended close.
Yet some first image of greatness trembles there,
And when the ambiguous crowded parts have met
The many-toned unity to which they moved,
The Artist's joy shall laugh at reason's rules;
The divine intention suddenly shall be seen,
The end vindicate intuition's sure technique.
A graph shall be of many meeting worlds,
A cube and union crystal of the gods;
A Mind shall think behind Nature's mindless mask,
A conscious Vast fill the old dumb brute Space.
This faint and fluid sketch of soul called man
Shall stand out on the background of long Time
A glowing epitome of eternity,
A little point reveal the infinitudes.
A Mystery's process is the universe.
At first was laid a strange anomalous base,
A void, a cipher of some secret Whole,
Where zero held infinity in its sum
And All and Nothing were a single term,
An eternal negative, a matrix Nought:
Into its forms the Child is ever born
Who lives for ever in the vasts of God.
A slow reversal's movement then took place:
A gas belched out from some invisible Fire,
Of its dense rings were formed these million stars;
Upon earth's new-born soil God's tread was heard.
Across the thick smoke of earth's ignorance
A Mind began to see and look at forms
And groped for knowledge in the nescient Night:
Caught in a blind stone-grip Force worked its plan
And made in sleep this huge mechanical world,
That Matter might grow conscious of its soul
And like a busy midwife the life-power
Deliver the zero carrier of the All.
Because eternal eyes turned on earth's gulfs
The lucent clarity of a pure regard
And saw a shadow of the Unknowable
Mirrored in the Inconscient's boundless sleep,
Creation's search for self began its stir.

A spirit dreamed in the crude cosmic whirl,
Mind flowed unknowing in the sap of life
And Matter's breasts suckled the divine Idea.
A miracle of the Absolute was born,
Infinity put on a finite soul,
All ocean lived within a wandering drop,
A time-made body housed the Illimitable.
To live this Mystery out our souls came here.

    A Seer within who knows the ordered plan
Concealed behind our momentary steps,
Inspires our ascent to viewless heights
As once the abysmal leap to birth and life.
His call had reached the Traveller in Time.
Apart in an unfathomed loneliness,
He travelled in his mute and single strength
Bearing the burden of the world's desire.
A formless Stillness called, a nameless Light.
Above him was the white immobile Ray,
Around him the eternal Silences.
No term was fixed to the high-pitched attempt;
World after world disclosed its guarded powers,
Heaven after heaven its deep beatitudes,
But still the invisible Magnet drew his soul.
A figure sole on Nature's giant stair,
He mounted towards an indiscernible end
On the bare summit of created things.

END OF CANTO ONE

THE KINGDOM OF SUBTLE MATTER

IN the impalpable field of secret self,
  This little outer being's vast support
Parted from vision by earth's solid fence,
He came into a magic crystal air
And found a life that lived not by the flesh,
A light that made visible immaterial things.
A fine degree in wonder's hierarchy,
The kingdom of subtle Matter's faery craft
Outlined against a sky of vivid hues,
Leaping out of a splendour-trance and haze,
The wizard revelation of its front.
A world of lovelier forms lies near to ours,
Where, undisguised by earth's deforming sight,
All shapes are beautiful and all things true.
In that lucent ambiance mystically clear
The eyes were doors to a celestial sense,
Hearing was music and the touch a charm
And the heart drew a deeper breath of power.
There dwell earth-nature's shining origins:
The perfect plans on which she moulds her works,
The distant outcomes of her travailing force
Repose in a framework of established fate.
Attempted vainly now or won in vain,
Already were mapped and scheduled there the time
And the figure of her future sovereignties
In the sumptuous lineaments traced by desire.
The golden issue of mind's labyrinth plots,
The riches unfound or still uncaught by our lives
Unsullied by the attaint of mortal thought
Abide in that pellucid atmosphere.

Our vague beginnings are overtaken there,
Our middle terms sketched out in prescient lines,
Our finished ends anticipated live.
This brilliant roof of our descending plane,
Intercepting the free boon of heaven's air,
Admits small inrushes of a mighty breath
Or fragrant circuits through gold lattices; *souls that are open*
It shields our ceiling of terrestrial mind
From deathless suns and the streaming of God's rain,
Yet canalises a strange irised glow,
And bright dews drip from the Immortal's sky.
A passage for the Powers that move our days,
Occult behind this grosser Nature's walls,
A gossamer marriage-hall of Mind with Form
Is hidden by a tapestry of dreams;
Heaven's meanings steal through it as through a veil,
Its inner sight sustains this outer scene.
A finer consciousness with happier lines,
It has a tact our touch cannot attain,
A purity of sense we never feel;
Its intercession with the eternal Ray
Inspires our transient earth's brief-lived attempts
At beauty and the perfect shape of things.
In rooms of the young divinity of power
And early play of the eternal Child
The embodiments of his outwinging thoughts
Laved in a bright everlasting wonder's tints
And lulled by whispers of that lucid air
Take dream-hued rest like birds on timeless trees
Before they dive to float on earth-time's sea.
All that here seems has lovelier semblance there.
Whatever our hearts conceive, our heads create,
Some high original beauty forfeiting,
Thence exiled here consents to an earthly tinge.
Whatever is here of visible charm and grace
Finds there its faultless and immortal lines;
All that is beautiful here is there divine.
Figures are there undreamed by mortal mind:
Bodies that have no earthly counterpart
Traverse the inner eye's illumined trance

95

And ravish the heart with their celestial tread
Persuading heaven to inhabit that wonder sphere.
The future's marvels wander in its gulfs;
Things old and new are fashioned in those depths:
A carnival of beauty crowds the heights
In that magic kingdom of ideal sight.
In its antechambers of splendid privacy
Matter and soul in conscious union meet
Like lovers in a lonely secret place:
In the clasp of a passion not yet unfortunate
They join their strength and sweetness and delight
And mingling make the high and low worlds one.
Intruder from the formless Infinite
Daring to break into the Inconscient's reign,
The spirit's leap towards body touches ground.
As yet unwrapped in earthly lineaments,
Already it wears outlasting death and birth,
Convincing the abyss by heavenly form,
A covering of its immortality
Alive to the lustre of the wearer's rank,
Fit to endure the rub of Change and Time.
A tissue mixed of the soul's radiant light
And Matter's substance of sign-burdened Force,—
Imagined vainly in our mind's thin air
An abstract phantasm mould of mental make,—
It feels what earthly bodies cannot feel
And is more real than this grosser frame.
After the falling of mortality's cloak
Lightened is its weight to heighten its ascent;
Refined to the touch of finer environments
It drops old patterned palls of denser stuff,
Cancels the grip of earth's descending pull
And bears the soul from world to higher world,
Till in the naked ether of the peaks
The spirit simplicity alone is left,
The eternal being's first transparent robe.
But when it must come back to its mortal load
And the hard ensemble of earth's experience,
Then its return resumes that heavier dress.
For long before earth's solid vest was forged

By the technique of the atomic Void,
A lucent envelope of self-disguise
Was woven round the secret spirit in things.
The subtle realms from those bright sheaths are made.
This wonder-world with all its radiant boon
Of vision and inviolate happiness,
Only for expression cares and perfect form;
Fair on its peaks, it has dangerous nether planes;
Its light draws towards the verge of Nature's lapse;
It lends beauty to the terror of the gulfs
And fascinating eyes to perilous Gods,
Invests with grace the demon and the snake.
Its trance imposes earth's inconscience,
Immortal it weaves for us death's sombre robe
And authorises our mortality.
This medium serves a greater Consciousness:
A vessel of its concealed autocracy,
It is the subtle ground of Matter's worlds,
It is the immutable in their mutable forms,
In the folds of its creative memory
It guards the deathless type of perishing things:
Its lowered potencies found our fallen strengths;
Its thought invents our reasoned ignorance;
Its sense fathers our body's reflexes.
Our secret breath of untried mightier force,
The lurking sun of an instant's inner sight,
Its fine suggestions are a covert fount
For our iridescent rich imaginings
Touching things common with transfiguring hues
Till even earth's mud grows rich and warm with the skies
And a glory gleams from the soul's decadence.
Its knowledge is our error's starting-point;
Its beauty dons our mud-mask ugliness,
Its artist good begins our evil's tale.
A heaven of creative truths above,
A cosmos of harmonious dreams between,
A chaos of dissolving forms below,
It plunges lost in our inconscient base.
Out of its fall our denser Matter came.

Thus taken was God's plunge into the Night.
This fallen world became a nurse of souls
Inhabited by concealed divinity.
A Being woke and lived in the meaningless void,
A world-wide Nescience strove towards life and thought,
A Consciousness plucked out from mindless sleep.
All here is driven by an insentient will.
Thus fallen, inconscient, frustrate, dense, inert,
Sunk into inanimate and torpid drowse
Earth lay, a drudge of sleep, forced to create
By a subconscient yearning memory
Left from a happiness dead before she was born,
An alien wonder on her senseless breast.
This mire must harbour the orchid and the rose,
From her blind unwilling substance must emerge
A beauty that belongs to happier spheres.
This is the destiny bequeathed to her,
As if a slain god left a golden trust
To a blind force and an imprisoned soul.
An immortal godhead's perishable parts
She must reconstitute from fragments lost,
Re-word from a document complete elsewhere
Her doubtful title to her divine Name.
A residue her sole inheritance,
All things she carries in her shapeless dust.
Her giant energy tied to petty forms
In the slow tentative motion of her power
With only frail blunt instruments for use,
She has accepted as her nature's need
And given to man as his stupendous work
A labour to the gods impossible.
A life living hardly in a field of death
Its portion claims of immortality;
A brute half-conscious body serves as means
A mind that must recover a knowledge lost
Held in stone-grip by the world's inconscience,
And wearing still these countless knots of Law
A spirit bound stand up as Nature's king.

A mighty kinship is this daring's cause.

All we attempt in this imperfect world,
Looks forward or looks back beyond Time's gloss
To its pure idea and firm inviolate type
In an absolute creation's flawless skill.
To seize the absolute in shapes that pass,
To feel the eternal's touch in time-made things,
This is the law of all perfection here.
A fragment here is caught of heaven's design;
Else could we never hope for greater life
And ecstasy and glory could not be.
Even in the littleness of our mortal state,
Even in this prison-house of outer form,
A brilliant passage for the infallible Flame
Is driven through gross walls of nerve and brain,
A Splendour presses or a Power breaks through,
Earth's great dull barrier is removed awhile,
The inconscient seal is lifted from our eyes
And we grow vessels of creative might.
The enthusiasm of a divine surprise
Pervades our life, a mystic stir is felt,
A joyful anguish trembles in our limbs;
A dream of beauty dances through the heart,
A thought from the eternal Mind draws near,
Intimations cast from the Invisible
Awaking from Infinity's sleep come down,
Symbols of That which never yet was made.
But soon the inert flesh responds no more,
Then sinks the sacred orgy of delight,
The blaze of passion and the tide of power
Are taken from us and, though a glowing form
Abides astonishing earth, imagined supreme,
Too little of what was meant has left a trace.
Earth's eyes half see, her forces half create;
Her rarest works are copies of heaven's art.
A radiance of a golden artifice,
A masterpiece of inspired device and rule,
Her forms hide what they house and only mime
The unseized miracle of self-born shapes
That live for ever in the Eternal's gaze.
Here in a difficult half-finished world

Is a slow toiling of unconscious Powers;
Here is man's ignorant divining mind,
His genius born from an inconscient soil.
To copy on earth's copies is his art.
For when he strives for things surpassing earth,
Too rude the workman's tools, too crude his stuff,
And hardly with his heart's blood he achieves
His transient house of the divine Idea,
His figure of a Time-inn for the Unborn.
Our being thrills with high far memories
And would bring down their dateless meanings here,
But, too divine for earthly Nature's scheme,
Beyond our reach the eternal marvels blaze.
Absolute they dwell, unborn, immutable,
Immaculate in the Spirit's deathless air,
Immortal in a world of motionless Time
And an unchanging muse of deep self-space.
Only when we have climbed above ourselves,
A line of the Transcendent meets our road
And joins us to the timeless and the true;
It brings to us the inevitable word,
The godlike act, the thoughts that never die.
A ripple of light and glory wraps the brain,
And travelling down the moment's vanishing route
The figures of eternity arrive.
As the mind's visitors or the heart's guests
They espouse our mortal brevity awhile,
Or seldom in some rare delivering glimpse
Are caught by our vision's delicate surmise.
Although beginnings only and first attempts,
These glimmerings point to the secret of our birth
And the hidden miracle of our destiny.
What we are there and here on earth shall be
Is imaged in a contact and a call.
As yet earth's imperfection is our sphere,
Our nature's glass shows not our real self;
That greatness still abides held back within.
Earth's doubting future hides our heritage:
The Light now distant shall grow native here,
The Strength that visits us our comrade power;

The Ineffable shall find a secret voice,
The Imperishable burn through Matter's screen
Making this mortal body godhead's robe.
The Spirit's greatness is our timeless source
And it shall be our crown in endless Time.
A vast Unknown is round us and within;
All things are wrapped in the dynamic One:
A subtle link of union joins all life.
Thus all creation is a single chain:
We are not left alone in a closed scheme
Between a driving of inconscient Force
And an incommunicable Absolute.
Our life is a spur in a sublime soul-range,
Our being looks beyond its walls of mind
And it communicates with greater worlds;
There are brighter earths and wider heavens than ours.
There are realms where Being broods in its own depths;
It feels in its immense dynamic core
Its nameless, unformed, unborn potencies
Cry for expression in the unshaped Vast:
Ineffable beyond Ignorance and death,
The images of its ever-living Truth
Look out from a chamber of its self-rapt soul:
As if to its own inner witness gaze
The Spirit holds up its mirrored self and works,
The power and passion of its timeless heart,
The figures of its formless ecstasy,
The grandeurs of its multitudinous might.
Thence comes the mystic substance of our souls
Into the prodigy of our nature's birth,
There is the unfallen height of all we are
And dateless fount of all we hope to be.
On every plane the hieratic Power,
Initiate of the unspoken verities,
Dreams to transcribe and make a part of life
In its own native style and living tongue
Some trait of the perfection of the Unborn,
Some vision seen in the omniscient Light,
Some far tune of the immortal rhapsodist Voice,
Some rapture of the all-creating Bliss,

Some form and plan of the Beauty unutterable.
Worlds are there nearer to those absolute realms,
Where the response to Truth is swift and sure
And spirit is not hampered by its frame
And hearts by sharp division seized and rent
And delight and beauty are inhabitants
And love and sweetness are the law of life.
A finer substance in a subtler mould
Embodies the divinity earth but dreams;
Its strength can overtake joy's running feet;
Overleaping the fixed hurdles set by Time,
The rapid net of an intuitive clasp
Captures the fugitive happiness we desire.
A Nature lifted by a larger breath,
Plastic and passive to the all-shaping Fire,
Answers the flaming Godhead's casual touch:
Immune from our inertia of response
It hears the word to which our hearts are deaf,
Adopts the seeing of immortal eyes
And, traveller on the roads of line and hue,
Pursues the spirit of beauty to its home.
Thus we draw near to the All-Wonderful
Following his rapture in things as sign and guide;
Beauty is his footprint showing us where he has passed,
Love is his heartbeats' rhythm in mortal breasts,
Happiness the smile on his adorable face.
A communion of spiritual entities,
A genius of creative Immanence,
Makes all creation deeply intimate:
A fourth dimension of aesthetic sense
Where all is in ourselves, ourselves in all,
To the cosmic wideness re-aligns our souls.
A kindling rapture joins the seer and seen;
The craftsman and the craft grown inly one
Achieve perfection by the magic throb
And passion of their close identity.
All that we slowly piece from gathered parts,
Or by long labour stumblingly evolve,
Is there self-born by its eternal right.
In us too the intuitive Fire can burn;

An agent Light, it is coiled in our folded hearts,
On the celestial levels is its home:
Descending, it can bring those heavens here.
But rarely burns the flame nor burns for long,
The joy it calls from those diviner heights
Brings brief magnificent reminiscences
And high splendid glimpses of interpreting thought,
But not the utter vision and delight.
A veil is kept, something is still held back,
Lest, captives of the beauty and the joy,
Our souls forget to the Highest to aspire.

In that fair subtle realm behind our own
The form is all and physical gods are kings.
The inspiring Light plays in fine boundaries;
A faultless beauty comes by Nature's grace;
There liberty is perfection's guarantee:
Although the absolute Image lacks, the Word
Incarnate, the sheer spiritual ecstasy,
All is a miracle of symmetric charm,
A fantasy of perfect line and rule.
There all feel satisfied in themselves and whole,
A rich completeness is by limit made,
Marvel in an utter littleness abounds,
An intricate rapture riots in a small space:
Each rhythm is kin to its environment,
Each line is perfect and inevitable,
Each object faultlessly built for charm and use.
All is enamoured of its own delight.
Intact it lives of its perfection sure
In a heaven-pleased self-glad immunity;
Content to be, it has need of nothing more.
Here was not futile effort's broken heart:
Exempt from the ordeal and the test,
Empty of opposition and of pain,
It was a world that could not fear nor grieve.
It had no grace of error or defeat,
It had no room for fault, no power to fail.
Out of some packed self-bliss it drew at once
Its form-discoveries of the mute Idea

And the miracle of its rhythmic thoughts and acts,
Its clear technique of firm and rounded lives,
Its gracious people of inanimate shapes
And glory of breathing bodies like our own.
Amazed, his senses ravished with delight,
He moved in a divine, yet kindred world
Admiring marvellous forms so near to ours
Yet perfect like the playthings of a god,
Deathless in the aspect of mortality.
In their narrow and exclusive absolutes
The finite's ranked supremacies throned abide;
It dreams not ever of what might have been;
Only in boundaries can this absolute live.
In a supremeness bound to its own plan
Where all was finished and no widths were left,
No space for shadows of the immeasurable,
No room for the incalculable's surprise,
A captive of its own beauty and ecstasy,
In a magic circle wrought the enchanted Might.
The spirit stood back effaced behind its frame.
Admired for the bright finality of its lines
A blue horizon limited the soul;
Thought moved in luminous facilities,
The outer ideal's shallows its swim-range:
Life in its boundaries lingered satisfied
With the small happiness of the body's acts.
Assigned as Force to a bound corner Mind,
Attached to the safe paucity of her room,
She did her little works and played and slept
And thought not of a greater work undone.
Forgetful of her violent vast desires,
Forgetful of the heights to which she rose,
Her walk was fixed within a radiant groove.
The beautiful body of a soul at ease,
Like one who laughs in sweet and sunlit groves,
Childlike she swung in her gold cradle of joy.
The spaces' call reached not her charmed abode,
She had no wings for wide and dangerous flight,
She faced no peril of sky or of abyss,
She knew no vistas and no mighty dreams,

No yearning for her lost infinitudes.
A perfect picture in a perfect frame,
This faery artistry could not keep his will:
Only a moment's fine release it gave;
A careless hour was spent in a slight bliss.
Our spirit tires of being's surfaces,
Transcended is the splendour of the form;
It turns to hidden powers and deeper states.
So now he looked beyond for greater light.
His soul's peak-climb abandoning in its rear
This brilliant courtyard of the House of Days,
He left that fine material Paradise.
His destiny lay beyond in larger Space.

END OF CANTO TWO

CANTO THREE

THE GLORY AND FALL OF LIFE

AN uneven broad ascent now lured his feet.
　　Answering a greater Nature's troubled call
He crossed the limits of embodied Mind
And entered wide obscure disputed fields
Where all was doubt and change and nothing sure,
A world of search and toil without repose.
As one who meets the face of the Unknown,
A questioner with none to give reply,
Attracted to a problem never solved,
Always uncertain of the ground he trod,
Always drawn on to an inconstant goal
He travelled through a land peopled by doubts
In shifting confines on a quaking base.
In front he saw a boundary ever unreached
And thought himself at each step nearer now,—
A far retreating horizon of mirage.
A vagrancy was there that brooked no home,
A journey of countless paths without a close.
Nothing he found to satisfy his heart;
A tireless wandering sought and could not cease.
There life is the manifest incalculable,
A movement of unquiet seas, a long
And venturesome leap of spirit into Space,
A vexed disturbance in the eternal Calm,
An impulse and passion of the Infinite.
Assuming whatever shape her fancy wills,
Escaped from the restraint of settled forms
She has left the safety of the tried and known.
Unshepherded by the fear that walks through Time,
Undaunted by Fate that dogs and Chance that springs,

166

She accepts disaster as a common risk;
Careless of suffering, heedless of sin and fall,
She wrestles with danger and discovery
In the unexplored expanses of the Soul.
To be seemed only a long experiment,
The hazard of a seeking ignorant Force
That tries all truths and, finding none supreme,
Moves on unsatisfied, unsure of its end.
As saw some inner mind, so life was shaped:
From thought to thought she passed, from phase to phase,
Tortured by her own powers or proud and blest,
Now master of herself, now toy and slave.
A huge inconsequence was her action's law,
As if all possibility must be drained
And anguish and bliss were pastimes of the heart.
In a gallop of thunder-hooved vicissitudes
She swept through the race-fields of Circumstance,
Or, swaying, she tossed between her heights and deeps,
Uplifted or broken on Time's incessant wheel.
Amid a tedious crawl of drab desires
She writhed, a worm mid worms in Nature's mud,
Then, Titan-statured, took all earth for food,
Ambitioned the seas for robe, for crown the stars
And shouting strode from peak to giant peak,
Clamouring for worlds to conquer and to rule.
Then wantonly enamoured of Sorrow's face,
She plunged into the anguish of the depths
And, wallowing, clung to her own misery.
In dolorous converse with her squandered self
She wrote the account of all that she had lost,
Or sat with grief as with an ancient friend.
A romp of violent raptures soon was spent,
Or she lingered tied to an inadequate joy
Missing the turns of fate, missing life's goal.
A scene was planned for all her numberless moods
Where each could be the law and way of life,
But none could offer a pure felicity;
Only a flickering zest they left behind
Or the fierce lust that brings a dead fatigue.
Amid her swift untold variety

Something remained dissatisfied ever the same
And in the new saw only a face of the old,
For every hour repeated all the rest
And every change prolonged the same unease.
A spirit of her self and aim unsure,
Tired soon of too much joy and happiness,
She needs the spur of pleasure and of pain
And the native taste of suffering and unrest:
She strains for an end that never can she win.
A perverse savour haunts her thirsting lips:
For the grief she weeps which came from her own choice,
For the pleasure yearns that racked with wounds her breast;
Aspiring to heaven she turns her steps towards hell.
Chance she has chosen and danger for playfellows;
Fate's dreadful swing she has taken for cradle and seat.
Yet pure and bright from the Timeless was her birth,
A lost world-rapture lingers in her eyes,
Her moods are faces of the Infinite:
Beauty and happiness are her native right,
And endless bliss is her eternal home.

This now revealed its antique face of joy,
A sudden disclosure to the heart of grief
Tempting it to endure and long and hope.
Even in changing worlds bereft of peace,
In an air racked with sorrow and with fear
And while his feet trod on a soil unsafe,
He saw the image of a happier state.
In an architecture of hieratic Space
Circling and mounting towards creation's tops,
At a blue height which never was too high
For warm communion between body and soul,
As far as heaven, as near as thought and hope,
Glimmered the kingdom of a griefless life.
Above him in a new celestial vault
Other than the heavens beheld by mortal eyes,
As on a fretted ceiling of the gods,
An archipelago of laughter and fire,
Swam stars apart in a rippled sea of sky.
Towered spirals, magic rings of vivid hue

And gleaming spheres of strange felicity
Floated through distance like a symbol world.
On the trouble and the toil they could not share,
On the unhappiness they could not aid,
Impervious to life's suffering, struggle, grief,
Untarnished by its anger, gloom and hate,
Unmoved, untouched, looked down great visioned planes
Blissful for ever in their timeless right.
Absorbed in their own beauty and content,
Of their immortal gladness they live sure.
Apart in their self-glory plunged, remote
Burning they swam in a vague lucent haze,
An everlasting refuge of dream-light,
A nebula of the splendours of the gods
Made from the musings of eternity.
Almost unbelievable by human faith,
Hardly they seemed the stuff of things that are.
As through a magic television's glass
Outlined to some magnifying inner eye
They shone like images thrown from a far scene
Too high and glad for mortal lids to seize.
But near and real to the longing heart
And to the body's passionate thought and sense
Are the hidden kingdoms of beatitude.
In some close unattained realm which yet we feel,
Immune from the harsh clutch of Death and Time,
Escaping the search of sorrow and desire,
In bright enchanted safe peripheries
For ever wallowing in bliss they lie.
In dream and trance and muse before our eyes,
Across a subtle vision's inner field,
Wide rapturous landscapes fleeting from the sight,
The figures of the perfect kingdom pass
And behind them leave a shining memory's trail.
Imagined scenes or great eternal worlds,
Dream-caught or sensed, they touch our hearts with their depths;
Unreal-seeming yet more real than life,
Happier than happiness, truer than things true
If dreams these were or captured images,
Dream's truth made false earth's vain realities.

In a swift eternal moment fixed there live
Or ever recalled come back to longing eyes
Calm heavens of imperishable Light,
Illumined continents of violet peace,
Oceans and rivers of the mirth of God
And griefless countries under purple suns.

     This, once a star of bright remote idea
Or imagination's comet trail of dream,
Took now a close shape of reality.
The gulf between dream-truth, earth-fact was crossed,
The wonder-worlds of life were dreams no more;
His vision made all they unveiled its own:
Their scenes, their happenings met his eyes and heart
And smote them with pure loveliness and bliss.
A breathless summit region drew his gaze
Whose boundaries jutted into a sky of Self
And dipped towards a strange ethereal base.
The quintessence glowed of Life's supreme delight.
On a spiritual and mysterious peak
Only a miracle's high transfiguring line
Divided life from the formless Infinite
And sheltered Time against eternity.
Out of that formless stuff Time mints his shapes;
The Eternal's quiet holds the cosmic act:
The protean images of the World-Force
Have drawn the strength to be, the will to last
From a deep ocean of dynamic peace.
Inverting the Spirit's apex towards life
She spends the plastic liberties of the One
To cast in acts the dreams of her caprice,
His wisdom's call steadies her careless feet,
He props her dance upon a rigid base,
His timeless still immutability
Must standardise her creation's miracle.
Out of the Void's unseeing energies
Inventing the scene of a concrete universe,
By his thought she has fixed its paces, in its blind acts
She sees by flashes of his all-knowing Light.
At her will the inscrutable Supermind leans down

To guide her force that feels but cannot know,
Its breadth of power controls her restless seas
And life obeys the governing Idea.
At her will, led by a luminous Immanence
The hazardous experimenting Mind
Pushes its way through obscure possibles
Mid chance formations of an unknowing world.
Our human ignorance moves towards the Truth
That Nescience may become omniscient:
Transmuted instincts shape to divine thoughts,
Thoughts house infallible immortal sight
And Nature climbs towards God's identity.
The Master of the worlds self-made her slave
Is the executor of her fantasies:
She has canalised the seas of omnipotence;
She has limited by her laws the Illimitable.
The Immortal bound himself to do her works;
He labours at the tasks her Ignorance sets,
Hidden in the cape of our mortality.
The worlds, the forms her goddess fancy makes
Have lost their origin on unseen heights:
Even severed, straying from their timeless source,
Even deformed, obscured, accursed and fallen,—
Since even fall has its perverted joy
And nothing she leaves out that serves delight,—
These too can to the peaks revert or here
Cut out the sentence of the spirit's fall,
Recover their forfeited divinity.
At once caught in an eternal vision's sweep
He saw her pride and splendour of highborn zones
And her regions crouching in the nether deeps.
Above was a monarchy of unfallen self,
Beneath was the gloomy trance of the abyss,
An opposite pole or dim antipodes.
There were vasts of the glory of life's absolutes:
All laughed in a safe immortality
And an eternal childhood of the soul
Before darkness came and pain and grief were born
Where all could dare to be themselves and one
And Wisdom played in sinless innocence

With naked Freedom in Truth's happy sun.
There were worlds of her laughter and dreadful irony,
There were fields of her taste of toil and strife and tears;
Her head lay on the breast of amorous Death,
Sleep imitated awhile extinction's peace.
The light of God she has parted from his dark
To test the savour of bare opposites.
Here mingling in man's heart their tones and hues
Have woven his being's mutable design,
His life a forward-rippling stream in Time,
His nature's constant fixed mobility,
His soul a moving picture's changeful film,
His cosmos-chaos of personality.
The grand creatrix with her cryptic touch
Has turned to pathos and power being's self-dream,
Made a passion-play of its fathomless mystery.

But here were worlds lifted half-way to heaven.
The Veil was there but not the Shadowy Wall;
In forms not too remote from human grasp
Some passion of the inviolate purity
Broke through, a ray of the original Bliss.
Heaven's joys might have been earth's if earth were pure.
There could have reached our divinised sense and heart
Some natural felicity's bright extreme,
Some thrill of supernature's absolutes:
All strengths could laugh and sport on earth's hard roads
And never feel her cruel edge of pain,
All love could play and nowhere Nature's shame.
But she has stabled her dreams in Matter's courts
And still her doors are barred to things supreme.
These worlds could feel God's breath visiting their tops;
Some glimmer of the Transcendent's hem was there.
Across the white aeonic silences
Immortal figures of embodied joy
Traversed wide spaces near to eternity's sleep.
Pure mystic voices in beatitude's hush
Appealed to Love's immaculate sweetnesses,
Calling his honeyed touch to thrill the worlds,
His blissful hands to seize on Nature's limbs,

His sweet intolerant might of union
To take all beings into his saviour arms,
Drawing to his pity the rebel and the waif
To force on them the happiness they refuse.
A chant hymeneal to the unseen Divine,
A flaming rhapsody of white desire
Lured an immortal music into the heart
And woke the slumbering ear of ecstasy.
A purer, fierier sense had there its home,
A burning urge no earthly limbs can hold.
One drew a large unburdened spacious breath
And the heart sped from beat to rapturous beat.
The voice of time sang of the Immortal's joy;
An inspiration and a lyric cry,
The moments came with ecstasy on their wings;
Beauty unimaginable moved heaven-bare
Absolved from boundaries in the vasts of dream;
The cry of the Birds of Wonder called from the skies
To the deathless people of the shores of Light.
Creation leaped straight from the hands of God;
Marvel and rapture wandered in the ways.
Only to be was a supreme delight,
Life was a happy laughter of the soul
And Joy was king with Love for minister.
The spirit's luminousness was bodied there.
Life's contraries were lovers or natural friends
And her extremes keen edges of harmony:
Indulgence with a tender purity came
And nursed the god on her maternal breast:
There none was weak, so falsehood could not live; ||
Ignorance was a thin shade protecting light,
Imagination the free-will of Truth,
Pleasure a candidate for heaven's fire;
The intellect was Beauty's worshipper,
Strength was the slave of calm spiritual law, ||
Power laid its head upon the breasts of Bliss.
There were summit glories inconceivable,
Autonomies of wisdom's still self-rule
And high dependencies of her virgin sun,
Illumined theocracies of the seeing soul

8

Throned in the power of the Transcendent's ray.
A vision of grandeurs, a dream of magnitudes
In sun-bright kingdoms moved with regal gait:
Assemblies, crowded senates of the gods,
Life's puissances reigned on seats of marble will,
High dominations and autocracies
And laurelled strengths and armed imperative mights.
All objects there were great and beautiful,
All beings wore a royal stamp of power.
There sat the oligarchies of natural Law,
Proud violent heads served one calm monarch brow:
All the soul's postures donned divinity.
There met the ardent mutual intimacies
Of mastery's joy and the joy of servitude
Imposed by Love on Love's heart that obeys
And Love's body held beneath a rapturous yoke.
All was a game of meeting kinglinesses.
For worship lifts the worshipper's bowed strength
Close to the god's pride and bliss his soul adores:
The ruler there is one with all he rules;
To him who serves with a free equal heart
Obedience is his princely training's school,
His nobility's coronet and privilege,
His faith is a high nature's idiom,
His service a spiritual sovereignty.
There were realms where Knowledge joined creative Power
In her high home and made her all his own:
The grand Illuminate seized her gleaming limbs
And filled them with the passion of his ray
Till all her body was its transparent house
And all her soul a counterpart of his soul.
Apotheosised, transfigured by wisdom's touch,
Her days became a luminous sacrifice;
An immortal moth in happy and endless fire,
She burned in his sweet intolerable blaze.
A captive Life wedded her conqueror.
In his wide sky she built her world anew;
She gave to mind's calm pace the motor's speed,
To thinking a need to live what the soul saw,
To living an impetus to know and see.

His splendour grasped her, her puissance to him clung;
She crowned the Idea a king in purple robes,
Put her magic serpent sceptre in Thought's grip,
Made forms his inward vision's rhythmic shapes
And her acts the living body of his will.
A flaming thunder, a creator flash,
His victor Light rode on her deathless Force :
A centaur's mighty gallop bore the god.
Life throned with mind, a double majesty.
Worlds were there of a happiness great and grave
And action tinged with dream, laughter with thought,
And passion there could wait for its desire
Until it heard the near approach of God.
Worlds were there of a childlike mirth and joy;
A carefree youthfulness of mind and heart
Found in the body a heavenly instrument;
It lit an aureate halo round desire
And freed the deified animal in the limbs
To divine gambols of love and beauty and bliss.
On a radiant soil that gazed at heaven's smile
A swift life-impulse stinted not nor stopped:
It knew not how to tire; happy were its tears.
There work was play and play the only work,
The tasks of heaven a game of godlike might:
A celestial bacchanal for ever pure,
Unstayed by faintness as in mortal frames
Life was an eternity of rapture's moods:
Age never came, care never lined the face.
Imposing on the safety of the stars
A race and laughter of immortal strengths,
The nude God-children in their play-fields ran
Smiting the winds with splendour and with speed;
Of storm and sun they made companions,
Sported with the white mane of tossing seas,
Slew distance trampled to death under their wheels
And wrestled in the arenas of their force.
Imperious in their radiance like the suns
They kindled heaven with the glory of their limbs
Flung like a divine largesse to the world.
A spell to force the heart to stark delight,

115

They carried the pride and mastery of their charm
As if Life's banner on the roads of Space.
Ideas were luminous comrades of the soul;
Mind played with speech, cast javelins of thought,
But needed not these instruments' toil to know;
Knowledge was Nature's pastime like the rest.
Investitured with the fresh heart's bright ray,
An early God-instinct's child inheritors,
Tenants of the perpetuity of Time
Still thrilling with the first creation's bliss,
They steeped existence in their youth of soul.
An exquisite and vehement tyranny,
The strong compulsion of their will to joy
Poured smiling streams of happiness through the world.
There reigned a breath of high immune content,
A fortunate gait of days in tranquil air,
A flood of universal love and peace.
A sovereignty of tireless sweetness lived
Like a song of pleasure on the lips of Time.
A large spontaneous order freed the will,
A sun-frank winging of the soul to bliss,
The breadth and greatness of the unfettered act
And the swift fire-heart's golden liberty.
There was no falsehood of soul-severance,
There came no crookedness of thought or word
To rob creation of its native truth;
All was sincerity and natural force.
There freedom was sole rule and highest law.
In a happy series climbed or plunged these worlds:
In realms of curious beauty and surprise,
In fields of grandeur and of titan power,
Life played at ease with her immense desires.
A thousand Edens she could build nor pause;
No bound was set to her greatness and to her grace
And to her heavenly variety.
Awake with a cry and stir of numberless souls,
Arisen from the breast of some deep Infinite,
Smiling like a new-born child at love and hope,
In her nature housing the Immortal's power,
In her bosom bearing the eternal Will,

No guide she needed but her luminous heart:
No fall debased the godhead of her steps,
No alien Night had come to blind her eyes.
There was no use for grudging ring or fence;
Each act was a perfection and a joy.
Abandoned to her rapid fancy's moods
And the rich coloured riot of her mind,
Initiate of divine and mighty dreams,
Magician builder of unnumbered forms
Exploring the measures of the rhythms of God,
At will she wove her wizard wonder-dance,
A Dionysian goddess of delight,
A Bacchant of creative ecstasy.

This world of bliss he saw and felt its call,
But found no way to enter into its joy;
Across the conscious gulf there was no bridge.
A darker air encircled still his soul
Tied to an image of unquiet life.
In spite of yearning mind and longing sense,
To a sad Thought by grey experience formed
And a vision dimmed by care and sorrow and sleep
All this seemed only a bright desirable dream
Conceived in a longing distance by the heart
Of one who walks in the shadow of earth-pain.
Although he once had felt the Eternal's clasp,
Too near to suffering worlds his nature lived,
And where he stood were entrances of Night.
Hardly, too close beset by the world's care,
Can the dense mould in which we have been made
Return sheer joy to joy, pure light to light.
For its tormented will to think and live
First to a mingled pain and pleasure woke
And still it keeps the habit of its birth:
A dire duality is our way to be.
In the crude beginnings of this mortal world
Life was not nor mind's play nor heart's desire.
When earth was built in the unconscious Void
And nothing was save a material scene,
Identified with sea and sky and stone

Her young gods yearned for the release of souls
Asleep in objects, vague, inanimate.
In that desolate grandeur, in that beauty bare,
In the deaf stillness, mid the unheeded sounds,
Heavy was the uncommunicated load
Of Godhead in a world that had no needs;
For none was there to feel or to receive.
This solid mass which brooked no throb of sense
Could not contain their vast creative urge:
Immersed no more in Matter's harmony,
The Spirit lost its statuesque repose.
In the uncaring trance it groped for sight,
Passioned for the movements of a conscious heart,
Famishing for speech and thought and joy and love,
In the dumb insensitive wheeling day and night
Hungered for the beat of yearning and response.
The poised inconscience shaken with a touch,
The intuitive silence trembling with a name,
They cried to Life to invade the senseless mould
And in brute forms awake divinity.
A voice was heard on the mute rolling globe,
A murmur moaned in the unlistening Void.
A being seemed to breathe where once was none:
Something pent up in dead insentient depths,
Denied conscious existence, lost to joy,
Turned as if one asleep since dateless time.
Aware of its own buried reality,
Remembering its forgotten self and right,
It yearned to know, to aspire, to enjoy, to live.
Life heard the call and left her native light.
Overflowing from her bright magnificent plane
On the rigid coil and sprawl of mortal space,
Here too the gracious great-winged Angel poured
Her splendour and her sweetness and her bliss,
Hoping to fill a fair new world with joy.
As comes a goddess to a mortal's breast
And fills his days with her celestial clasp,
She stooped to make her home in transient shapes;
In Matter's womb she cast the Immortal's fire,
In the unfeeling Vast woke thought and hope,

Smote with her charm and beauty flesh and nerve
And forced delight on earth's insensible frame.
Alive and clad with trees and herbs and flowers
Earth's great brown body smiled towards the skies,
Azure replied to azure in the sea's laugh;
New sentient creatures filled the unseen depths,
Life's glory and swiftness ran in the beauty of beasts,
Man dared and thought and met with his soul the world.
But while the magic breath was on its way,
Before her gifts could reach our prisoned hearts,
A dark ambiguous Presence questioned all.
The secret Will that robes itself with Night
And offers to spirit the ordeal of the flesh,
Imposed a mystic mask of death and pain.
Interned now in the slow and suffering years
Sojourns the winged and wonderful wayfarer
And can no more recall her happier state,
But must obey the inert Inconscient's law,
Insensible foundation of a world
In which blind limits are on beauty laid
And sorrow and joy as struggling comrades live.
A dim and dreadful muteness fell on her:
Abolished was her subtle mighty spirit
And slain her boon of child-god happiness,
And all her glory into littleness turned
And all her sweetness into a maimed desire.
To feed death with her works is here life's doom.
So veiled was her immortality that she seemed,
Inflicting consciousness on unconscious things,
An episode in an eternal death,
A myth of being that must for ever cease.
Such was the evil mystery of her change.

END OF CANTO THREE

CANTO FOUR

THE KINGDOMS OF THE LITTLE LIFE

A QUIVERING trepidant uncertain world
    Born from that dolorous meeting and eclipse
Appeared in the emptiness where her feet had trod,
A quick obscurity, a seeking stir.
There was a writhing of half-conscious force
Hardly awakened from inconscient sleep
And tied to an instinct-driven Ignorance,
To find itself and find its hold on things.
Inheritor of poverty and loss,
Assailed by memories that fled when seized,
Haunted by a forgotten uplifting hope,
It strove with a blindness as of groping hands
To fill the aching and disastrous gap
Between earth-pain and the bliss from which Life fell.
A world that ever seeks for something missed,
Hunting for a joy that earth has failed to keep,
Too near to our gates its unappeased unrest
For peace to live on the inert solid globe.
It has joined its hunger to the hunger of earth,
It has given the law of craving to our lives,
It has made our spirit's need a fathomless gulf.
An Influence entered mortal night and day,
A shadow overcast the time-born race;
In the troubled stream where leaps a blind heart-pulse
And the nerve-beat of feeling wakes in sense
Dividing Matter's sleep from conscious Mind,
There strayed a call that knew not why it came.
A Power beyond earth's scope has touched the earth;
The repose that might have been can be no more;
A formless yearning passions in man's heart,

120

A cry is in his blood for happier things:
Else could he roam on a free sunlit soil
With the childlike pain-forgetting mind of beasts
Or live happy, unmoved, like flowers and trees.
The Might that came upon the earth to bless
Has stayed on earth to suffer and aspire.
The infant laugh that rang through time is hushed:
Man's natural joy of life is overcast
And sorrow is his nurse of destiny.
The animal's thoughtless joy is left behind,
Care and reflection burden his daily walk:
He has risen to greatness and to discontent,
He is awake to the Invisible.
Insatiate seeker, he has all to learn:
He has exhausted now life's surface acts,
His being's hidden realms remain to explore.
He becomes a mind, he becomes a spirit and self;
In his fragile tenement he grows Nature's lord.
In him Matter wakes from its long obscure trance,
In him earth feels the Godhead drawing near.
An eyeless Power that sees no more its aim,
A restless hungry energy of Will,
Life cast her seed in the body's indolent mould;
It woke from happy torpor a blind Force
Compelling it to sense and seek and feel.
In the enormous labour of the Void
Perturbing with her dreams the vast routine
And dead roll of a slumbering universe
The mighty prisoner struggled for release.
Alive with her yearning woke the inert cell,
In the heart she kindled a fire of passion and need,
Amid the deep calm of inanimate things
Arose her great voice of toil and prayer and strife.
A groping consciousness in a voiceless world,
A guideless sense was given her for her road;
Thought was withheld and nothing now she knew
But all the unknown was hers to feel and clasp.
Obeying the push of unborn things towards birth
Out of her seal of insentient life she broke:
In her substance of unthinking mute soul-strength

That cannot utter what its depths divine,
Awoke a blind necessity to know.
The chain that bound her she made her instrument;
Instinct was hers, the chrysalis of Truth,
And effort and growth and striving nescience.
Inflicting on the body desire and hope,
Imposing on inconscience consciousness
She brought into Matter's dull tenacity
Her anguished claim to her lost sovereign right,
Her tireless search, her vexed uneasy heart,
Her wandering unsure steps, her cry for change.
Adorer of a joy without a name,
In her obscure cathedral of delight
To dim dwarf gods she offers secret rites.
But vain unending is the sacrifice,
The priest an ignorant mage who only makes
Futile mutations in the altar's plan
And casts blind hopes into a powerless flame.
A burden of transient gains weighs down her steps
And hardly under that load can she advance;
But the hours cry to her, she travels on
Passing from thought to thought, from want to want;
Her greatest progress is a deepened need.
Matter dissatisfies, she turns to Mind;
She conquers earth, her field, then claims the heavens.
Insensible, breaking the work she has done
The stumbling ages over her labour pass,
And still no great transforming light came down
And no revealing rapture touched her fall.
Only a glimmer sometimes splits mind's sky
Justifying the ambiguous providence
That makes of night a path to unknown dawns
Or a dark clue to some diviner state.
In Nescience began her mighty task,
In Ignorance she pursues the unfinished work;
For Knowledge gropes, but meets not Wisdom's face.
Ascending slowly with unconscious steps,
A foundling of the gods she wanders here
Like a child-soul left near the gates of Hell

Fumbling through fog in search of Paradise.

 In this slow ascension he must follow her pace
Even from her faint and dim subconscious start:
So only can earth's last salvation come.
For so only could he know the obscure cause
Of all that holds us back and baffles God
In the jail-delivery of the imprisoned soul.
Along swift paths of fall through dangerous gates
He chanced into a grey obscurity
Teeming with instincts from the mindless gulfs
That pushed to wear a form and win a place.
Life here was intimate with Death and Night
And ate Death's food that she might breathe awhile;
She was their inmate and adopted waif.
Accepting subconscience, in dumb darkness' reign
A sojourner, she hoped not any more.
There far away from Truth and luminous thought
He saw the original seat, the separate birth
Of the dethroned, deformed and suffering Power.
An unhappy face of falsity made true,
A contradiction of our divine birth,
Indifferent to beauty and to light,
Parading she flaunted her animal disgrace
Unhelped by camouflage, brutal and bare,
An authentic image recognised and signed
Of her outcast force exiled from heaven and hope,
Fallen, glorying in the vileness of her state,
The grovel of a strength once half divine,
The graceless squalor of her beast desires,
The staring visage of her ignorance,
The naked body of her poverty.
Here first she crawled out from her cabin of mud
Where she had lain insconscient, rigid, mute:
Its narrowness and torpor held her still,
A darkness clung to her uneffaced by Light.
There neared no touch redeeming from above:
The upward look was alien to her sight,
Forgotten the fearless godhead of her walk;
Renounced was the glory and felicity,

123

The adventure in the dangerous fields of Time:
Hardly she availed, wallowing, to bear and live.

A wide unquiet mist of seeking space,
A rayless region swallowed in vague swathes,
That seemed, unnamed, unbodied and unhoused,
A swaddled visionless and formless mind,
Asked for a body to translate its soul.
Its prayer denied, it fumbled after thought.
As yet not powered to think, hardly to live,
It opened into a weird and pigmy world
Where this unhappy magic had its source.
On dim confines where Life and Matter meet
He wandered among things half-seen, half-guessed,
Pursued by ungrasped beginnings and lost ends.
There life was born but died before it could live.
There was no solid ground, no constant drift;
Only some flame of mindless Will had power.
Himself was dim to himself, half-felt, obscure,
As if in a struggle of the Void to be.
In strange domains where all was living sense
But mastering thought was not nor cause nor rule,
Only a crude child-heart cried for toys of bliss,
Mind flickered, a disordered infant-glow,
And random shapeless energies drove towards form
And took each wisp-fire for a guiding sun.
This blindfold force could place no thinking step;
Asking for light she followed darkness' clue.
An inconscient Power groped towards consciousness,
Matter smitten by Matter glimmered to sense,
Blind contacts, slow reactions beat out sparks
Of instinct from a cloaked subliminal bed,
Sensations crowded, dumb substitutes for thought,
Perception answered Nature's waking blows
But still was a mechanical response,
A jerk, a leap, a start in Nature's dream,
And rude unchastened impulses jostling ran
Heedless of every motion but their own
And, darkling, clashed with darker than themselves,
Free in a world of settled anarchy.

He = Ushwapati

The need to exist, the instinct to survive
Engrossed the tense precarious moment's will
And an unseeing desire felt out for food.
The gusts of Nature were the only law,
Force wrestled with force but no result remained:
Only were achieved a nescient grasp and drive
And feelings and instincts knowing not their source,
Sense-pleasures and sense-pangs soon caught, soon lost,
And the brute motion of unthinking lives.
It was a vain unnecessary world
Whose will to be brought poor and sad results
And meaningless suffering and a grey unease.
Nothing seemed worth the labour to become.

But judged not so his spirit's wakened eye. || *Ushwapati*
As shines a solitary witness star
That burns apart, Light's lonely sentinel,
In the drift and teeming of a mindless Night,
A single thinker in an aimless world
Awaiting some tremendous dawn of God,
He saw the purpose in the works of Time.
Even in that aimlessness a work was done
Pregnant with magic will and change divine.
The first writhings of the cosmic serpent Force /*Kundalini*
Uncoiled from the mystic ring of Matter's trance; *Job*
It raised its head in the warm air of life. *Leviathan*
It could not cast off yet Night's stiffening sleep
Or wear as yet mind's wonder-flecks and streaks,
Put on its jewelled hood the crown of soul
Or stand erect in the blaze of spirit's sun.
As yet were only seen foulness and force,
The secret crawl of consciousness to light
Through a fertile slime of lust and battening sense,
Beneath the body's crust of thickened self
A tardy fervent working in the dark,
The turbid yeast of Nature's passionate change,
Ferment of the soul's creation out of mire.
A heavenly process donned this grey disguise,
A fallen ignorance in its covert night
Laboured to achieve its dumb unseemly work,

Root Chakra (margin note left)

125

A camouflage of the Inconscient's need
To release the glory of God in Nature's mud.
His sight, spiritual in embodying orbs,
Could pierce through the grey phosphorescent haze
And scan the secrets of the shifting flux
That animates these mute and solid cells
And leads the thought and longing of the flesh
And the keen lust and hunger of its will.
This too he tracked along its hidden stream
And traced its acts to a miraculous fount.
A mystic Presence none can probe nor rule,
Creator of this game of ray and shade
In this sweet and bitter paradoxical life,
Asks from the body the soul's intimacies
And by the swift vibration of a nerve
Links its mechanic throbs to light and love.
It summons the spirit's sleeping memories
Up from subconscient depths beneath Time's foam;
Oblivious of their flame of happy truth,
Arriving with heavy eyes that hardly see,
They come disguised as feelings and desires,
Like weeds upon the surface float awhile
And rise and sink on a somnambulist tide.
Impure, degraded though her motions are,
Always a heaven-truth broods in life's deeps;
In our obscurest members burns that fire.
A touch of God's rapture in creation's acts,
A lost remembrance of felicity
Lurks still in the dumb roots of death and birth,
The world's senseless beauty mirrors God's delight.
That rapture's smile is secret everywhere;
It flows in the wind's breath, in the tree's sap,
Its hued magnificence blooms in leaves and flowers.
When life broke through its half-drowse in the plant
That feels and suffers but cannot move or cry,
In beast and in winged bird and thinking man
It made of the heart's rhythm its music's beat;
It forced the unconscious tissues to awake
And ask for happiness and earn the pang
And thrill with pleasure and laughter of brief delight,

And quiver with pain and crave for ecstasy.
Imperative, voiceless, ill-understood,
Too far from light, too close to being's core,
Born strangely in Time from the eternal Bliss,
It presses on heart's core and vibrant nerve;
Its sharp self-seeking tears our consciousness;
Our pain and pleasure have that sting for cause;
Instinct with it, but blind to its true joy
The soul's desire leaps out towards passing things.
All Nature's longing drive none can resist,
Comes surging through the blood and quickened sense;
An ecstasy of the infinite is her cause.
It turns in us to finite loves and lusts,
The will to conquer and have, to seize and keep,
To enlarge life's room and scope and pleasure's range,
To battle and overcome and make one's own,
The hope to mix one's joy with other's joy,
A yearning to possess and be possessed,
To enjoy and be enjoyed, to feel, to live.
Here was its early brief attempt to be,
Its rapid end of momentary delight
Whose stamp of failure haunts all ignorant life.
Inflicting still its habit on the cells
The phantom of a dark and evil start
Ghostlike pursues all that we dream and do.
Although on earth are firm established lives,
A working of habit or a sense of law,
A steady repetition in the flux,
Yet are its roots of will ever the same;
These passions are the stuff of which we are made.
This was the first cry of the awaking world.
It clings around us still and clamps the god.
Even when reason is born and soul takes form,
In beast and reptile and in thinking man
It lasts and is the fount of all their life.
This too was needed that breath and living might be.
The spirit in a finite ignorant world
Must rescue so its prisoned consciousness
Forced out in little jets at quivering points
From the Inconscient's sealed infinitude.

Then slowly it gathers mass, looks up at Light.
This Nature lives tied to her origin,
A clutch of nether force is on her still;
Out of unconscious depths her instincts leap;
A neighbour is her life to insentient Nought.
Under this law an ignorant world was made.
    In the enigma of the darkened Vasts,
In the passion and self-loss of the Infinite
When all was plunged in the negating Void,
Non-Being's night could never have been saved
If Being had not plunged into the dark
Carrying with it its triple mystic cross.
Invoking in world-time the timeless truth,
Bliss changed to sorrow, knowledge made ignorant,
God's force turned into a child's helplessness
Can bring down heaven by their sacrifice.
A contradiction founds the base of life:
The eternal, the divine Reality
Has faced itself with its own contraries;
Being became the Void and Conscious-Force
Nescience and walk of a blind Energy
And Ecstasy took the figure of world-pain.
In a mysterious dispensation's law
A Wisdom that prepares its far-off ends
Planned so to start her slow aeonic game.
A blindfold search and wrestle and fumbling clasp
Of a half-seen Nature and a hidden Soul,
A game of hide and seek in twilit rooms,
A play of love and hate and fear and hope
Continues in the nursery of mind
Its hard and heavy romp of self-born twins.
At last the struggling Energy can emerge
And meet the voiceless Being in wider fields;
Then can they see and speak and, breast to breast,
In a larger consciousness, a clearer light,
The Two embrace and strive and each know each
Regarding closer now the playmate's face.
Even in these formless coilings he could feel
Matter's response to an infant stir of soul.

In Nature he saw the mighty Spirit concealed,
Watched the weak birth of a tremendous Force,
Pursued the riddle of Godhead's tentative pace,
Heard the faint rhythms of a great unborn Muse.

Then came a fiercer breath of waking life,
And there arose from the dim gulf of things
The strange creations of a thinking sense,
Existences half-real and half-dream.
A life was there that hoped not to survive:
Beings were born who perished without trace,
Events that were a formless drama's limbs
And actions driven by a blind creature will.
A seeking Power found out its road to form,
Patterns were built of love and joy and pain
And symbol figures for the moods of Life.
An insect hedonism fluttered and crawled
And basked in a sunlit Nature's surface thrills,
And dragon raptures, python agonies
Crawled in the marsh and mire and licked the sun.
Huge armoured strengths shook the frail quaking ground,
Great puissant creatures with a dwarfish brain,
And pigmy tribes imposed their small life-drift.
In a dwarf model of humanity
Nature now launched the extreme experience
And master-point of her design's caprice,
Luminous result of her half-conscious climb
On rungs twixt her sublimities and grotesques
To massive from infinitesimal shapes,
To a subtle balancing of body and soul,
To an order of intelligent littleness.
Around him in the moment-beats of Time
The kingdom of the animal self arose,
Where deed is all and mind is still half-born
And the heart obeys a dumb unseen control.
The Force that works by the light of Ignorance,
Her animal experiment began,
Crowding with conscious creatures her world-scheme;
But to the outward only were they alive,
Only they replied to touches and surfaces

129

9

And to the prick of need that drove their lives.
A body that knew not its own soul within,
There lived and longed, had wrath and joy and grief;
A mind was there that met the objective world
As if a stranger or enemy at its door:
Its thoughts were kneaded by the shocks of sense;
It captured not the spirit in the form,
It entered not the heart of what it saw;
It looked not for the power behind the act,
It studied not the hidden motive in things
Nor strove to find the meaning of it all.
Beings were there who wore a human form;
Absorbed they lived in the passion of the scene,
But knew not who they were or why they lived:
Life had for them no aim save Nature's joy
And the stimulus and delight of outer things;
They worked for the body's wants, they craved no more,
Content to breathe, to feel, to sense, to act,
Identified with the spirit's outward shell.
The veiled spectator watching from their depths
Fixed not his inward eye upon himself
Nor turned to find the author of the plot,
He saw the drama only and the stage.
There was no brooding stress of deeper sense,
The burden of reflection was not borne:
Mind looked on Nature with unknowing eyes,
Adored her boons and feared her monstrous strokes.
It pondered not on the magic of her laws,
It thirsted not for the secret wells of Truth,
But made a register of crowding facts
And strung sensations on a vivid thread:
It hunted and it fled and sniffed the winds,
Or slothed inert in sunshine and soft air:
It sought the engrossing contacts of the world,
But only to feed the surface sense with bliss.
These felt life's quiver in the outward touch,
They could not feel behind the touch the soul.
To guard their form of self from Nature's harm
To enjoy and to survive was all their care.
The narrow horizon of their days was filled

With things and creatures that could help and hurt:
The world's values hung upon their little self.
Isolated, cramped in the vast unknown,
To save their small lives from surrounding Death
They made a tiny circle of defence
Against the siege of the huge universe:
They preyed upon the world and were its prey,
But never dreamed to conquer and be free.
Obeying the World-Power's hints and firm taboos
A scanty part they drew from her rich store;
There was no conscious code and no life-plan:
The patterns of thinking of a little group
Fixed a traditional behaviour's law.
Ignorant of soul save as a wraith within,
Tied to a mechanism of unchanging lives
And to a dull usual sense and feeling's beat,
They turned in grooves of animal desire.
In walls of stone fenced round they worked and warred,
Did by a banded selfishness a small good
Or wrought a dreadful wrong and cruel pain
On sentient lives and thought they did no ill.
Ardent from the sack of happy peaceful homes
And gorged with slaughter, plunder, rape and fire,
They made of human selves their helpless prey,
A drove of captives led to lifelong woe
Or torture a spectacle made and holiday,
Mocking or thrilled by their torn victim's pangs;
Admiring themselves as titans and as gods
Proudly they sang their high and glorious deeds
And praised their victory and their splendid force.
An animal in the instinctive herd
Pushed by life impulses, forced by common needs,
Each in his own kind saw his ego's glass;
All served the aim and action of the pack.
Those like himself, by blood or custom kin,
To him were parts of his life, his adjunct selves,
His personal nebula's constituent stars,
Satellite companions of his solar I.
A master of his life's environment,
A leader of a huddled human mass

131

Herding for safety on a dangerous earth
He gathered them round him as if minor Powers
To make a common front against the world,
Or, weak and sole on an indifferent earth,
As a fortress for his undefended heart,
Or else to heal his body's loneliness.
In others than his kind he sensed a foe,
An alien unlike force to shun and fear,
A stranger and adversary to hate and slay.
Or he lived as lives the solitary brute;
At war with all he bore his single fate.
Absorbed in the present act, the fleeting days,
None thought to look beyond the hour's gains,
Or dreamed to make this earth a fairer world,
Or felt some touch divine surprise his heart.
The gladness that the fugitive moment gave,
The desire grasped, the bliss, the experience won,
Movement and speed and strength were joy enough
And bodily longings shared and quarrel and play,
And tears and laughter and the need called love.
In war and clasp these life-wants joined the All-Life,
Wrestlings of a divided unity
Inflicting mutual grief and happiness
In ignorance of the Self for ever one.
Arming its creatures with delight and hope
A half-awakened Nescience struggled there
To know by sight and touch the outside of things.
Instinct was formed; in memory's crowded sleep
The past lived on as in a bottomless sea:
Inverting into half-thought the quickened sense
She felt around for truth with fumbling hands,
Clutched to her the little she could reach and seize
And put aside in her subconscient cave.
So must the dim being grow in light and force
And rise to his higher destiny at last,
Look up to God and round at the universe,
And learn by failure and progress by fall
And battle with environment and doom,
By suffering discover his deep soul
And by possession grow to his own vasts.

Half-way she stopped and found her faith no more.
Still nothing was achieved but to begin,
Yet finished seemed the circle of her force,
Only she had beaten out sparks of ignorance,
Only the life could think and not the mind,
Only the sense could feel and not the soul,
Only was lit some heat of the flame of Life,
Some joy to be, some rapturous leaps of sense.
All was an impetus of half-conscious Force,
A spirit sprawling drowned in dense life-foam,
A vague self grasping at the shape of things.
Behind all moved seeking for vessels to hold
A first raw vintage of the grapes of God,
On earth's mud a spilth of the supernal Bliss,
Intoxicating the stupefied soul and mind
A heady wine of rapture dark and crude,
Dim, uncast yet into spiritual form,
Obscure inhabitant of the world's blind core,
An unborn godhead's will, a mute desire.

    A third creation now revealed its face.
A mould of body's early mind was made.
A glint of light kindled the obscure World-Force;
It dowered a driven world with the seeing Idea
And armed the act with Thought's dynamic point:
A small thinking being watched the works of Time.
A difficult evolution from below
Called a masked intervention from above;
Else this great, blind inconscient universe
Could never have disclosed its hidden mind,
Or even in blinkers worked in beast and man
The Intelligence that devised the cosmic scheme.
At first he saw a dim obscure mind-power
Moving concealed by Matter and dumb life.
A current thin, it streamed in life's vast flow
Tossing and drifting under a drifting sky
Amid the surge and glimmering tremulous wash,
Released in splash of sense and feeling's waves.
In the deep midst of an unconscious world
Its huddled waves and foam of consciousness ran

Pressing and eddying through a narrow strait,
Carrying experience in its crowded pace.
It flowed emerging into upper light
From the deep pool of its subliminal birth
To reach some high existence still unknown.
There was no thinking self, aim there was none:
All was unrecognised stress and seekings vague.
Only to the unstable surface rose
Sensations, stabs and edges of desire
And passion's leaps and brief emotion's cries,
A casual colloquy of flesh with flesh,
A murmur of heart to longing wordless heart,
Glimmerings of knowledge with no shape of thought
And jets of subconscious will or hunger's pulls.
All was dim sparkle on a foaming top:
It whirled around a drifting shadow-self
In an inconscient flood of Force in Time.
Then came the pressure of a seeing Power
That drew all into a dancing turbid mass
Circling around a single luminous point,
Centre of reference in a conscious field,
Figure of a unitary Light within.
It lit the impulse of the half-sentient flood,
Even an illusion gave of fixity
As if a sea could serve as a firm soil.
That strange observing Power imposed its sight.
It forced on flux a limit and a shape,
It gave its stream a lower narrow bank,
Drew lines to snare the spirit's formlessness.
It fashioned the life-mind of bird and beast,
The answer of the reptile and the fish,
The primitive pattern of the thoughts of man.
A finite movement of the Infinite
Came winging its way through a wide air of Time;
A march of Knowledge moved in Nescience
And guarded in the form a separate soul.
Its right to be immortal it reserved,
But built a wall against the siege of death
And threw a hook to clutch eternity.
A thinking entity appeared in Space.

A little ordered world broke into view
Where being had prison-room for act and sight,
A floor to walk, a clear but scanty range.
An instrument-personality was born,
And a restricted clamped intelligence
Consented to restrain in narrow bounds
Its seeking; it tied the thought to visible things,
Prohibiting the adventure of the Unseen
And the soul's tread through unknown infinities.
A reflex reason, Nature-habit's glass
Illumined life to know and fix its field,
Accepting a dangerous ignorant brevity
And the inconclusive purpose of its walk,
And profit by the hour's precarious chance
In the allotted boundaries of its fate.
A little joy and knowledge satisfied
This little being tied into a knot
And hung on a bulge of its environment,
A little curve cut off in measureless Space,
A little span of life in all vast Time.
A thought was there that planned, a will that strove,
But for small aims within a narrow scope,
Wasting unmeasured toil on transient things.
It knew itself a creature of the mud;
It asked no larger law, no loftier air;
It had no inward look, no upward gaze.
A backward scholar on logic's rickety bench
Indoctrinated by the erring sense,
It took appearance for the face of God,
For casual lights the marching of the suns,
For heaven a starry strip of doubtful blue;
Aspects of being feigned to be the whole.
There was a voice of busy interchange,
A market-place of trivial thoughts and acts:
A life soon spent, a mind the body's slave
Here seemed the brilliant crown of Nature's works,
And tiny egos took the world as means
To sate awhile dwarf lusts and brief desires,
In a death-closed passage saw life's start and end
As though a blind alley were creation's sign,

As if for this the soul had coveted birth
In the wonderland of a self-creating world
And the opportunities of cosmic Space.
This creature passionate only to survive,
Fettered to puny thoughts with no wide range
And to the body's needs and pangs and joys,
This fire growing by its fuel's death,
Increased by what it seized and made its own:
It gathered and grew and gave itself to none.
Only it hoped for greatness in its den
And pleasure and victory in small fields of power
And conquest of life-room for self and kin,
An animal limited by its feeding-space.
It knew not the Immortal in its house,
It had no greater deeper cause to live.
In limits only it was powerful;
Acute to capture truth for outward use,
Its knowledge was the body's instrument;
Absorbed in the little works of its prison-house
It turned around the same unchanging points
In the same circle of interest and desire,
But thought itself the master of its jail.
Although for action, not for wisdom made,
Thought was its apex or its gutter's rim:
It saw an image of the external world
And saw its surface self, but knew no more.
Out of a slow confused embroiled self-search
Mind grew to a clarity cut out, precise,
A gleam enclosed in a stone ignorance.
In this bound thinking's narrow leadership
Tied to the soil, inspired by common things,
Attached to a confined familiar world,
Amid the multitude of her motived plots,
Her changing actors and her million masks,
Life was a play monotonously the same.
There were no vast perspectives of the spirit,
No swift invasions of unknown delight,
No golden distances of wide release.
This petty state resembled our human days
But fixed to eternity of changeless type,

A moment's movement doomed to last through Time.
Existence bridge-like spanned the inconscient gulfs,
A half-illumined building in a mist
Which from a void of Form arose to sight
And jutted out into a void of Soul.
A little light in a great darkness born,
Life knew not where it went nor whence it came.
Around all floated still the nescient haze.

END OF CANTO FOUR

THE GODHEADS OF THE LITTLE LIFE

A FIXED and narrow power with rigid forms,
    He saw the empire of the little life,
An unhappy corner in eternity.
It lived upon the margin of the Idea
Protected by Ignorance as in a shell.
Then, hoping to learn the secret of this world
He peered across its scanty fringe of sight,
To disengage from its surface-clear obscurity
The Force that moved it and the Idea that made
Imposing smallness on the Infinite,
The ruling spirit of its littleness,
The divine law that gave it right to be,
Its claim on Nature and its need in Time.
He plunged his gaze into the siege of mist
That held this ill-lit straitened continent
Ringed with the skies and seas of ignorance
And kept it safe from Truth and Self and Light.
As when a search-light stabs the Night's blind breast
And dwellings and trees and figures of men appear
As if revealed to an eye in Nothingness,
All lurking things were torn out of their veils
And held up in his vision's sun-white blaze.
A busy restless uncouth populace
Teemed in their dusky unnoted thousands there.
In a mist of secrecy wrapping the world-scene
The little deities of Time's nether act
Who work remote from Heaven's controlling eye,
Plotted, unknown to the creatures whom they move,
The small conspiracies of this petty reign
Amused with the small contrivings, the brief hopes

And little eager steps and little ways
And reptile wallowings in the dark and dust,
And the crouch and ignominy of creeping life.
A trepidant and motley multitude,
A strange pell-mell of magic artisans
Was seen moulding the plastic clay of life,
An elfin brood, an elemental kind.
Astonished by the unaccustomed glow,
As if immanent in the shadows started up
Imps with wry limbs and carved beast visages,
Sprite prompters goblin-wizened or faery-small,
And genii fairer but unsouled and poor
And fallen beings, their heavenly portion lost,
And errant divinities trapped in Time's dust.
Ignorant and dangerous wills but armed with power,
Half-animal, half-god their mood, their shape.
Out of the greyness of a dim background
Their whispers come, an inarticulate force,
Awake in mind an echoing thought or word,
To their sting of impulse the heart's sanction draw,
And in that little Nature do their work
And fill its powers and creatures with unease.
Its seed of joy they curse with sorrow's fruit,
Put out with error's breath its scanty lights
And turn its surface truths to falsehood's ends,
Its small emotions spur, its passions drive
To the abyss or through the bog and mire:
Or else with a goad of hard dry lusts they prick,
While jogs on devious ways that nowhere lead
Life's cart finding no issue from ignorance.
To sport with good and evil is their law;
Luring to failure and meaningless success,
All models they corrupt, all measures cheat,
Make knowledge a poison, virtue a pattern dull
And lead the endless cycles of desire
Through semblances of sad or happy chance
To an inescapable fatality.
All by their influence is enacted there.
Nor there alone is their empire or their role:
Wherever are soulless minds and guideless lives

And in a small body self is all that counts,
Wherever love and light and largeness lack,
These crooked fashioners take up their task.
To all half-conscious worlds they extend their reign.
Here too these godlings drive our human hearts,
Our nature's twilight is their lurking place.
Here too the darkened primitive heart obeys
The veiled suggestions of a hidden Mind
That dogs our knowledge with misleading light
And stands between us and the truth that saves.
It speaks to us with the voices of the Night:
Our darkened lives to greater darkness move;
Our seekings listen to calamitous hopes.
A structure of unseeing thoughts is built
And reason used by an irrational Force.
This earth alone is not our teacher and nurse;
The powers of all the worlds have entrance here.
In their own fields they follow the wheel of law
And cherish the safety of a settled type;
On earth out of their changeless orbit thrown
Their law is kept, lost their fixed form of things.
Into a creative chaos they are cast
Where all asks order but is driven by Chance;
Strangers to earth-nature, they must learn earth's ways,
Aliens or opposites, they must unite:
They work and battle and with pain agree:
These join, those part, all parts and joins anew,
Till all have found their divine harmony.
Our life's uncertain way winds circling on,
Our mind's unquiet search asks always light,
Till they have learnt their secret in their source,
In the light of the Timeless and its spaceless home,
In the joy of the Eternal sole and one.
But now the Light supreme is far away:
Our conscious life obeys the inconscience' laws;
To ignorant purposes and blind desires
•Our hearts are moved by an ambiguous force;
Even our mind's conquests wear a battered crown.
A slowly changing order binds our will.
This is our doom until our souls are free.

A mighty Hand then rolls mind's firmaments back,
Infinity takes up the finite's acts
And Nature steps into the eternal Light.
Then only ends this dream of nether life.

At the outset of this enigmatic world
Which seems at once an enormous brute machine
And a slow unmasking of the Spirit in things,
In this revolving chamber without walls
In which God sits impassive everywhere
As if unknown to himself and by us unseen
In a miracle of inconscient secrecy,
Yet is all here his action and his will.
In this whirl and sprawl through infinite vacancy
The Spirit became Matter and lay in the whirl,
A body sleeping without sense or soul.
A mass phenomenon of visible shapes
Supported by the silence of the Void
Appeared in the eternal Consciousness
And seemed an outward and insensible world.
There was none there to see and none to feel;
Only the miraculous Inconscient,
A subtle wizard skilled, was at its task.
Inventing ways for magical results,
Managing creation's marvellous device,
Marking mechanically dumb wisdom's points,
Using the unthought inevitable Idea,
It did the works of God's intelligence
Or wrought the will of some supreme Unknown.
Still consciousness was hidden in Nature's womb,
Unfelt was the Bliss whose rapture dreamed the worlds.
Being was an inert substance driven by Force.
At first was only an etheric Space:
Its huge vibrations circled round and round
Housing some unconceived initiative:
Upheld by a supreme original Breath
Expansion and contraction's mystic act
Created touch and friction in the void,
Into abstract emptiness brought clash and clasp:
Parent of an expanding universe

In a matrix of disintegrating force,
By spending it conserved an endless sum.
On the hearth of Space it kindled a viewless Fire
That, scattering worlds as one might scatter seeds,
Whirled out the luminous order of the stars.
An ocean of electric Energy
Formlessly formed its strange wave-particles
Constructing by their dance this solid scheme,
Its mightiness in the atom shut to rest;
Masses were forged or feigned and visible shapes;
Light flung the photon's swift revealing spark
And showed, in the minuteness of its flash
Imaged, this cosmos of apparent things.
Thus has been made this real impossible world,
An obvious miracle or convincing show.
Or so it seems to man's audacious mind
Who seats his thought as the arbiter of truth,
His personal vision as impersonal fact,
As witnesses of an objective world
His erring sense and his instruments' artifice.
Thus must he work life's tangible riddle out
In a doubtful light, by error seize on Truth
And slowly part the visage and the veil.
Or else, forlorn of faith in mind and sense,
His knowledge a bright body of ignorance,
He sees in all things strangely fashioned here
The unwelcome jest of a deceiving Force,
A parable of Maya and her might.
This vast perpetual motion caught and held
In the mysterious and unchanging change
Of the persistent movement we call Time
And ever renewing its recurrent beat,
These mobile rounds that stereotype a flux,
These static objects in the cosmic dance
That are but Energy's self-repeating whirls
Prolonged by the spirit of the brooding Void,
Awaited life and sense and waking Mind.
A little the Dreamer changed his pose of stone.
But when the Inconscient's scrupulous work was done
And Chance coerced by fixed immutable laws,

A scene was set for Nature's conscious play.
Then stirred the Spirit's mute immobile sleep;
The Force concealed broke dumbly, slowly out.
A dream of living woke in Matter's heart,
A will to live moved in the Inconscient's dust,
A freak of living startled vacant Time,
Ephemeral in a blank eternity,
Infinitesimal in a dead Infinite.
A subtler breath quickened dead Matter's forms;
The world's set rhythm changed to a conscious cry;
A serpent Power twinned the insensible Force.
Islands of living dotted lifeless space
And germs of living formed in formless air.
A life was born that followed Matter's law,
Ignorant of the motives of its steps;
Ever inconstant, yet for ever the same,
It repeated the paradox that gave it birth:
Its restless and unstable stabilities
Recurred incessantly in the flow of Time
And purposeful movements in unthinking forms
Betrayed the heavings of an imprisoned Will.
Waking and sleep lay locked in mutual arms;
Helpless and indistinct came pleasure and pain
Trembling with the first faint thrills of a World-Soul.
A strength of life that could not cry or move,
Yet broke into beauty signing some deep delight:
An inarticulate sensibility,
Throbs of the heart of an unknowing world,
Ran through its somnolent torpor and there stirred
A vague uncertain thrill, a wandering beat,
A dim unclosing as of secret eyes.
Infant self-feeling grew and birth was born.
A godhead woke but lay with dreaming limbs;
Her house refused to open its sealed doors.
Insentient to our eyes that only see
The form, the act and not the imprisoned God,
Life hid in her pulse occult of growth and power
A consciousness with mute stifled beats of sense,
A mind suppressed that knew not yet of thought,
An inert spirit that could only be.

143

At first she raised no voice, no motion dared:
Charged with world-power, instinct with living force,
Only she clung with her roots to the safe earth,
Thrilled dumbly to the shocks of ray and breeze
And put out tendril fingers of desire;
The strength in her yearning for sun and light
Felt not the embrace that made her breathe and live;
Absorbed she dreamed content with beauty and hue.
At last the charmed Immensity looked forth:
Astir, vibrant, hungering, she groped for mind;
Then slowly sense quivered and thought peered out;
She forced the reluctant mould to grow aware.
The magic was chiselled of a conscious form;
Its tranced vibrations rhythmed a quick response,
And luminous stirrings prompted brain and nerve,
Awoke in Matter spirit's identity
And in a body lit the miracle
Of the heart's love and the soul's witness-gaze.
Impelled by an unseen Will there could break out
Fragments of some vast impulse to become
And vivid glimpses of a secret self,
And the doubtful seeds and force of shapes to be
Awoke from the inconscient swoon of things.
An animal creation crept and ran
And flew and called between the earth and sky,
Hunted by death but hoping still to live
And glad to breathe if only for a while.
Then man was moulded from the original brute.
A thinking mind had come to lift life's moods,
A keen-edged tool of a Nature mixed and vague,
An intelligence half-witness, half-machine.
This seeming driver of her wheel of works
Missioned to motive and record her drift
And fix its law on her inconstant powers,
This master-spring of a delicate enginery,
Aspired to enlighten its user and refine
Lifting to a vision of the indwelling Power
The absorbed mechanic's crude initiative:
He raised his eyes; Heaven-light mirrored a Face.
Amazed at the works wrought in her mystic sleep,

She looked upon the world that she had made:
Wondering now seized the great automaton;
She paused to understand her self and aim,
Pondering she learned to act by conscious rule,
A visioned measure guided her rhythmic steps;
Thought bordered her instincts with a frame of will
And lit with the idea her blinded urge.
On her mass of impulses, her reflex acts,
On the Inconscient's pushed or guided drift
And mystery of unthinking accurate steps
She stuck the specious image of a Self,
A living idol of disfigured spirit;
On Matter's acts she imposed a patterned law;
She made a thinking body from chemic cells
And moulded a being out of a driven force.
To be what she was not inflamed her hope:
She turned her dream towards some high Unknown;
A breath was felt below of One supreme.
An opening looked up to spheres above
And coloured shadows limned on mortal ground
The passing figures of immortal things;
 A quick celestial flash could sometimes come:
The illumined soul-ray fell on heart and flesh
And touched with semblances of ideal light
The stuff of which our earthly dreams are made.
A fragile human love that could not last,
Ego's moth-wings to lift the seraph soul,
Appeared, a surface glamour of brief date
Extinguished by a scanty breath of Time;
Joy that forgot mortality for a while
Came, a rare visitor who left betimes,
And made all things seem beautiful for an hour,
Hopes that soon fade to drab realities
And passions that crumble to ashes while they blaze
Kindled the common earth with their brief flame.
A creature insignificant and small
Visited, uplifted by an unknown Power,
Man laboured on his little patch of earth
For means to last, to enjoy, to suffer and die.
A spirit that perished not with the body and breath

Was there like a shodow of the Unmanifest
And stood behind the little personal form
But claimed not yet this earthly embodiment.
Assenting to Nature's long slow-moving toil,
Watching the works of his own ignorance,
Unknown, unfelt the mighty Witness lives
And nothing shows the Glory that is here.
A Wisdom governing the mystic world,
A Silence listening to the cry of Life,
It sees the hurrying crowd of moments stream
Towards the still greatness of a distant hour.

   This huge world unintelligibly turns
In the shadow of a mused Inconscience;
It hides a key to inner meanings missed,
It locks in our hearts a voice we cannot hear.
An enigmatic labour of the Spirit,
An exact machine of which none knows the use,
An art and ingenuity without sense,
This minute elaborate orchestrated life
For ever plays its motiveless symphonies.
The mind learns and knows not, turning its back to truth;
It studies surface laws by surface thought,
Life's steps surveys and Nature's process sees,
Not seeing for what she acts or why we live;
It marks her tireless care of just device,
Her patient intricacy of fine detail,
The ingenious spirit's brave inventive plan
In her great futile mass of endless works,
Adds purposeful figures to her purposeless sum,
Its gabled storeys piles, its climbing roofs
On the close-carved foundations she has laid,
Imagined citadels reared in mythic air
Or mounts a stair of dream to a mystic moon:
Transient creations point and hit the sky:
A world-conjecture's scheme is laboured out
On the dim floor of mind's incertitude,
Or painfully built a fragmentary whole.
Impenetrable, a mystery recondite
Is the vast plan of which we are a part;

Its harmonies are discords to our view,
Because we know not the great theme they serve.
Inscrutable work the cosmic agencies.
Only the fringe of a wide surge we see;
Our instruments have not that greater light,
Our will tunes not with the eternal Will,
Our heart's sight is too blind and passionate.
Impotent to share in Nature's mystic tact,
Inapt to feel the pulse and core of things,
Our reason cannot sound life's mighty sea
And only counts its waves and scans its foam;
It knows not whence these motions touch and pass,
It sees not whither sweeps the hurrying flood:
Only it strives to canalise its powers
And hopes to turn its course to human ends:
But all its means come from the Inconscient's store.
Unseen here act dim huge world-energies
And only trickles and currents are our share.
Our mind lives far off from the authentic Light
Catching at little fragments of the Truth,
In a small corner of infinity,
Our lives are inlets of an ocean's force.
Our conscious movements have sealed origins
But with those shadowy seats no converse hold;
No understanding binds our comrade parts;
Our acts emerge from a crypt our minds ignore.
Our deepest depths are ignorant of themselves;
Even our body is a mystery shop;
As our earth's roots lurk screened below our earth,
So lie unseen our roots of mind and life.
Our springs are kept close hid beneath, within;
Our souls are moved by powers behind the wall.
In the subterranean reaches of the spirit
A puissance acts and recks not what it means;
Using unthinking monitors and scribes,
It is the cause of what we think and feel.
The troglodytes of the subconscious Mind,
Ill-trained slow stammering interpreters,
Only of their small task's routine aware
And busy with the record in our cells,

147

Concealed in the subliminal secrecies
Mid an obscure occult machinery,
Capture the mystic Morse whose measured lilt
Transmits the messages of the cosmic Force.
A whisper falls into life's inner ear
And echoes from the dun subconscient caves,
Speech leaps, thought quivers, the heart vibrates, the will
Answers and tissue and nerve obey the call.
Our lives translate these subtle intimacies;
All is the commerce of a secret Power.
  A thinking puppet is the mind of life:
Its choice is the work of elemental strengths
That know not their own birth and end and cause
And glimpse not the immense intent they serve.
In this nether life of man drab-hued and dull,
Yet filled with poignant small ignoble things,
The conscious Doll is pushed a hundred ways
And feels the push but not the hands that drive.
For none can see the masked ironic troupe
To whom our figure-selves are marionettes,
Our deeds unwitting movements in their grasp,
Our passionate strife an entertainment's scene.
Ignorant themselves of their own fount of strength
They play their part in the enormous Whole.
Agents of darkness imitating light,
Spirits obscure and moving things obscure,
Unwillingly they serve a mightier Power.
Ananke's engines organising Chance,
Channels perverse of a stupendous Will,
Tools of the Unknown who use us as their tools,
Invested with Power in Nature's nether state,
Into the actions mortals think their own
They bring the incoherences of Fate,
Or make a doom of Time's slipshod caprice
And toss the lives of men from hand to hand
In an inconsequent and devious game.
Against all higher Truth their stuff rebels;
Only to Titan force their will lies prone.
Inordinate their hold on human hearts,
In all our nature's turns they intervene.

Insignificant architects of low-built lives
And engineers of interest and desire,
Out of crude earthiness and muddy thrills
And coarse reactions of material nerve
They build our huddled structures of self-will
And the ill-lighted mansions of our thought,
Or with the ego's factories and marts
Surround the beautiful temple of the soul.
Artists minute of the hues of littleness,
They set the mosaic of Life's comedy
Or plan the trivial tragedy of our days,
Arrange the deed, combine the circumstance
And the fantasia of the moods costume.
These unwise prompters of man's ignorant heart
And tutors of his stumbling speech and will,
Movers of petty wraths and lusts and hates
And changeful thoughts and shallow emotion's starts,
These slight illusion-makers with their masks,
Painters of the decor of a dull-hued stage
And nimble scene-shifters of the human play,
Ever are busy with this ill-lit scene.
Ourselves incapable to build our fate
Only as actors speak and strut our parts
Until the piece is done and we pass off
Into a brighter Time and subtler Space.
Thus they inflict their little pigmy law
And curb the mounting slow uprise of man,
Then his too scanty walk with death they close.

    This is the ephemeral creature's daily life.
As long as the human animal is lord
And a dense nether nature screens the soul,
As long as intellect's outward-gazing sight
Serves earthy interest and creature joys,
An incurable littleness pursues his days,
Ever since consciousness was born on earth,
Life is the same in insect, ape and man,
Its stuff unchanged, its way the common route.
If new designs, if richer details grow
And thought is added and more tangled cares,

If little by little it wears a brighter face,
Still even in man the plot is mean and poor.
A gross content prolongs his fallen state;
His small successes are failures of the soul,
His little pleasures punctuate frequent griefs:
Hardship and toil are the heavy price he pays
For the right to live and his last wages death.
An inertia sunk towards inconscience,
A sleep that imitates death is his repose.
A puny splendour of creative force
Is made his spur to fragile human works
Which yet outlast their brief creator's breath.
He dreams sometimes of the revels of the gods
And sees the Dionysian gesture pass,—
A leonine greatness that would tear his soul
If through his failing limbs and fainting heart
The sweet and joyful mighty madness swept:
Trivial amusements stimulate and waste
The energy given to him to grow and be.
His little hour is spent in little things.
A brief companionship with many jars,
A little love and jealousy and hate,
A touch of friendship mid indifferent crowds
Draw his heart-plan on life's diminutive map.
If something great awakes, too frail his pitch
To reveal its zenith tension of delight,
His thought to eternise its ephemeral soar,
Art's brilliant gleam is a pastime for his eyes,
A thrill that smites the nerves is music's spell.
Amidst his harassed toil and welter of cares,
Pressed by the labour of his crowding thoughts,
He draws sometimes around his aching brow
Nature's calm mighty hands to heal his life-pain.
He is saved by her silence from his rack of self;
In her tranquil beauty is his purest bliss.
A new life dawns, he looks out from vistas wide;
The Spirit's breath moves him but soon retires:
His strength was not made to hold that puissant guest.
All dulls down to convention and routine
Or a fierce excitement brings him vivid joys:

His days are tinged with the red hue of strife
And lust's hot glare and passion's crimson stain;
Battle and murder are his tribal game.
Time has he none to turn his eyes within
And look for his lost self and his dead soul.
His motion on too short an axis wheels;
He cannot soar but creeps on his long road
Or if, impatient of the trudge of Time,
He would make a splendid haste on Fate's slow road,
His heart that runs soon pants and tires and sinks;
Or he walks ever on and finds no end.
Hardly a few can climb to greater life.
All tunes to a low scale and conscious pitch.
His knowledge dwells in the house of Ignorance;
His force nears not even once the Omnipotent,
Rare are his visits of heavenly ecstasy.
The bliss which sleeps in things and tries to wake,
Breaks out in him in a small joy of life:
This scanty grace is his persistent stay;
It lightens the burden of his many ills
And reconciles him to his little world.
He is satisfied with his common average kind;
Tomorrow's hopes and his old rounds of thought,
His old familiar interests and desires
He has made a thick and narrowing hedge
Defending his small life from the Invisible;
His being's kinship to infinity
He has shut away from him into inmost self,
Fenced off the greatnesses of hidden God.
His being was formed to play a trivial part
In a little drama on a petty stage;
In a narrow plot he has pitched his tent of life
Beneath the wide gaze of the starry Vast.
He is the crown of all that has been done:
Thus is creation's labour justified;
This is the world's result, Nature's last poise!
And if this were all and nothing more were meant,
If what now seems were the whole of what must be,
If this were not a stade through which we pass
On our road from Matter to eternal Self,

To the Light that made the worlds, the Cause of things,
Well might interpret our mind's limited view
Existence as an accident in Time,
Illusion or phenomenon or freak,
The paradox of a creative Thought
Which moves between unreal opposites,
Inanimate Force struggling to feel and know,
Matter that chanced to read itself by Mind,
Inconscience monstrously engendering soul.
At times all looks unreal and remote:
We seem to live in a fiction of our thoughts
Pieced from sensation's fanciful traveller's tale,
Or caught on the film of the recording brain,
A figment or circumstance in cosmic sleep.
A somnambulist walking under the moon,
An image of ego treads through an ignorant dream
Counting the moments of a spectral Time.
In a false perspective of effect and cause,
Trusting to a specious prospect of world-space,
It drifts incessantly from scene to scene,
Whither it knows not, to what fabulous verge.
All here is dreamed or doubtfully exists,
But who the dreamer is and whence he looks
Is still unknown or only a shadowy guess.
Or the world is real but ourselves too small,
Insufficient for the mightiness of our stage.
A thin life-curve crosses the titan whirl
Of the orbit of a soulless universe,
And in the belly of the sparse rolling mass
A mind looks out from a small casual globe
And wonders what itself and all things are.
And yet to some interned subjective sight
That strangely has formed in Matter's sightless stuff,
A pointillage minute of little self
Takes figure as world-being's conscious base.
Such is our scene in the half-light below.
This is the sign of Matter's infinite,
This the weird purport of the picture shown
To Science the giantess, measurer of her field,
As she pores on the record of her close survey

And mathematises her huge external world,
To Reason bound within the circle of sense,
Or in Thought's broad impalpable Exchange
A speculator in tenuous vast ideas,
Abstractions in the void her currency
We know not with what firm values for its base.
Only religion in this bankruptcy
Presents its dubious riches to our hearts
Or signs unprovisioned cheques on the Beyond:
Our poverty shall there have its revenge.
Our spirits depart discarding a futile life
Into the black unknown or with them take
Death's passport into immortality.

Yet was this only a provisional scheme,
A false appearance sketched by limiting sense,
Mind's insufficient self-discovery,
An early attempt, a first experiment.
This was a toy to amuse the infant earth;
But knowledge ends not in these surface powers
That live upon a ledge in the Ignorance
And dare not look into the dangerous depths
Or to stare upward measuring the Unknown.
There is a deeper seeing from within
And, when we have left these small purlieus of mind,
A greater vision meets us on the heights
In the luminous wideness of the Spirit's gaze.
At last there wakes in us a witness Soul
That looks at truths unseen and scans the Unknown;
Then all assumes a new and marvellous face.
The world quivers with a God-light at its core,
In Time's deep heart high purposes move and live,
Life's borders crumble and join infinity.
This broad, confused, yet rigid scheme becomes
A magnificent imbroglio of the Gods,
A game, a work ambiguously divine.
Our seekings are short-lived experiments
Made by a wordless and inscrutable Power
Testing its issues from inconscient Night
To meet its luminous self of Truth and Bliss.

It peers at the Real through the apparent form;
It labours in our mortal mind and sense;
Amid the figures of the Ignorance,
In the symbol pictures drawn by word and thought,
It seeks the truth to which all figures point;
It looks for the source of Light with vision's lamp;
It works to find the doer of all works,
The unfelt Self within who is the guide,
The unknown Self above who is the goal.
All is not here a blinded Nature's task:
A Word, a Wisdom watches us from on high,
A Witness sanctioning her will and works,
An Eye unseen in the unseeing vast;
There is an Influence from a Light above,
There are thoughts remote and sealed eternities;
A mystic motive drives the stars and suns.
In this passage from a deaf unknowing Force
To struggling consciousness and transient breath
A mighty supernature waits on Time.
The world is other than we now think and see,
Our lives a deeper mystery than we have dreamed;
Our minds are starters in the race to God,
Our souls deputed selves of the Supreme.
Across the cosmic field through narrow lanes
Asking a scanty dole from Fortune's hands
And garbed in beggar's robes there walks the One.
Even in the theatre of these small lives
Behind the act a secret sweetness breathes,
An urge of miniature divinity.
A mystic passion from the wells of God
Flows through the guarded spaces of the soul;
A force that helps, supports the suffering earth,
An unseen nearness and a hidden joy.
There are muffled throbs of laughter's undertones,
The murmur of an occult happiness,
An exultation in the depths of sleep,
A heart of bliss within a world of pain.
An Infant nursed on Nature's covert breast,
An Infant playing in the magic woods,
Fluting to rapture by the Spirit's streams,

Awaits the hour when we shall turn to his call.
In this investiture of fleshly life
A soul that is a spark of God survives
And sometimes it breaks through the sordid screen
And kindles a fire that makes us half-divine.
In our body's cells there sits a hidden Power
That sees the unseen and plans eternity,
Our smallest parts have room for deepest needs;
There too the golden Messengers can come:
A door is cut in the mud wall of self;
Across the lowly threshold with bowed heads
Angels of ecstasy and self-giving pass,
And lodged in an inner sanctuary of dream
The makers of the image of deity live.
Pity is there and fire-winged sacrifice,
And flashes of sympathy and tenderness
Cast heaven-lights from the heart's secluded shrine.
A work is done in the deep silences;
A glory and wonder of spiritual sense,
A laughter in beauty's everlasting space
Transforming world-experience into joy,
Inhabit the mystery of the untouched gulfs;
Lulled by Time's beats eternity sleeps in us.
In the sealed hermetic heart, the happy core,
Unmoved behind this outer shape of death
The eternal Entity prepares within
Its matter of divine felicity,
Its reign of heavenly phenomenon.
Even in our sceptic mind of ignorance
A foresight comes of some immense release,
Our will lifts towards it slow and shaping hands.
Each part in us desires its absolute:
Our thoughts covet the everlasting Light,
Our strength derives from an omnipotent Force,
And since from a veiled God-joy the worlds were made
And since eternal beauty asks for form
Even here where all is made of being's dust,
Our hearts are captured by ensnaring shapes,
Our very senses blindly seek for bliss.
Our error crucifies Reality

155

To force its birth and divine body here,
Compelling, incarnate in a human form
And breathing in limbs that one can touch and clasp,
Its knowledge to rescue ancient Ignorance,
Its saviour light the inconscient universe.
And when that greater Self comes sea-like down
To fill this image of our transience,
All shall be captured by delight, transformed:
In waves of undreamed ecstasy shall roll
Our mind and life and sense and laugh in a light
Other than this hard limited human day,
The body's tissues thrill apotheosised,
Its cells sustain bright metamorphosis.
This little being of Time, this shadow-soul,
This living dwarf figure-head of darkened spirit
Out of its traffic of petty dreams shall rise.
Its shape of person and its ego face
Divested of this mortal travesty,
Like a clay troll kneaded into a god,
New-made in the image of the eternal Guest,
It shall be caught to the breast of a white Force
And, flaming with the paradisal touch
In a rose-fire of sweet spiritual grace,
In the red passion of its infinite change,
Quiver, awake, and shudder with ecstasy.
As if reversing a deformation's spell,
Released from the black magic of the Night,
Renouncing servitude to the dark Abyss,
It shall learn at last who lived within unseen
And seized with marvel in the adoring heart
To the enthroned Child-Godhead kneel aware,
Trembling with beauty and delight and love.
But first the spirit's ascent we must achieve
Out of the chasm from which our nature rose.
The soul must soar sovereign above the form
And climb to summits beyond mind's half-sleep;
Our hearts we must inform with heavenly strength,
Surprise the animal with the occult god.
Then kindling the gold tongue of sacrifice,
Calling the powers of a bright hemisphere,

We shall shed the discredit of our mortal state,
Make the abysm a road for Heaven's descent,
Acquaint our depths with the supernal Ray
And cleave the darkness with the mystic Fire.

Adventuring once more in the natal mist
Across the dangerous haze, the pregnant stir,
He through the astral chaos shore a way
Mid the grey faces of its demon gods,
Questioned by whispers of its flickering ghosts,
Besieged by sorceries of its fluent force.
As one who walks unguided through strange fields
Tending he knows not where nor with what hope,
He trod a soil that failed beneath his feet
And journeyed in stone strength to a fugitive end.
His trail behind him was a vanishing line
Of glimmering points in a vague immensity;
A bodiless murmur travelled at his side
In the wounded gloom complaining against light.
A huge obstruction its immobile heart,
The watching opacity multiplied as he moved
Its hostile mass of dead and staring eyes;
The darkness glimmered like a dying torch.
Around him an extinguished phantom glare
Peopled with shadowy and misleading shapes
The vague Inconscient's dark and measureless cave.
His only sunlight was his spirit's flame.

END OF CANTO FIVE

CANTO SIX

THE KINGDOMS AND GODHEADS OF THE GREATER LIFE

A S one who between dim receding walls
Towards the far gleam of a tunnel's mouth,
Hoping for light, walks now with freer pace
And feels approach a breath of wider air,
So he escaped from that grey anarchy.
Into an ineffectual world he came,
A purposeless region of arrested birth
Where being from non-being fled and dared
To live but had no strength long to abide.
Above there gleamed a pondering brow of sky
Tormented, crossed by wings of doubtful haze
Adventuring with a voice of roaming winds
And crying for a direction in the void
Like blind souls looking for the selves they lost
And wandering through unfamiliar worlds;
Wings of vague questioning met the query of Space.
After denial dawned a dubious hope,
A hope of self and form and leave to live
And the birth of that which never yet could be,
And joy of the mind's hazard, the heart's choice,
Grace of the unknown and hands of sudden surprise
And a touch of sure delight in unsure things:
To a strange uncertain tract his journey came
Where consciousness played with unconscious self
And birth was an attempt or episode.
A charm drew near that could not keep its spell,
An eager Power that could not find its way,
A Chance that chose a strange arithmetic
But could not bind with it the forms it made,

158

A multitude that could not guard its sum
Which less than zero grew and more than one.
Arriving at a large and shadowy sense
That cared not to define its fleeting drift
Life laboured in a strange and mythic air
Denuded of her sweet magnificent suns.
In worlds imagined, never yet made true,
A lingering glimmer on creation's verge,
One strayed and dreamed and never stopped to achieve:
To achieve would have destroyed that magic Space.
The marvels of a twilight wonderland,
Full of a beauty strangely, vainly made,
A surge of fanciful realities,
Dim tokens of a Splendour sealed above,
Awoke the passion of the eyes' desire,
Compelled belief on the enamoured thought
And drew the heart but led it to no goal.
A magic flowed as if of moving scenes
That kept awhile their fugitive delicacy
Of sparing lines limned by an abstract art
In a rare scanted light with faint dream-brush
On a silver background of incertitude.
An infant glow of heavens near to morn,
A fire intense conceived but never lit,
Caressed the air with ardent hints of day.
The perfect longing for imperfection's charm,
The illumined caught by the snare of Ignorance,
Ethereal creatures drawn by body's lure
To that region of promise, beating invisible wings,
Came hungry for the joy of finite life
But too divine to tread created soil
And share the fate of perishable things.
The Children of the unembodied Gleam
Arisen from a formless thought in the soul
And chased by an imperishable desire,
Traversed the field of the pursuing gaze.
A will that unpersisting failed, worked there:
Life was a search but finding never came.
There nothing satisfied, but all allured,
Things seemed to be that never wholly are,

Images were seen that looked like living acts
And symbols hid the sense they claimed to show,
Pale dreams grew real to the dreamer's eyes.
The souls came there that vainly strive for birth,
And spirits entrapped might wander through all time,
Yet never find the truth by which they live.
All ran like hopes that hunt a lurking chance;
Nothing was solid, nothing felt complete:
All was unsafe, miraculous and half-true.
It seemed a realm of lives that had no base.

Then dawned a greater seeking, broadened sky,
A journey under wings of brooding Force.
First came the kingdom of the morning star:
A twilight beauty trembled under its spear
And the throb of promise of a wider Life.
Then slowly rose a great and doubting sun
And in its light she made of self a world.
A spirit was there that sought for its own deep self,
Yet was content with fragments pushed in front
And parts of living that belied the Whole
But, pieced together, might one day be true.
Yet something seemed to be achieved at last.
A growing volume of the will to be,
A text of living and a graph of force,
A script of acts, a song of conscious forms
Burdened with meanings fugitive from thought's grasp
And crowded with undertones of life's rhythmic cry,
Could write itself on the hearts of living things.
In an outbreak of the might of secret Spirit,
In Life and Matter's answer of delight,
Some face of deathless beauty could be caught
That gave immortality to a moment's joy,
Some word that could incarnate highest Truth
Leaped out from a chance tension of the soul,
Some hue of the Absolute could fall on life,
Some glory of knowledge and intuitive sight,
Some passion of the rapturous heart of Love.
A hierophant of the bodiless Secrecy
Interned in an unseen spiritual sheath,

The Will that pushes sense beyond its scope
To feel the light and joy intangible,
Half found its way into the Ineffable's peace,
Half captured a sealed sweetness of desire
That yearned from a bosom of mysterious Bliss,
Half manifested veiled Reality.
A soul not wrapped into its cloak of mind
Could glimpse the true sense of a world of forms;
Illumined by a vision in the thought,
Upbuoyed by the heart's understanding flame,
It could hold in the conscious ether of the spirit
The divinity of a symbol universe.

This realm inspires us with our vaster hopes;
Its forces have made landings on our globe,
Its signs have stamped their patterns on our lives:
It lends a sovereign movement to our fate,
Its errant waves motive our life's high surge.
All that we seek for is prefigured there
And all we have not known nor even sought
Which yet one day must be born in human hearts
That the Timeless may fulfil itself in things.
Incarnate in the mystery of the days,
Eternal in an unclosed Infinite,
A mounting endless possibility
Climbs high upon a topless ladder of dream
Forever in the Being's conscious trance.
All on that ladder mounts to an unseen end.
An Energy of perpetual transience makes
The journey from which no return is sure,
The pilgrimage of Nature to the Unknown.
As if in her ascent to her lost source
She hoped to unroll all that could ever be,
Her high procession moves from stage to stage,
A progress leap from sight to greater sight,
A process march from form to ampler form,
A caravan of the inexhaustible
Formations of a boundless Thought and Force.
Her timeless Power that lay once on the lap
Of a beginningless and endless Calm,
Now severed from the Spirit's immortal bliss,

11

Erects the type of all the joys she has lost;
Compelling transient substance into shape,
She hopes by the creative act's release
To o'erleap sometimes the gulf she cannot fill,
To heal awhile the wound of severance,
Escape from the moment's prison of littleness
And meet the Eternal's wide sublimities
In the uncertain time-field portioned here.
Almost she nears what never can be attained;
She shuts eternity into an hour
And fills a little soul with the Infinite;
The Immobile leans to the magic of her call;
She stands on a shore in the Illimitable,
Perceives the formless Dweller in all forms
And feels around her infinity's embrace.
Her task no ending knows, she serves no aim
But labours driven by a nameless Will
That came from some unknowable formless Vast.
This is her secret and impossible task
To catch the boundless in a net of birth,
To cast the spirit into physical form,
To lend speech and thought to the Ineffable;
She is pushed to reveal the ever Unmanifest.
Yet by her skill the impossible has been done:
She follows her sublime irrational plan,
Invents devices of her magic art
To find new bodies for the Infinite
And images of the Unimaginable;
She has lured the Eternal into the arms of Time.
Even now herself she knows not what she has done.
For all is wrought beneath a baffling mask:
A semblance other than its hidden truth
The aspect wears of an illusion's trick,
A feigned time-driven unreality,
The unfinished creation of a changing soul
In a body changing with the inhabitant.
Insignificant her means, infinite her work;
On a great field of shapeless consciousness
In little finite strokes of mind and sense
An endless truth she endlessly unfolds;

A timeless mystery works out in Time.
The greatness she has dreamed her acts have missed,
Her labour is a passion and a pain,
A rapture and pang, her glory and her curse;
And yet she cannot choose but labours on;
Her mighty heart forbids her to desist.
As long as the world lasts her failure lives
Astonishing and foiling Reason's gaze,
A folly and a beauty unspeakable,
A superb madness of the will to live,
A daring, a delirium of delight.
This is her being's law, its sole resource;
She sates, though satisfaction never comes,
Her hungry will to lavish everywhere
Her many-imaged fictions of the Self
And thousand fashions of one Reality.
A world she made touched by truth's fleeing hem,
A world cast into a dream of what it seeks,
An icon of truth, a conscious mystery's shape.
It lingered not like the earth-mind hemmed in
In solid barriers of apparent fact;
It dared to trust the dream-mind and the soul.
A hunter of spiritual verities
Still only thought or guessed or held by faith,
It seized in imagination and confined
A painted bird of paradise in a cage.
This greater life is enamoured of the Unseen;
It calls to some highest Light beyond its reach,
It can feel the Silence that absolves the soul;
It feels a saviour touch, a ray divine:
Beauty and good and truth its godheads are.
It is near to heavenlier heavens than earth's eyes see,
A direr darkness than man's life can bear.
It has kinship with the demon and the god.
A strange enthusiasm has moved its heart;
It hungers for heights, it passions for the supreme.
It hunts for the perfect word, the perfect shape,
It leaps to the summit thought, the summit light.
For by the form the Formless is brought close
And all perfection fringes the Absolute.

A child of heaven who never saw his home,
Its impetus meets the eternal at a point:
It can only near and touch, it cannot hold;
It can only strain towards some bright extreme:
Its greatness is to seek and to create.

On every plane, this Greatness must create.
On earth, in heaven, in hell she is the same;
Of every fate she takes her mighty part.
A guardian of the fire that lights the suns,
She triumphs in her glory and her might:
Opposed, oppressed she bears God's urge to be born:
The spirit survives upon non-being's ground,
World-force outlasts world-disillusion's shock:
Dumb, she is still the Word, inert the Power.
Here fallen, a slave of death and ignorance,
To things deathless she is driven to aspire
And moved to know even the Unknowable.
Even nescient, null, her sleep creates a world.
When most unseen, most mightily she works;
Housed in the atom, buried in the clod
Her quick creative passion cannot cease.
Inconscience is her long gigantic pause,
Her cosmic swoon is a stupendous phase:
Time-born, she hides her immortality;
In death, her bed, she waits the hour to rise.
Even with the Light denied that sent her forth
And the hope dead she needed for her task,
Even when her brightest stars are quenched in Night,
Nourished by hardship and calamity
And with pain for her body's handmaid, masseuse, nurse,
Her tortured invisible spirit continues still
To toil though in darkness, to create though with pangs;
She carries crucified God upon her breast.
In chill insentient depths where joy is none,
Immured, oppressed by the resisting Void
Where nothing moves and nothing can become,
Still she remembers, still invokes the skill
The Wonder-Worker gave her at her birth,
Imparts to drowsy formlessness a shape,
Reveals a world where nothing was before.

In realms confined to a prone circle of death,
To a dark eternity of Ignorance,
A quiver in an inert inconscient mass,
Or imprisoned in immobilised whorls of Force,
By Matter's blind compulsion deaf and mute
She reposes motionless in its dust of sleep.
Then, for her rebel waking's punishment
Given only hard mechanic Circumstance
As the enginery of her magic craft,
She fashions godlike marvels out of mud;
In the plasm she sets her dumb immortal urge,
Helps the live tissue to think, the closed sense to feel,
Flashes through the frail nerves poignant messages,
In a heart of flesh miraculously loves,
To brute bodies gives a soul, a will, a voice.
Ever she summons as by a sorcerer's wand
Beings and shapes and scenes innumerable,
Torch-bearers of her pomps through Time and Space.
This world is her long journey through the night,
The suns and planets lamps to light her road,
Our reason is the confidante of her thoughts,
Our senses are her vibrant witnesses.
There drawing her signs from things half true, half false,
She labours to replace by realised dreams
The memory of her lost eternity.

These are her deeds in this huge world-ignorance:
Till the veil is lifted, till the night is dead,
In light or dark she keeps her tireless search;
Time is her road of endless pilgrimage.
One mighty passion motives all her works.
Her eternal Lover is her action's cause;
For him she leaped forth from the unseen Vasts
To move here in a stark unconscious world.
Its acts are her commerce with her hidden Guest,
His moods she takes for her heart's passionate moulds;
In beauty she treasures the sunlight of his smile.
Ashamed of her rich cosmic poverty,
She cajoles with her small gifts his mightiness,
Holds with her scenes his look's fidelity
And woos his large-eyed wandering thoughts to dwell

In figures of her million-impulsed Force.
Only to attract her veiled companion
And keep him close to her breast in her world-cloak
Lest from her arms he turn to his formless peace,
Is her heart's business and her clinging care.
Yet when he is most near, she feels him far.
For contradiction is her nature's law.
Although she is ever in him and he in her,
As if unaware of the eternal tie,
Her will is to shut God into her works
And keep him as her cherished prisoner
That never they may part again in Time.
A sumptuous chamber of the Spirit's sleep
At first she made, a deep interior room,
Where he slumbers as if a forgotten guest.
But now she turns to break the oblivious spell,
Awakes the sleeper on the sculptured couch;
She finds again the Presence in the form
And in the light that wakes with him recovers
A meaning in the hurry and trudge of Time,
And through this mind that once obscured the soul
Passes a glint of unseen deity.
Across a luminous dream of spirit-space
She builds creation like a rainbow bridge
Between the original Silence and the Void.
A net is made of the mobile universe;
She weaves a snare for the conscious Infinite.
A knowledge is with her that conceals its steps
And seems a mute omnipotent Ignorance.
A might is with her that makes wonders true;
The incredible is her stuff of common fact.
Her purposes, her workings riddles prove;
Examined, they grow other than they were,
Explained, they seem yet more inexplicable.
Even in our world a mystery has reigned
Earth's cunning screen of trivial plainness hides;
Her larger levels are of sorceries made.
There the enigma shows its splendid prism,
There is no deep disguise of commonness;
Occult, profound comes all experience,

Marvel is ever new, miracle divine.
There is a screened burden, a mysterious touch,
There is a secrecy of hidden sense.
Although no earthen mask weighs on her face,
Into herself she flees from her own sight.
All forms are tokens of some veiled idea
Whose covert purpose lurks from mind's pursuit,
Yet is a womb of sovereign consequence.
There every thought and feeling is an act,
And every act a symbol and a sign,
And every symbol hides a living power.
A universe she builds from truths and myths,
But what she needed most she cannot build;
All shown is a figure or copy of the Truth,
But the Real veils from her its mystic face.
All else she finds, there lacks eternity;
All is sought out but missed the Infinite.

A consciousness lit by a Truth above
Was felt; it saw the light but not the Truth:
It caught the Idea and built from it a world;
It made an Image there and called it God.
Yet something true and inward harboured there.
The beings of that world of greater life,
Tenants of a larger air and freer space,
Live not by the body or in outward things:
A deeper living was their seat of self.
In that intense domain of intimacy
Objects dwell as companions of the soul;
The body's actions are a minor script,
The surface rendering of a life within.
All forces are Life's retinue in that world
And thought and body as her handmaids move.
The universal widenesses give her room:
All feel the cosmic movement in their acts
And are the instruments of her cosmic might.
Or their own self they make their universe.
In all who have risen to a greater Life
A voice of unborn things whispers to the ear,
To their eyes visited by some high sunlight

Aspiration shows the image of a crown:
To work out a seed that she has thrown within,
To achieve her power in them her creatures live.
Each is a greatness growing towards the heights
Or from his inner centre oceans out;
In circling ripples of concentric power
They swallow, glutted, their environment.
Even of that largeness many a cabin make;
In narrower breadths and briefer vistas pent
They live content with some small greatness won.
To rule the little empire of themselves,
To be a figure in their private world
And make the milieu's joys and griefs their own
And satisfy their life-motives and life-wants
Is charge enough and office for this strength,
A steward of the Person and his fate.
This was transition-line and starting-point,
A first immigration into heavenliness,
For all who cross into that brilliant sphere:
These are the kinsmen of our earthly race;
This region borders on our mortal state.

This wider world our greater movements gives,
Its strong formations build our growing selves;
Its creatures are our brighter replicas,
Complete the types we only initiate
And are securely what we strive to be.
As if thought-out eternal characters,
Entire, not pulled as we by contrary tides,
They follow the unseen leader in the heart,
Their lives obey the inner nature's law.
There is kept grandeur's store, the hero's mould;
The soul is the watchful builder of its fate;
None is a spirit indifferent and inert;
They choose their side, they see the god they adore.
A battle is joined between the true and false,
A pilgrimage sets out to the divine Light.
For even Ignorance there aspires to know
And shines with the lustre of a distant star;
There is a knowledge in the heart of sleep
And Nature comes to them as a conscious force.

An ideal is their leader and their king:
Aspiring to the monarchy of the sun
They call in Truth for their high government,
Hold her incarnate in their daily acts
And fill their thoughts with her inspired voice
And shape their lives into her breathing form,
Till in her sun-gold godhead they too share.
Or to the truth of Darkness they subscribe;
Whether for Heaven or Hell they must wage war:
Warriors of Good, they serve a shining cause
Or are Evil's soldiers in the pay of Sin.
For evil and good an equal tenure keep
Wherever Knowledge is Ignorance's twin.
All powers of Life towards their godhead tend
In the wideness and the daring of that air,
Each builds its temple and expands its cult,
And Sin too there is a divinity.
Affirming the beauty and splendour of her law
She claims life as her natural domain,
Assumes the world's throne or dons the papal robe:
Her worshippers proclaim her sacred right.
A red-tiaraed falsehood they revere,
Worship the shadow of a crooked god,
Admit the black Idea that twists the brain
Or lie with the harlot Power that slays the Soul.
A mastering virtue statuesques the pose,
Or a titan passion goads to a proud unrest:
At Wisdom's altar they are kings and priests
Or their life a sacrifice to an idol of Power.
Or Beauty shines on them like a wandering star;
Too far to reach, passionate they follow her light;
In Art and Life they catch the All-Beautiful's ray
And make the world their radiant treasure house:
Even common figures are with marvel robed;
A charm and greatness locked in every hour
Awakes the joy which sleeps in all things made.
A mighty victory or a mighty fall,
A throne in heaven or a pit in hell,
The dual Energy they have justified
And marked their souls with her tremendous seal:

Whatever Fate may do to them they have earned;
Something they have done, something they have been, they live.
There Matter is soul's result and not its cause.
In a contrary balance to earth's truth of things
The gross weighs less, the subtle counts for more;
On inner values hangs the outer plan.
As quivers with the thought the expressive word,
As yearns the act with the passion of the soul
This world's apparent sensible design
Looks vibrant back to some interior might.
A Mind not limited by external sense
Gave figures to the spirit's imponderables,
The world's impacts without channels registered
And turned into the body's concrete thrill
The vivid workings of a bodiless Force;
Powers here subliminal that act unseen
Or in ambush crouch waiting behind the wall
Came out in front uncovering their face.
The occult grew there overt, the obvious kept
A covert turn and shouldered the unknown;
The unseen was felt and jostled visible shapes.
In the communion of two meeting minds
Thought looked at thought and had no need of speech;
Emotion clasped emotion in two hearts,
They felt each other's thrill in the flesh and nerves
Or melted each in each and grew immense
As when two houses burn and fire joins fire:
Hate grappled hate and love broke in on love,
Will wrestled with will on mind's invisible ground;
Others' sensations passing through like waves
Left quivering the subtle body's frame,
Their anger rushed galloping in brute attack,
A charge of trampling hooves on shaken soil;
One felt another's grief invade the breast,
Another's joy exulting ran through the blood:
Hearts could draw close through distance, voices near
That spoke upon the shore of alien seas.
There beat a throb of living interchange:
Being felt being even when afar
And consciousness replied to consciousness.

And yet the ultimate oneness was not there.
There was a separateness of soul from soul:
An inner wall of silence could be built,
An armour of conscious might protect and shield;
The being could be closed in and solitary;
One could remain apart in self, alone.
Identity was not yet nor union's peace.
All was imperfect still, half-known, half-done:
The miracle of Inconscience overpassed,
The miracle of the Superconscient still
Unknown, self-wrapped, unfelt, unknowable,
Looked down on them, origin of all they were.
As forms they came of the formless Infinite,
As names lived of a nameless Eternity.
The beginning and the end were there occult;
A middle term worked unexplained, abrupt:
They were words that spoke to a vast wordless Truth,
They were figures crowding an unfinished sum.
None truly knew himself or knew the world
Or the Reality living there enshrined:
Only they knew what Mind could take and build
Out of the secret Supermind's huge store.
A darkness under them, a bright Void above,
Uncertain they lived in a great climbing space;
By mysteries they explained a Mystery,
A riddling answer met the riddle of things.
As he moved in this ether of ambiguous life,
Himself he grew a riddle to himself;
As symbols he saw all and sought their sense.

  Across the leaping springs of death and birth
And over shifting borders of soul-change,
A hunter on the Spirit's creative track,
He followed in life's fine and mighty trails
Pursuing her sealed formidable delight
In a perilous adventure without close.
At first no aim appeared in these large steps:
Only the wide source he saw of all things here
Looking towards a wider source beyond.
For as she drew away from earthly lines,

A tenser drag was felt from the Unknown,
A higher context of delivering thought
Drove her towards marvel and discovery;
There came a high release from pettier cares,
A mightier image of desire and hope,
A vaster formula, a greater scene.
Ever she circled towards some far-off Light:
Her signs still covered more than they revealed;
But tied to some immediate sight and will
They lost their purport in the joy of use,
Till stripped of their infinite meaning they became
A cipher gleaming with unreal sense.
Armed with a magical and haunted bow
She aimed at a target kept invisible
And ever deemed remote though always near.
As one who spells illumined characters,
The key-book of a crabbed magician text,
He scanned her subtle tangled weird designs
And the screened difficult theorem of her clues,
Traced in the monstrous sands of desert Time
The thread beginnings of her titan works,
Watched her charade of action for some hint,
Read the No-gestures of her silhouettes,
And strove to capture in their burdened drift
The dance-fantasia of her sequences
Escaping into rhythmic mystery,
A glimmer of fugitive feet on fleeing soil.
In the labyrinth pattern of her thoughts and hopes
And the byways of her intimate desires,
In the complex corners crowded with her dreams
And rounds crossed by an intrigue of irrelevant rounds,
A wanderer straying amid fugitive scenes
He lost its signs and chased each failing guess.
Ever he met key-words, ignorant of their key.
A sun that dazzled its own eye of sight,
A luminous enigma's brilliant hood
Lit the dense purple barrier of thought's sky:
A dim large trance showed to the night her stars.
As if sitting near an open window's gap,
He read by lightning-flash on crowding flash

Chapters of her metaphysical romance
Of the soul's search for lost Reality
And her fictions drawn from spirit's authentic fact,
Her caprices and conceits and meanings locked,
Her rash unseizable freaks and mysteried turns.
The magnificent wrappings of her secrecy
That fold her desirable body out of sight,
The strange significant forms woven on her robe,
Her meaningful outlines of the souls of things
He saw, her false transparencies of thought-hue,
Her rich brocades with imaged fancies sewn
And mutable masks and broideries of disguise.
A thousand baffling faces of the Truth
Looked at him from her forms with unknown eyes
And wordless mouths unrecognisable,
Spoke from the figures of her masquerade,
Or peered from the recondite magnificence
And subtle splendour of her draperies.
In sudden scintillations of the unknown,
Inexpressive sounds became veridical,
Ideas that seemed unmeaning flashed out truth;
Voices that came from unseen waiting worlds
Uttered the syllables of the Unmanifest
To clothe the body of the mystic Word,
And wizard diagrams of the occult Law
Sealed some precise unreadable harmony,
Or used hue and figure to reconstitute
The herald blazon of Time's secret things.
In her green wildernesses and lurking depths,
In her thickets of joy where danger clasps delight,
He glimpsed the hidden wings of her songster hopes,
A glimmer of blue and gold and scarlet fire.
In her covert lanes, bordering her chance field-paths
And by her singing rivulets and calm lakes
He found the glow of her golden fruits of bliss
And the beauty of her flowers of dream and muse.
As if a miracle of heart's change by joy
He watched in the alchemist radiance of her suns
The crimson outburst of one secular flower
On the tree of sacrifice of spiritual love.

In the sleepy splendour of her noons he saw,
A perpetual repetition through the hours,
Thought's dance of dragon-flies on mystery's stream
That skim but never test its murmurs' race,
And heard the laughter of her rose desires
Running as if to escape from longed-for hands,
Jingling sweet anklet-bells of fantasy.
Amidst live symbols of her occult power
He moved and felt them as close real forms:
In that life more concrete than the lives of men
Throbbed heart-beats of the hidden reality:
Embodied was there what we but think and feel,
Self-framed what here takes outward borrowed shapes.
A comrade of Silence on her austere heights
Accepted by her mighty loneliness,
He stood with her on meditating peaks
Where life and being are a sacrament
Offered to the Reality beyond,
And saw her loose into Infinity
Her hooded eagles of significance,
Messengers of Thought to the Unknowable.
Identified in soul-vision and soul-sense,
Entering into her depths as into a house,
All he became that she was or longed to be,
He thought with her thoughts and journeyed with her steps,
Lived with her breath and scanned all with her eyes
That he might learn the secret of her soul.
A witness overmastered by his scene,
He admired her splendid front of pomp and play
And the marvels of her rich and delicate craft,
And thrilled to the insistence of her cry;
Impassioned he bore the sorceries of her might,
Felt laid on him her abrupt mysterious will,
Her hands that knead fate in their violent grasp,
Her touch that moves, her powers that seize and drive.
But this too he saw, her soul that wept within,
Her seekings vain that clutch at fleeing truth,
Her hopes whose sombre gaze mates with despair,
The passion that possessed her longing limbs,
The trouble and rapture of her yearning breasts,

174

Her mind that toils unsatisfied with its fruits,
Her heart that captures not the one Beloved.
Always he met a veiled and seeking Force,
An exiled goddess building mimic heavens,
A Sphinx whose eyes look up to a hidden Sun.

    Ever he felt near a spirit in her forms:
Its passive presence was her nature's strength;
This sole is real in apparent things,
Even upon earth the spirit is life's key,
But her solid outsides nowhere bear its trace.
Its stamp on her acts is undiscoverable.
A pathos of lost heights is its appeal.
Only sometimes is caught a shadowy line
That seems a hint of veiled reality.
Life stared at him with vague confused outlines
Offering a picture the eyes could not keep,
A story that was yet not written there.
As in a fragmentary half-lost design
Life's meanings fled from the pursuing eye.
Life's visage hides life's real self from sight;
Life's secret sense is written within, above.
The thought that gives it sense lives far beyond;
It is not seen in its half-finished design.
In vain we hope to read the baffling signs
Or find the word of the half-played charade.
Only in that greater life a cryptic thought
Is found, is hinted some interpreting word
That makes the earth-myth a tale intelligible.
Something was seen at last that looked like truth.
In a half-lit air of hazardous mystery
The eye that looks at the dark half of truth
Made out an image mid a vivid blur
And peering through a mist of subtle tints
He saw a half-blind chained divinity
Bewildered by the world in which he moved,
Yet conscious of some light prompting his soul.
Attracted to strange far-off shimmerings,
Led by the fluting of a distant Player
He sought his way amid life's laughter and call

And the index chaos of her myriad steps
Towards some total deep infinitude.
Around crowded the forest of her signs:
At hazard he read by arrow-leaps of Thought
That hit the mark by guess or luminous chance,
Her changing coloured road-lights of idea
And her signals of uncertain swift event,
The hieroglyphs of her symbol pageantries
And her landmarks in the tangled paths of Time.
In her mazes of approach and of retreat
To every side she draws him and repels,
But drawn too near escapes from his embrace;
All ways she leads him but no way is sure.
Allured by the many-toned marvel of her chant,
Attracted by the witchcraft of her moods
And moved by her casual touch to joy and grief,
He loses himself in her but wins her not.
A fugitive paradise smiles at him from her eyes:
He dreams of her beauty made for ever his,
He dreams of his mastery her limbs shall bear,
He dreams of the magic of her breasts of bliss.
In her illumined script, her fanciful
Translation of God's pure original text,
He thinks to read the Scripture Wonderful,
Hieratic key to unknown beatitudes.
But the Word of Life is hidden in its script,
The chant of Life has lost its divine note.
Unseen, a captive in a house of sound,
The spirit lost in the splendour of a dream
Listens to a thousand-voiced illusion's ode.
A delicate weft of sorcery steals the heart
Or a fiery magic tints her tones and hues,
Yet they but wake a thrill of transient grace;
A vagrant march struck by the wanderer Time
They call to a brief unsatisfied delight
Or wallow in ravishments of mind and sense,
But miss the luminous answer of the soul.
A blind heart-throb that reaches joy through tears,
A yearning towards peaks for ever unreached,
An ecstasy of unfulfilled desire

Track the last heavenward climbings of her voice.
Transmuted are past suffering's memories
Into an old sadness's sweet escaping trail:
Turned are her tears to gems of diamond pain,
Her sorrow into a magic crown of song.
Brief are her snatches of felicity
That touch the surface, then escape or die:
A lost remembrance echoes in her depths,
A deathless longing is hers, a veiled self's call;
A prisoner in the mortal's limiting world,
A spirit wounded by life sobs in her breast;
A cherished suffering is her deepest cry.
A wanderer on forlorn despairing routes,
Along the roads of sound a frustrate voice
Forsaken cries to a forgotten bliss.
Astray in the echo caverns of Desire,
It guards the phantoms of a soul's dead hopes
And keeps alive the voice of perished things
Or lingers upon sweet and errant notes
Hunting for pleasure in the heart of pain.
A fateful hand has touched the cosmic chords
And the intrusion of a troubled strain
Covers the inner music's hidden key
That guides unheard the surface cadences.
Yet is it joy to live and to create
And joy to love and labour though all fails,
And joy to seek though all we find deceives
And all on which we lean betrays our trust;
Yet something in its depths was worth the pain,
A passionate memory haunts with ecstasy's fire.
Even grief has joy hidden beneath its roots:
For nothing is truly vain the One has made:
In our defeated hearts God's strength survives
And victory's star still lights our desperate road;
Our death is made a passage to new worlds.
This to Life's music gives its anthem swell.
To all she lends the glory of her voice;
Heaven's raptures whisper to her heart and pass,
Earth's transient yearnings cry from her lips and fade.
Alone the God-given hymn escapes her art

That came with her from her spiritual home
But stopped half-way and failed, a silent word
Awake in some deep pause of waiting worlds,
A murmur suspended in eternity's hush:
But no breath comes from the supernal peace:
A sumptuous interlude occupies the ear
And the heart listens and the soul consents;
An evanescent music it repeats
Wasting on transience Time's eternity.
A tremolo of the voices of the hours
Oblivious screens the high intended theme
The self-embodying spirit came to play
On the vast clavichord of Nature-Force.
Only a mighty murmur here and there
Of the eternal Word, the blissful Voice
Or Beauty's touch transfiguring heart and sense,
A wandering splendour and a mystic cry,
Recalls the strength and sweetness heard no more.

Here is the gap, here stops or sinks life's force;
This deficit paupers the magician's skill:
This want makes all the rest seem thin and bare.
A half-sight draws the horizon of her acts:
Her depths remember what she came to do,
But the mind has forgotten or the heart mistakes:
In Nature's endless lines is lost the God.
In knowledge to sum up omniscience,
In action to erect the Omnipotent,
To create her Creator here was her heart's conceit,
To invade the cosmic scene with utter God.
Toiling to transform the still far Absolute
Into an all-fulfilling epiphany,
Into an utterance of the Ineffable,
She would bring the glory here of the Absolute's force,
Change poise into creation's rhythmic swing,
Marry with a sky of calm a sea of bliss.
A fire to call eternity into Time,
Make body's joy as vivid as the soul's,
Earth she would lift to neighbourhood with heaven,
Labours life to equate with the Supreme

And reconcile the Eternal and the Abyss.
Her pragmatism of the transcendent Truth
Fills silence with the voices of the gods,
But in the cry the single Voice is lost.
For Nature's vision climbs beyond her acts.
A life of gods in heaven she sees above,
A demi-god emerging from an ape
Is all she can in our mortal element.
Here the half-god, the half-titan are her peak:
This greater life wavers twixt earth and sky.
A poignant paradox pursues her dreams:
Her hooded energy moves an ignorant world
To look for a joy her own strong clasp puts off:
In her embrace it cannot turn to its source.
Immense her power, endless her act's vast drive,
Astray is its significance and lost.
Although she carries in her secret breast
The law and journeying curve of all things born
Her knowledge partial seems, her purpose small;
On a soil of yearning tread her sumptuous hours.
A leaden Nescience weighs the wings of Thought,
Her power oppresses the being with its garbs,
Her action prisons its immortal gaze.
A sense of limit haunts her masteries
And nowhere is assured content or peace:
For all the depth and beauty of her work
A wisdom lacks that sets the spirit free.
An old and faded charm had now her face
And palled for him her quick and curious lore;
His wide soul asked a deeper joy than hers.
Out of her daedal lines he sought escape;
But neither gate of horn nor ivory
He found nor postern of spiritual sight.
There was no issue from that dreamlike space.
Our being must move eternally through Time;
Death helps us not, vain is the hope to cease;
A secret Will compels us to endure.
Our life's repose is in the Infinite;
It cannot end, its end is Life supreme.
Death is a passage, not the goal of our walk:

179

Some ancient deep impulsion labours on:
Our souls are dragged as with a hidden leash,
Carried from birth to birth, from world to world,
Our acts prolong after the body's fall
The old perpetual journey without pause.
No silent peak is found where Time can rest.
This was a magic stream that reached no sea.
However far he went, wherever turned,
The wheel of works ran with him and outstripped;
Always a farther task was left to do.
A beat of action and a cry of search
For ever grew in that unquiet world;
A busy murmur filled the heart of Time.
All was contrivance and unceasing stir.
A hundred ways to live were tried in vain:
A sameness that assumed a thousand forms
Strove to escape from its long monotone
And made new things that soon were like the old.
A curious decoration lured the eye
And novel values furbished ancient themes
To cheat the mind with the idea of change.
A different picture that was still the same
Appeared upon the cosmic vague background.
Only another labyrinthine house
Of creatures and their doings and events,
A city of the traffic of bound souls,
A market of creation and her wares
Was offered to the labouring mind and heart.
A circuit ending where it first began
Is dubbed the forward and eternal march
Of progress on perfection's unknown road.
Each final scheme leads to a sequel plan.
Yet every new departure seems the last,
Inspired evangel, theory's ultimate peak,
Proclaiming a panacea for all Time's ills
Or carrying thought in its ultimate zenith flight
And trumpeting supreme discovery;
Each brief idea, a structure perishable,
Publishes the immortality of its rule,
Its claim to be the perfect form of things,

Truth's last epitome, Time's golden best.
But nothing has been achieved of infinite worth:
A world made ever anew, never complete,
Piled always half-attempts on lost attempts
And saw a fragment as the eternal Whole.
In the aimless mounting total of things done
Existence seemed a vain necessity's act,
A wrestle of eternal opposites
In a clasped antagonism's close-locked embrace,
A play without denouement or idea,
A hunger march of lives without a goal,
Or, written on a bare black board of Space,
A futile and recurring sum of souls,
A hope that failed, a light that never shone,
The labour of an unaccomplished Force
Tied to its acts in a dim eternity.
There is no end or none can yet be seen:
Although defeated, life must struggle on;
Always she sees a crown she cannot grasp;
Her eyes are fixed beyond her fallen state.
There quivers still within her breast and ours
A glory that was once and is no more,
Or there calls to us from some unfulfilled beyond
A greatness yet unreached by the halting world.
In a memory behind our mortal sense
A dream persists of larger happier air
Breathing around free hearts of joy and love,
Forgotten by us, immortal in lost Time.
A ghost of bliss pursues her haunted depths;
For she remembers still though now so far
Her realm of golden ease and glad desire
And the beauty and strength and happiness that were hers
In the sweetness of her glowing paradise,
In her kingdom of immortal ecstasy
Half-way between God's silence and the Abyss.
This knowledge in our hidden parts we keep;
Awake to a vague mystery's appeal,
We meet a deep unseen Reality
Far truer than the world's face of present Truth:
We are chased by a self we cannot now recall

And moved by a Spirit we must still become.
As one who has lost the kingdom of his soul,
We look back to some god-phase of our birth
Other than this imperfect creature here
And hope in this or a diviner world
To recover yet from Heaven's patient guard
What by our mind's forgetfulness we miss,
Our being's natural felicity,
Our heart's delight we have exchanged for grief,
The body's thrill we bartered for mere pain,
The bliss for which our mortal nature yearns
As yearns an obscure moth to blazing Light.
Our life is a march to a victory never won.
This wave of being longing for delight,
This eager turmoil of unsatisfied strengths,
These long far files of forward-striving hopes
Lift worshipping eyes to the blue Void called heaven
Looking for the golden Hand that never came,
The advent for which all creation waits,
The beautiful visage of Eternity
That shall appear upon the roads of Time.
Yet still to ourselves we say rekindling faith,
"Oh, surely one day he shall come to our cry,
One day he shall create our life anew
And utter the magic formula of peace
And bring perfection to the scheme of things.
One day he shall descend to life and earth,
Leaving the secrecy of the eternal doors,
Into a world that cries to him for help,
And bring the truth that sets the spirit free,
The joy that is the baptism of the soul,
The strength that is the outstretched arm of Love.
One day he shall lift his beauty's dreadful veil,
Impose delight on the world's beating heart
And bare his secret body of light and bliss."
But now we strain to reach an unknown goal:
There is no end of seeking and of birth,
There is no end of dying and return;
The life that wins its aim asks greater aims,
The life that fails and dies must live again;

Till it has found itself it cannot cease.
All must be done for which life and death were made.
But who shall say that even then is rest?
Or there repose and action are the same
In the deep breast of God's supreme delight.
In a high state where ignorance is no more,
Each movement is a wave of peace and bliss,
Repose God's motionless creative force,
Action a ripple in the Infinite
And birth a gesture of Eternity.
A sun of transfiguration still can shine
And Night can bare its core of mystic light;
The self-cancelling, self-afflicting paradox
Into a self-luminous mystery might change,
The imbroglio into a joyful miracle.
Then God could be visible here, here take a shape;
Disclosed would be the spirit's identity;
Life would reveal her true immortal face.
But now a termless labour is her fate:
In its recurrent decimal of events
Birth, death appear as its vibrating points;
The old question-mark margins each finished page,
Each volume of her effort's history.
A limping Yes through the aeons journeys still
Accompanied by an eternal No.
All seems in vain, yet endless is the game.
Impassive turns the ever-circling Wheel,
Life has no issue, death brings no release.
A prisoner of itself the being lives
And keeps its futile immortality;
Extinction is denied, its sole escape.
An error of the gods has made the world.
Or indifferent the Eternal watches Time.

END OF CANTO SIX

THE DESCENT INTO NIGHT

A MIND absolved from life, made calm to know,
    A heart divorced from the blindness and the pang,
The seal of tears, the bond of ignorance,
He turned to find that wide world-failure's cause.
Away he looked from Nature's visible face
And sent his gaze into the viewless Vast,
The formidable unknown Infinity,
Asleep behind the endless coil of things,
That carries the universe in its timeless breadths
And the ripples of its being are our lives.
The worlds are built by its unconscious Breath
And Matter and Mind are its figures or its powers,
Our waking thoughts the output of its dreams.
The veil was rent that covers Nature's depths:
He saw the fount of the world's lasting pain
And the mouth of the black pit of Ignorance;
The evil guarded at the roots of life
Raised up its head and looked into his eyes.
On a dim bank where dies subjective Space,
From a stark ridge overlooking all that is,
A tenebrous awakened Nescience,
Her wide blank eyes wondering at Time and Form,
Stared at the inventions of the living Void
And the Abyss whence our beginnings rose.
Behind appeared a grey carved mask of Night
Watching the birth of all created things.
A hidden Puissance conscious of its force,
A vague and lurking Presence everywhere,
A contrary Doom that threatens all things made,
A Death figuring as the dark seed of life,

Seemed to engender and to slay the world.
Then from the sombre mystery of the gulfs
And from the hollow bosom of the Mask
Something crept forth that seemed a shapeless Thought.
A fatal Influence upon creatures stole
Whose lethal touch pursued the immortal spirit,
On life was laid the haunting finger of Death
And overcast with error, grief and pain
The soul's native will for truth and joy and light.
A deformation coiled that claimed to be
The being's very turn, Nature's true drive.
A hostile and perverting Mind at work
In every corner ensconced of conscious life
Corrupted Truth with her own formulas;
Intercepter of the listening of the soul,
Afflicting knowledge with the hue of doubt
It captured the oracles of the occult gods,
Effaced the signposts of Life's pilgrimage,
Cancelled the firm rock-edicts graved by Time,
And on the foundations of the cosmic Law
Erected its bronze pylons of misrule.
Even Light and Love by that cloaked danger's spell
Turned from the brilliant nature of the gods
To fallen angels and misleading suns,
Became themselves a danger and a charm,
A perverse sweetness, heaven-born malefice:
Its power could deform divinest things.
A wind of sorrow breathed upon the world;
All thought with falsehood was besieged, all act
Stamped with defect or with frustration's sign,
All high attempt with failure or vain success,
But none could know the reason of his fall.
The grey Mask whispered and though no sound was heard,
Yet in the ignorant heart a seed was sown
That bore black fruit of suffering, death and bale.
Out of the chill steppes of a bleak Unseen
Invisible, wearing the Night's grey mask,
Arrived the shadowy dreadful messengers,
Invaders from a dangerous world of power,
Ambassadors of evil's absolute.

In silence the inaudible voices spoke,
Hands that none saw planted the fatal grain,
No form was seen, yet a dire work was done,
An iron decree in crooked uncials written
Imposed a law of sin and adverse fate.
Life looked at him with changed and sombre eyes:
Her beauty he saw and the yearning heart in things
That with a little happiness is content,
Answering to a small ray of truth or love;
He saw her gold sunlight and her far blue sky,
Her green of leaves and hue and scent of flowers
And the charm of children and the love of friends
And the beauty of women and kindly hearts of men,
But saw too the dreadful Powers that drive her moods
And the anguish she has strewn upon her ways,
Fate waiting on the unseen steps of men
And her evil and sorrow and last gift of death.
A breath of disillusion and decadence
Corrupting watched for Life's maturity
And made to rot the full grain of the soul:
Progress became a purveyor of Death.
A world that clung to the law of a slain Light
Cherished the putrid corpses of dead truths,
Hailed twisted forms as things free, new and true,
Beauty from ugliness and evil drank
Feeling themselves guests at a banquet of the gods
And tasted corruption like a high-spiced food.
A darkness settled on the heavy air;
It hunted the bright smile from Nature's lips
And slew the native confidence in her heart
And put fear's crooked look into her eyes.
The lust that warps the spirit's natural good
Replaced by a manufactured virtue and vice
The frank spontaneous impulse of the soul:
Afflicting Nature with the dual's lie,
Their twin values whetted a forbidden zest,
Made evil a relief from spurious good,
The ego battened on righteousness and sin
And each became an instrument of Hell.
In rejected heaps by a monotonous road

The old simple delights were left to lie
On the wasteland of life's descent to Night.
All glory of life dimmed tarnished into a doubt,
All beauty ended in an aging face;
All power was dubbed a tyranny cursed by God
And Truth a fiction needed by the mind;
The chase of joy was now a tired hunt;
All knowledge was left a questioning Ignorance.

As from a womb obscure he saw emerge
The body and visage of a dark Unseen
Hidden behind the fair outside of life.
Its dangerous commerce is our suffering's cause.
Its breath is a subtle poison in men's hearts;
All evil starts from that ambiguous face.
A peril haunted now the common air;
The world grew full of menacing Energies,
And wherever turned for help or hope his eyes,
In field and house, in street and camp and mart,
He met the prowl and stealthy come and go
Of armed disquieting bodied Influences.
A march of goddess figures dark and nude
Alarmed the air with grandiose unease;
Appalling footsteps drew invisibly near,
Shapes that were threats invaded the dream-light,
And ominous beings passed him on the road
Whose very gaze was a calamity:
A charm and sweetness sudden and formidable,
Faces that raised alluring lips and eyes
Approached him armed with beauty like a snare,
But hid a fatal meaning in each line
And could in a moment dangerously change.
But he alone discerned that screened attack.
A veil upon the inner vision lay,
A force was there that hid its dreadful steps;
All was belied, yet thought itself the truth;
All were beset but knew not of the siege:
For none could see the authors of their fall.

Aware of some dark wisdom still withheld
That was the seal and warrant of this strength,

He followed the track of dim tremendous steps
Returning to the night from which they came.
A tract he reached unbuilt and owned by none:
There all could enter but none stay for long.
It was a no-man's-land of evil air,
A crowded neighbourhood without one home,
A borderland between the world and hell.
There unreality was Nature's lord:
It was a space where nothing could be true,
For nothing was what it had claimed to be:
A high appearance wrapped a spacious void.
Yet nothing would confess its own pretence
Even to itself in the ambiguous heart:
A vast deception was the law of things;
Only by that deception they could live.
An unsubstantial Nihil guaranteed
The falsehood of the forms this Nature took
And made them seem awhile to be and live.
A borrowed magic drew them from the Void;
They took a shape and stuff that was not theirs
And showed a colour that they could not keep,
Mirrors to a fantasm of reality.
Each rainbow brilliance was a splendid lie;
A beauty unreal graced a glamour face.
Nothing could be relied on to remain:
Joy nurtured tears and good an evil proved,
But never out of evil one plucked good:
Love ended early in hate, delight killed with pain,
Truth into falsity grew and death ruled life.
A Power that laughed at the mischief of the world,
An irony that joined the world's contraries
And flung them into each other's arms to strive,
Put a sardonic rictus on God's face.
Aloof, its influence entered everywhere
And left a cloven hoof-mark on the breast;
A twisted heart and a strange sombre smile
Mocked at the sinister comedy of life.
Announcing the advent of a perilous Form
An ominous tread softened its dire footfall
That none might understand or be on guard;

None heard until a dreadful grasp was close.
Or else all augured a divine approach,
An air of prophecy felt, a heavenly hope,
Listened for a gospel, watched for a new star.
The Fiend was visible, but cloaked in light;
He seemed a helping angel from the skies:
He armed untruth with Scripture and the Law;
He deceived with wisdom, with virtue slew the soul
And led to perdition by the heavenward path.
A lavish sense he gave of power and joy,
And when arose the warning from within,
He reassured the ear with dulcet tones,
Or took the mind captive in its own net;
His rigorous logic made the false seem true.
Amazing the elect with holy lore
He spoke as with the very voice of God.
The air was full of treachery and ruse;
Truth-speaking was a stratagem in that place;
Ambush lurked in a smile and peril made
Safety its cover, trust its entry's gate:
Falsehood came laughing with the eyes of truth;
Each friend might turn an enemy or spy,
The hand one clasped ensleeved a dagger's stab
And an embrace could be Doom's iron cage.
Agony and danger stalked their trembling prey
And softly spoke as to a timid friend:
Attack sprang suddenly vehement and unseen;
Fear leaped upon the heart at every turn
And cried out with an anguished dreadful voice;
It called for one to save but none came near.
All warily walked, for death was ever close;
Yet caution seemed a vain expense of care,
For all that guarded proved a deadly net,
And when after long suspense salvation came
And brought a glad relief disarming strength,
It served as a smiling passage to worse fate.
There was no truce and no safe place to rest;
One dared not slumber or put off one's arms:
It was a world of battle and surprise.
All who were there lived for themselves alone;

All warred against all, but with a common hate
Turned on the mind that sought some higher good;
Truth was exiled lest she should dare to speak
And hurt the heart of darkness with her light
Or bring her pride of knowledge to blaspheme
The settled anarchy of established things.

   Then the scene changed, but kept its dreadful core:
Altering its form the life remained the same.
A capital was there without a State:
It had no ruler, only groups that strove.
He saw a city of ancient Ignorance
Founded upon a soil that knew not Light.
There each in his own darkness walked alone:
Only they agreed to differ in Evil's paths,
To live in their own way for their own selves
Or to enforce a common lie and wrong;
There Ego was lord upon his peacock seat
And falsehood sat by him, his mate and queen:
The world turned to them as Heaven to Truth and God.
Injustice justified by firm decrees
The sovereign weights of Error's legalised trade,
But all the weights were false and none the same;
Ever she watched with her balance and a sword
Lest any sacrilegious word expose
The sanctified formulas of her old misrule.
In high professions wrapped self-will walked wide
And licence stalked prating of order and right:
There was no altar raised to Liberty;
True freedom was abhorred and hunted down:
Harmony and tolerance nowhere could be seen;
Each group proclaimed its dire and naked Law.
A frame of ethics knobbed with scriptural rules
Or a theory passionately believed and praised
A table seemed of high Heaven's sacred code.
A formal practice mailed and iron-shod
Gave to a rude and ruthless warrior kind
Drawn from the savage bowels of the earth
A proud stern poise of harsh nobility,
A civic posture rigid and formidable.

But all their private acts belied the pose:
Power and utility were their Truth and Right,
An eagle rapacity clawed its coveted good,
Beaks pecked and talons tore all weaker prey.
In their sweet secrecy of pleasant sins
Nature they obeyed and not a moralist God.
Inconscient traders in bundles of contraries,
They did what in others they would persecute;
When their eyes looked upon their fellow's vice,
An indignation flamed, a virtuous wrath;
Oblivious of their own deep-hid offence,
Moblike they stoned a neighbour caught in sin.
A pragmatist judge within passed false decrees,
Posed worst iniquities on equity's base,
Reasoned ill actions just, sanctioned the scale
Of the merchant ego's interest and desire.
Thus was a balance kept, the world could live.
A zealot fervour pushed their ruthless cults,
All faith not theirs bled scourged as heresy;
They questioned, captived, tortured, burned or smote
And forced the soul to abandon right or die.
Amid her clashing creeds and warring sects
Religion sat upon a blood-stained throne.
A hundred tyrannies oppressed and slew
And founded unity upon fraud and force.
Only what seemed was prized as real there:
The ideal was a cynic ridicule's butt:
Hooted by the crowd, mocked by enlightened wits,
Spiritual seeking wandered outcasted,—
A dreamer's self-deceiving web of thought
Or mad chimera deemed or hypocrite's fake,
Its passionate instinct trailed through minds obscure
Lost in the circuits of the Ignorance.
A lie was there the truth and truth a lie.
Here must the traveller of the upward way—
For daring Hell's kingdoms winds the heavenly route—
Pause or pass slowly through that perilous space,
A prayer upon his lips and the great Name.
If probed not all discernment's keen spear-point,
He might stumble into falsity's endless net.

Over his shoulder often he must look back
Like one who feels on his neck an enemy's breath;
Else stealing up behind a treasonous blow
Might prostrate cast and pin to unholy soil,
Pierced through his back by Evil's poignant stake.
So might one fall on the Eternal's road
Forfeiting the spirit's lonely chance in Time
And no news of him reach the waiting gods,
Marked "missing" in the register of souls,
His name the index of a failing hope,
The position of a dead remembered star.
Only were safe who kept God in their hearts:
Courage their armour, faith their sword, they must walk,
The hand ready to smite, the eye to scout,
Casting a javelin regard in front,
Heroes and soldiers of the army of Light.
Hardly even so, the grisly danger past,
Released into a calmer purer air,
They dared at length to breathe and smile once more.
Once more they moved beneath a real sun.
Though Hell claimed rule, the spirit still had power.
This No-man's-land he passed without debate;
Him the heights missioned, him the Abyss desired:
None stood across his way, no voice forbade.
For swift and easy is the downward path,
And now towards the Night was turned his face.

A greater darkness waited, a worse reign,
If worse can be where all is evil's extreme;
Yet to the cloaked the uncloaked is naked worst.
There God and Truth and the supernal Light
Had never been or else had power no more.
As when one slips in a deep moment's trance
Over mind's border into another world,
He crossed a boundary whose stealthy trace
Eye could not see but only the soul feel.
Into an armoured fierce domain he came
And saw himself wandering like a lost soul
Amid grimed walls and savage slums of Night.
Around him crowded grey and squalid huts

Neighbouring proud palaces of perverted Power,
Inhuman quarters and demoniac wards.
A pride in evil hugged its wretchedness;
A misery haunting splendour pressed those fell
Dun suburbs of the cities of dream-life.
There Life displayed to the spectator soul
The shadow depths of her strange miracle.
A strong and fallen goddess without hope,
Obscured, deformed by some dire Gorgon spell,
As might a harlot empress in a bouge,
Nude, unashamed, exulting she upraised
Her evil face of perilous beauty and charm
And, drawing panic to a shuddering kiss
Twixt the magnificence of her fatal breasts,
Allured to their abyss the spirit's fall.
Across the field of sight she multiplied
As on a scenic film or moving plate
The implacable splendour of her nightmare pomps.
On the dark background of a soulless world
She staged between a lurid light and shade
Her dramas of the sorrow of the depths
Written on the agonised nerves of living things:
Epics of horror and grim majesty,
Wry statues spat and stiffened in life's mud,
A glut of hideous forms and hideous deeds
Paralysed pity in the hardened breast.
In booths of sin and night-repairs of vice
Styled infamies of the body's concupiscence
And sordid imaginations etched in flesh,
Turned lust into a decorative art:
Abusing Nature's gift her pervert skill
Immortalised the sown grain of living death,
In a mud goblet poured the bacchic wine,
To a satyr gave the thyrsus of a god.
Impure, sadistic, with grimacing mouths,
Grey foul inventions gruesome and macabre
Came televisioned from the gulfs of Night.
Her craft ingenious in monstrosity,
Impatient of all natural shape and poise,
A gape of nude exaggerated lines,

Gave caricature a stark reality,
And art-parades of weird distorted forms,
And gargoyle masks obscene and terrible
Trampled to tormented postures the torn sense.
An inexorable evil's worshipper,
She made vileness great and sublimated filth;
A dragon power of reptile energies
And strange epiphanies of grovelling Force
And serpent grandeurs couching in the mire
Drew adoration to a gleam of slime.
All Nature pulled out of her frame and base
Was twisted into an unnatural pose:
Repulsion stimulated inert desire;
Agony was made a red-spiced food for bliss,
Hatred was trusted with the work of lust
And torture took the form of an embrace;
A ritual anguish consecrated death;
Worship was offered to the Undivine.
A new aesthesis of Inferno's art
That trained the mind to love what the soul hates,
Imposed allegiance on the quivering nerves
And forced the unwilling body to vibrate.
Too sweet and too harmonious to excite
In this regime that soiled the being's core,
Beauty was banned, the heart's feeling dulled to sleep
And cherished in their place sensation's thrills;
The world was probed for jets of sense-appeal.
Here cold material intellect was the judge
And needed sensual prick and jog and lash
That its hard dryness and dead nerves might feel
Some passion and power and acrid point of life.
A new philosophy theorised evil's rights,
Gloried in the shimmering rot of decadence,
Or gave to a python force persuasive speech
And armed with knowledge the primeval brute.
Over life and Matter only brooding bowed,
Mind changed to the image of a rampant beast;
It scrambled into the pit to dig for truth
And lighted its search with the subconscient's flares.
Thence bubbling rose sullying the upper air,

The filth and festering secrets of the Abyss:
This it called positive fact and real life.
This now composed the fetid atmosphere.
A wild-beast passion crept from secret Night
To watch its prey with fascinating eyes:
Around him like a fire with sputtering tongues
There lolled and laughed a bestial ecstasy;
The air was packed with longings brute and fierce;
Crowding and stinging in a monstrous swarm
Pressed with a noxious hum into his mind
Thoughts that could poison Nature's heavenliest breath,
Forcing reluctant lids assailed the sight
Acts that revealed the mystery of Hell.
All that was there was on this pattern made.

A race possessed inhabited those parts.
A force demoniac lurking in man's depths
That heaves suppressed by the heart's human law,
Awed by the calm and sovereign eyes of Thought,
Can in a fire and earthquake of the soul
Arise and, calling to its native night,
Overthrow the reason, occupy the life
And stamp its hoof on Nature's shaking ground:
This was for them their being's flaming core.
A mighty energy, a monster god,
Hard to the strong, implacable to the weak,
It stared at the harsh unpitying world it made
With the stony eyelids of its fixed idea.
Its heart was drunk with a dire hunger's wine,
In others' suffering felt a thrilled delight
And of death and ruin the grandiose music heard.
To have power, to be master, was sole virtue and good:
It claimed the whole world for Evil's living room,
Its party's grim totalitarian reign
The cruel destiny of breathing things.
All on one plan was shaped and standardised
Under a dark dictatorship's breathless weight.
In street and house, in councils and in courts
Beings he met who looked like living men
And climbed in speech upon high wings of thought

But harboured all that is subhuman, vile
And lower than the lowest reptile's crawl.
The reason meant for nearness to the gods
And uplift to heavenly scale by the touch of mind
Only enhanced by its enlightening ray
Their inborn nature's wry monstrosity.
Often a familiar visage studying
Joyfully encountered at some dangerous turn,
Hoping to recognise a look of light,
His vision warned by the spirit's inward eye
Discovered suddenly Hell's trade-mark there,
Or saw with the inner sense that cannot err,
In the semblance of a fair or virile form
The demon and the goblin and the ghoul.
An insolence reigned of cold stone-hearted strength
Mighty, obeyed, approved by the Titan's law,
The huge laughter of a giant cruelty
And fierce glad deeds of ogre violence.
In that wide cynic den of thinking beasts
One looked in vain for a trace of pity and love;
There was no touch of sweetness anywhere,
But only Force and its acolytes, greed and hate:
There was no help for suffering, none to save,
None dared resist or speak a noble word.
Armed with the aegis of tyrannic Power,
Signing the edicts of her dreadful rule
And using blood and torture as a seal,
Darkness proclaimed her slogans to the world.
A servile blinkered silence hushed the mind
Or only it repeated lessons taught,
While mitred, holding the good shepherd's staff,
Falsehood enthroned on awed and prostrate hearts
The cults and creeds that organise living death
And slay the soul on the altar of a lie.
All were deceived or served their own deceit;
Truth in that stifling atmosphere could not live.
There wretchedness believed in its own joy
And fear and weakness hugged their abject depths;
All that is low and sordid-thoughted, base,
All that is drab and poor and miserable,

Breathed in a laxed content its natural air
And felt no yearning of divine release:
Arrogant, gibing at more luminous states
The people of the gulfs despised the sun.
A barriered autarchy excluded light;
Fixed in its will to be its own grey self,
It vaunted its norm unique and splendid type:
It soothed its hunger with a plunderer's dream;
Flaunting its cross of servitude like a crown,
It clung to its dismal harsh autonomy.
A bull-throat bellowed with its brazen tongue;
Its hard and shameless clamour filling space
And threatening all who dared to listen to truth
Claimed the monopoly of the battered ear;
A deafened acquiescence gave its vote,
And braggart dogmas shouted in the night
Kept for the fallen soul once deemed a god
The pride of its abysmal absolute.

    A lone discoverer in these menacing realms
Guarded like termite cities from the sun,
Oppressed mid crowd and tramp and noise and flare,
Passing from dusk to deeper dangerous dusk,
He wrestled with powers that snatched from mind its light
And smote from him their clinging influences.
Soon he emerged in a dim wall-less space.
For now the peopled tracts were left behind;
He walked between wide banks of failing eve.
Around him grew a gaunt spiritual blank,
A threatening waste, a sinister loneliness
That left mind bare to an unseen assault,
An empty page on which all that willed could write
Stark monstrous messages without control.
A travelling dot on downward roads of Dusk
Mid barren fields and barns and straggling huts
And a few crooked and phantasmal trees,
He faced a sense of death and conscious Void.
But still a hostile Life unseen was there
Whose deathlike poise resisting light and truth
Made living a bleak gap in nullity.

He heard the grisly voices that deny;
Assailed by thoughts that swarmed like spectral hordes,
A prey to the staring phantoms of the gloom
And terror approaching with its lethal mouth,
Driven by a strange will down ever down,
The sky above a communiqué of Doom,
He strove to shield his spirit from despair,
But felt the horror of the growing Night
And the Abyss rising to claim his soul.
Then ceased the abodes of creatures and their forms
And solitude wrapped him in its voiceless folds.
All vanished suddenly like a thought expunged;
His spirit became an empty listening gulf
Void of the dead illusion of a world:
Nothing was left, not even an evil face;
He was alone with the grey python Night.
A dense and nameless Nothing conscious, mute,
Which seemed alive but without body or mind,
Lusted all being to annihilate
That it might be for ever nude and sole.
As in a shapeless beast's intangible jaws,
Gripped, strangled by that lusting, viscous blot,
Attracted to some black and giant mouth
And swallowing throat and a huge belly of doom,
His being from its own vision disappeared
Drawn towards depths that hungered for its fall.
A formless void suppressed his struggling brain,
A darkness grim and cold oppressed his flesh,
A whispered grey suggestion chilled his heart;
Haled by a serpent-force from its warm home
And dragged to extinction in blank vacancy
Life clung to its seat with cords of gasping breath;
Lapped was his body by a tenebrous tongue.
Existence smothered travailed to survive;
Hope strangled perished in his empty soul,
Belief and memory abolished died
And all that helps the spirit in its course.
There crawled through every tense and aching nerve
Leaving behind its poignant quaking trail
A nameless and unutterable fear.

As a sea nears a victim bound and still,
The approach alarmed his mind for ever dumb
Of an implacable eternity
Of pain inhuman and intolerable.
This he must bear, his hope of heaven estranged;
He must ever exist without extinction's peace
In a slow suffering Time and tortured Space,
An anguished nothingness his endless state.
A lifeless vacancy was now his breast,
And in the place where once was luminous thought,
Only remained like a pale motionless ghost
An incapacity for faith and hope
And the dread conviction of a vanquished soul
Immortal still but with its godhead lost,
Self lost and God and touch of happier worlds.
But he endured, stilled the vain terror, bore
The smothering coils of agony and affright;
Then peace returned and the soul's sovereign gaze.
To the blank horror a calm Light replied:
Immutable, undying and unborn,
Mighty and mute the Godhead in him woke
And faced the pain and danger of the world.
He mastered the tides of Nature with a look:
He met with his bare spirit naked Hell.

END OF CANTO SEVEN

CANTO EIGHT

THE WORLD OF FALSEHOOD, THE MOTHER
OF EVIL AND THE SONS OF DARKNESS

THEN could he see the hidden heart of Night:
    The labour of its stark unconsciousness
Revealed the endless terrible Inane.
A spiritless blank Infinity was there;
A Nature that denied the eternal Truth
In the vain braggart freedom of its thought
Hoped to abolish God and reign alone.
There was no sovereign Guest, no witness Light;
Unhelped it would create its own bleak world.
Its large blind eyes looked out on demon acts,
Its deaf ears heard the untruth its dumb lips spoke;
Its huge misguided fancy took vast shapes,
Its mindless sentience quivered with fierce conceits;
Engendering a brute principle of life
Evil and pain begot a monstrous soul.
The Anarchs of the formless depths arose,
Great titan beings and demoniac powers,
World-egos racked with lust and thought and will,
Vast minds and lives without a spirit within:
Impatient architects of error's house,
Leaders of the cosmic ignorance and unrest
And sponsors of sorrow and mortality
Embodied the dark Ideas of the Abyss.
A shadow substance into emptiness came,
Dim forms were born in the unthinking Void
And eddies met and made an adverse Space
In whose black folds Being imagined Hell.
His eyes piercing the triple-plated gloom
Identified their sight with its blind stare:

Accustomed to the unnatural dark, they saw
Unreality made real and conscious Night.
A violent, fierce and formidable world,
An ancient womb of huge calamitous dreams,
Coiled like a larva in the obscurity
That keeps it from the spear-points of Heaven's stars.
It was the gate of a false Infinite,
An eternity of disastrous absolutes,
An immense negation of spiritual things.
All once self-luminous in the spirit's sphere
Turned now into their own dark contraries:
Being collapsed into a pointless void
That yet was a zero parent of the worlds;
Inconscience swallowing up the cosmic Mind
Produced a universe from its lethal sleep;
Bliss into black coma fallen, insensible,
Coiled back to itself and God's eternal joy
Through a false poignant figure of grief and pain
Still dolorously nailed upon a cross
Fixed in the soil of a dumb insentient world
Where birth was a pang and death an agony,
Lest all too soon should change again to bliss.
Thought sat, a priestess of Perversity,
On her black tripod of the triune Snake
Reading by opposite signs the eternal script,
A sorceress reversing Life's God-frame.
In darkling aisles with evil eyes for lamps
And fatal voices chanting from the apse,
In strange infernal dim basilicas
Intoning the magic of the unholy Word,
The ominous profound Initiate
Performed the ritual of her mysteries.
There suffering was Nature's daily food
Alluring to the anguished heart and flesh,
And torture was the formula of delight,
Pain mimicked the celestial ecstasy.
There Good, a faithless gardener of God,
Watered with virtue the world's upas-tree
And, careful of the outward word and act,
Engrafted his hypocrite blooms on native ill.

All high things served their nether opposite:
The forms of Gods sustained a demon cult;
Heaven's face became a mask and snare of Hell.
There in the heart of vain phenomenon,
In an enormous action's writhen core
He saw a shape illimitable and vague
Sitting on Death who swallows all things born.
A chill fixed face with dire and motionless eyes,
Her dreadful strident in her shadowy hand
Outstretched, she pierced all creatures with one fate.

When nothing was save Matter without soul
And a spiritless hollow was the heart of Time,
Then Life first touched the insensible Abyss;
Awaking the stark Void to hope and grief
Her pallid beam smote the unfathomed Night
In which God hid himself from his own view.
In all things she sought their slumbering mystic truth,
The unspoken Word that inspires unconscious forms;
She groped in his deeps for an invisible Law,
Fumbled in the dim subconscient for his mind
And strove to find a way for spirit to be.
But from the Night another answer came.
A seed was in that nether matrix cast,
A dumb unprobed husk of perverted truth,
A cell of an insentient infinite.
A monstrous birth prepared its cosmic form
In Nature's titan embryo, Ignorance.
Then in a fatal and stupendous hour
Something that sprang from the stark Inconscient's sleep
Unwillingly begotten by the mute Void,
Lifted its ominous head against the stars;
Overshadowing earth with its huge body of Doom
It chilled the heavens with the menace of a face.
A nameless Power, a shadowy Will arose
Immense and alien to our universe.
In the inconceivable Purpose none can gauge
A vast Non-Being robed itself with shape,
The boundless Nescience of the unconscious depths
Covered eternity with Nothingness.

A seeking Mind replaced the seeing Soul:
Life grew into a huge and hungry death,
The Spirit's bliss was changed to cosmic pain.
Assuring God's self-cowled neutrality
A mighty opposition conquered Space.
A sovereign ruling falsehood, death and grief,
It pressed its fierce hegemony on earth;
Disharmonising the original style
Of the architecture of her fate's design,
It falsified the primal cosmic Will
And bound to struggle and dread vicissitudes
The long slow process of the patient Power.
Implanting error in the stuff of things
It made an Ignorance of the all-wise Law;
It baffled the sure touch of life's hid sense,
Kept dumb the intuitive guide in Matter's sleep,
Deformed the insect's instinct and the brute's,
Disfigured man's thought-born humanity.
A shadow fell across the simple Ray:
Obscured was the Truth-light in the cavern heart
That burns unwitnessed in the altar crypt
Behind the still velamen's secrecy
Companioning the Godhead of the shrine.
Thus was the dire antagonist Energy born
Who mimes the eternal Mother's mighty shape
And mocks her luminous infinity
With a grey distorted silhouette in the Night.
Arresting the passion of the climbing soul,
She forced on life a slow and faltering pace;
Her hand's deflecting and retarding weight
Is laid on the mystic evolution's curve:
The tortuous line of her deceiving mind
The Gods see not and man is impotent;
Oppressing the God-spark within the soul
She forces back to the beast the human fall.
Yet in her formidable instinctive mind
She feels the One grow in the heart of Time
And sees the Immortal shine through the human mould.
Alarmed for her rule and full of fear and rage
She prowls around each light that gleams through the dark

Casting its ray from the Spirit's lonely tent,
Hoping to enter with fierce stealthy tread
And in the cradle slay the divine Child.
Incalculable are her strength and ruse,
Her touch is a fascination and a death;
She kills her victim with his own delight;
Even Good she makes a hook to drag to Hell.
For her the world runs to its agony.
Often the pilgrim on the Eternal's road
Ill-lit from clouds by the pale moon of Mind,
Or in devious by-ways wandering alone,
Or lost in deserts where no path is seen,
Falls overpowered by her lion leap,
A conquered captive under her dreadful paws.
Intoxicated by a burning breath
And amorous groan of a destroying mouth,
Once a companion of the sacred Fire,
The mortal perishes to God and Light,
An adversary governs heart and brain,
A Nature hostile to the Mother-force.
The self of life yields up its instruments
To Titan and demoniac agencies
That aggrandise earth-nature and disframe:
A cowled fifth-columnist is now thought's guide;
His subtle defeatist murmur slays the faith
And, lodged in the breast or whispering from outside,
A lying inspiration fell and dark
A new order substitutes for the divine.
A silence falls upon the spirit's heights,
From the veiled sanctuary the God retires,
Empty and cold is the chamber of the Bride;
The golden Nimbus now is seen no more,
No longer burns the white spiritual ray
And hushed for ever is the secret Voice.
Then by the Angel of the Vigil Tower
A name is struck from the recording book;
A flame that sang in Heaven sinks quenched and mute,
In ruin ends the epic of a soul.
This is the tragedy of the inner death
When forfeited is the divine element

And only a mind and body live to die.

For terrible agencies the Spirit allows
And there are subtle and enormous Powers
That shield themselves with the covering Ignorance.
Offspring of the gulfs, agents of the shadowy Force,
Haters of light, intolerant of peace,
Aping to the thought the shining Friend and Guide,
Opposing in the heart the eternal Will,
They veil the occult, uplifting Harmonist.
His wisdom's oracles are made our bonds;
The doors of God they have locked with keys of creed
And shut out by the Law his tireless Grace.
Along all Nature's lines they have set their posts
And intercept the caravans of Light;
Wherever the Gods act, they intervene.
A yoke is laid upon the world's dim heart;
Masked are its beats from the supernal Bliss,
And the closed peripheries of brilliant Mind
Block the fine entries of celestial Fire.
Always the dark Adventurers seem to win;
Nature they fill with evil's institutes,
Turn into defeats the victories of Truth,
Proclaim as falsehoods the eternal laws,
And load the dice of Doom with wizard lies;
The world's shrines they have occupied, usurped its thrones.
In scorn of the dwindling chances of the Gods
They claim creation as their conquered fief
And crown themselves the iron Lords of Time.
Adepts of the illusion and the mask,
The artificers of Nature's fall and pain
Have built their altars of triumphant Night
In the clay temple of terrestrial life.
In the vacant precincts of the sacred Fire,
In front of the reredos in the mystic rite
Facing the dim velamen none can pierce,
Intones his solemn hymn the mitred priest
Invoking their dreadful presence in his breast:
Attributing to them the awful Name
He chants the syllables of the magic text

205

And summons the unseen communion's act,
While twixt the incense and the muttered prayer
All the fierce bale with which the world is racked
Is mixed in the foaming chalice of man's heart
And poured to them like sacramental wine.
Assuming names divine they guide and rule.
Opponents of the Highest they have come
Out of their world of soulless thought and power
To serve by enmity the cosmic scheme.
Night is their refuge and strategic base.
Against the sword of Flame, the luminous Eye,
Bastioned they live in massive forts of gloom,
Calm and secure in sunless privacy:
No wandering ray of Heaven can enter there.
Armoured, protected by their lethal masks,
As in a studio of creative Death
The giant sons of Darkness sit and plan
The drama of the earth, their tragic stage.
All who would raise the fallen world must come
Under the dangerous arches of their power;
For even the radiant children of the gods
To darken their privilege is and dreadful right.
None can reach heaven who has not passed through hell.

This too the traveller of the worlds must dare.
A warrior in the dateless duel's strife,
He entered into dumb despairing Night
Challenging the darkness with his luminous soul.
Alarming with his steps the threshold gloom
He came into a fierce and dolorous realm
Peopled by souls who never had tasted bliss;
Ignorant like men born blind who know not light,
They could equate worst ill with highest good,
Virtue was to their eyes a face of sin
And evil and misery were their natural state.
A dire administration's penal code
Making of grief and pain the common law,
Decreeing universal joylessness
Had changed life into a stoic sacrament
And torture into a daily festival.

An act was passed to chastise happiness;
Laughter and pleasure were banned as deadly sins:
A questionless mind was ranked as wise content,
A dull heart's silent apathy as peace:
Sleep was not there, torpor was the sole rest,
Death came but neither respite gave nor end;
Always the soul lived on and suffered more.
Ever he deeper probed that kingdom of pain;
Around him grew the terror of a world
Of agony followed by worse agony,
And in the terror a great wicked joy
Glad of one's own and others' calamity.
There thought and life were a long punishment,
The breath a burden and all hope a scourge,
The body a field of torment, a massed unease;
Repose was a waiting between pang and pang.
This was the law of things none dreamed to change:
A hard sombre heart, a harsh unsmiling mind
Rejected happiness like a cloying sweet;
Tranquillity was a tedium and ennui:
Only by suffering life grew colourful;
It needed the spice of pain, the salt of tears.
If one could cease to be, all would be well;
Else only fierce sensations gave some zest:
A fury of jealousy burning the gnawed heart,
The sting of murderous spite and hate and lust,
The whisper that lures to the pit and treachery's stroke
Threw vivid spots on the dull aching hours.
To watch the drama of infelicity,
The writhing of creatures under the harrow of doom
And sorrow's tragic gaze into the night
And horror and the hammering heart of fear
Were the ingredients in Time's heavy cup
That pleased and helped to enjoy its bitter taste.
Of such fierce stuff was made up life's long hell:
These were the threads of the dark spider's web
In which the soul was caught, quivering and wrapt;
This was religion, this was Nature's rule.
In a fell chapel of iniquity
To worship a black pitiless image of Power

Kneeling one must cross hard-hearted stony courts,
A pavement like a floor of evil fate.
Each stone was a keen edge of ruthless force
And glued with the chilled blood from tortured breasts;
The dry gnarled trees stood up like dying men
Stiffened into a pose of agony,
And from each window peered an ominous priest
Chanting Te Deums for slaughter's crowning grace,
Cities uprooted, blasted human homes,
Burned writhen bodies, the bombshell's massacre.
"Our enemies are fallen, are fallen", they sang,
"All who once stayed our will are smitten and dead;
How great we are, how merciful art Thou."
Thus thought they to reach God's impassive throne
And Him command whom all their acts opposed,
Magnifying their deeds to touch his skies,
And make him an accomplice of their crimes.
There no relenting pity could have place,
But ruthless strength and iron moods had sway,
A dateless sovereignty of terror and gloom:
This took the figure of a darkened God
Revered by the racked wretchedness he had made,
Who held in thrall a miserable world,
And helpless hearts nailed to unceasing woe
Adored the feet that trampled them into mire.
It was a world of sorrow and of hate,
Sorrow with hatred for its lonely joy,
Hatred with others' sorrow as its feast;
A bitter rictus curled the suffering mouth;
A tragic cruelty saw its ominous chance.
Hate was the black archangel of that realm;
It glowed, a sombre jewel in the heart
Burning the soul with its malignant rays,
And wallowed in its fell abysm of might.
These passions even objects seemed to exude,—
For mind overflowed into the inanimate
That answered with the wickedness it received,—
Against their users used malignant powers,
Hurt without hands and strangely, suddenly slew,
Appointed as instruments of an unseen doom.

Or they made themselves a fateful prison wall
Where men condemned wake through the creeping hours
Counted by the tollings of an ominous bell.
An evil environment worsened evil souls:
All things were conscious there and all perverse.
In this infernal realm he dared to press
Even into its deepest pit and darkest core,
Perturbed its tenebrous base, dared to contest
Its ancient privileged right and absolute force:
In Night he plunged to know her dreadful heart,
In Hell he sought the root and cause of Hell.
Its anguished gulfs opened in his own breast;
He listened to clamours of its crowded pain,
The heart-beats of its fatal loneliness.
Above was a chill deaf eternity.
In vague tremendous passages of Doom
He heard the goblin voice that guides to slay,
And faced the enchantments of the demon Sign,
And traversed the ambush of the opponent Snake.
In menacing tracts, in tortured solitudes
Companionless he roamed through desolate ways
Where the red Wolf waits by the fordless stream
And Death's black eagles scream to the precipice,
And met the hounds of bale who hunt men's hearts
Baying across the veldts of Destiny,
In footless battlefields of the Abyss
Fought shadowy combats in mute eyeless depths,
Assaults of Hell endured and Titan strokes
And bore the fierce inner wounds that are slow to heal.
A prisoner of a hooded magic Force,
Captured and trailed in Falsehood's lethal net
And often strangled in the noose of grief,
Or cast on the grim morass of swallowing doubt,
Or shut into pits of error and despair,
He drank her poison draughts till none was left.
In a world where neither hope nor joy could come
The ordeal he suffered of evil's absolute reign,
Yet kept intact his spirit's radiant truth.
Incapable of motion or of force,
In Matter's blank denial gaoled and blind,

Pinned to the black inertia of our base
He treasured between his hands his flickering soul.
His being ventured into mindless Void,
Intolerant gulfs that knew not thought nor sense;
Thought ceased, sense failed, his soul still saw and knew.
In atomic parcellings of the Infinite
Near to the dumb beginnings of lost Self,
He felt the curious small futility
Of the creation of material things.
Or, stifled in the Inconscient's hollow dusk,
He sounded the mystery dark and bottomless
Of the enormous and unmeaning deeps
Whence struggling life in a dead universe rose.
There in the stark identity lost by mind
He felt the sealed sense of the insensible world
And a mute wisdom in the unknowing Night.
Into the abysmal secrecy he came
Where darkness peers from her mattress, grey and nude
And stood on the last locked subconscient's floor
Where Being slept unconscious of its thoughts
And built the world not knowing what it built.
There waiting its hour the future lay unknown,
There is the record of the vanished stars.
There in the slumber of the cosmic Will
He saw the secret key of Nature's change.
A light was with him, an invisible hand
Was laid upon the error and the pain
Till it became a quivering ecstasy,
The shock of sweetness of an arm's embrace.
He saw in Night the Eternal's shadowy veil,
Knew death for a cellar of the house of life,
In destruction felt creation's hasty pace,
Knew loss as the price of a celestial gain
And hell as a short cut to heaven's gates.
Then in Illusion's occult factory
And in the Inconscient's magic printing house
Torn were the formats of the primal Night
And shattered the stereotypes of Ignorance.
Alive, breathing a deep spiritual breath,
Nature expunged her stiff mechanical code

And the articles of the bound soul's contract,
Falsehood gave back to Truth her tortured shape.
Annulled were the tables of the law of pain,
And in their place grew luminous characters.
The skilful Penman's unseen finger wrote
His swift intuitive calligraphy;
Earth's forms were made his divine documents,
The wisdom embodied mind could not reveal,
Inconscience chased from the world's voiceless breast;
Transfigured were the fixed schemes of reasoning Thought.
Arousing consciousness in things inert,
He imposed upon dark atom and dumb mass
The diamond script of the Imperishable,
Inscribed on the dim heart of fallen things
A paean-song of the free Infinite
And the Name, foundation of eternity,
And traced on the awake exultant cells
In the ideographs of the Ineffable
The lyric of the love that waits through Time
And the mystic volume of the Book of Bliss
And the message of the superconscient Fire.
Then Life beat pure in the corporeal frame;
The infernal Gleam died and could slay no more.
Hell split across its huge abrupt façade
As if a magic building were undone,
Night opened and vanished like a gulf of dream.
Into being's gap scooped out as empty Space
In which she has filled the place of absent God,
There poured a wide intimate and blissful Dawn,
Healed were all things that Time's torn heart had made
And sorrow could live no more in Nature's breast:
Division ceased to be, for God was there.
The soul lit the conscious body with its ray,
Matter and Spirit mingled and were one.

END OF CANTO EIGHT

CANTO NINE

THE PARADISE OF THE LIFE-GODS

AROUND him shone a great felicitous Day.
A lustre of some rapturous Infinite,
It held in the splendour of its golden laugh
Regions of the heart's happiness set free,
Intoxicated with the wine of God,
Immersed in light, perpetually divine.
A favourite and intimate of the Gods
Obeying the divine command to joy,
It was the sovereign of its own delight
And master of the kingdoms of its force.
Assured of the bliss for which all forms were made,
Unmoved by fear and grief and the shocks of Fate
And unalarmed by the breath of fleeting Time
And unbesieged by adverse circumstance,
It breathed in a sweet secure unguarded ease
Free from our body's frailty inviting death,
Far from our danger zone of stumbling Will.
It needed not to curb its passionate beats;
Thrilled by the clasp of the warm satisfied sense
And the swift wonder-rush and flame and cry
Of the life-impulse's red magnificent race,
It lived in a jewel-rhythm of the laughter of God
And lay on the breast of universal love.
Immune the unfettered Spirit of Delight
Pastured his gleaming sun-herds and moon-flocks
Along the lyric speed of griefless streams
In fragrance of the unearthly asphodel.
A silence of felicity wrapped the heavens,
A ceaseless radiance smiled upon the heights;
A murmur of inarticulate ravishment

Trembled in the winds and touched the enchanted soil;
Incessant in the arms of ecstasy
Repeating its sweet involuntary note
A sob of rapture flowed along the hours.
Advancing under an arch of glory and peace,
Traveller on plateau and on musing ridge,
As one who sees in the World-Magician's glass
A miracled imagery of soul-scapes flee
He traversed scenes of an immortal joy
And gazed into abysms of beauty and bliss.
Around him was a light of conscious suns
And a brooding gladness of great symbol things;
To meet him crowded plains of brilliant calm,
Mountains and violet valleys of the Blest,
Deep glens of joy and crooning waterfalls
And woods of quivering purple solitude;
Below him lay like gleaming jewelled thoughts
Rapt dreaming cities of Gandharva kings.
Across the vibrant secrecies of Space
A dim and happy music sweetly stole,
Smitten by unseen hands he heard heart-close
The harp's cry of the heavenly minstrels pass,
And voices of unearthly melody
Chanted the glory of eternal love
In the white-blue moonbeam air of Paradise.
A summit and core of all that marvellous world,
Apart stood high Elysian nameless hills,
Burning like sunsets in a trance of eve.
As if to some new unsearched profundity,
Into a joyful stillness plunged their base;
Their slopes through a hurry of laughter and voices sank,
Crossed by a throng of singing rivulets,
Adoring blue heaven with their happy hymn,
Down into woods of shadowy secrecy:
Lifted into wide voiceless mystery
Their peaks climbed towards a greatness beyond life.
The shining Edens of the vital gods
Received him in their deathless harmonies.
All things were perfect there that flower in Time;
Beauty was there creation's native mould,

Peace was a thrilled voluptuous purity.
There Love fulfilled her gold and roseate dreams
And Strength her crowned and mighty reveries;
Desire climbed up, a swift omnipotent flame,
And Pleasure had the stature of the gods;
Dream walked along the highway of the stars;
Sweet common things turned into miracles:
Overtaken by the spirit's sudden spell,
Smitten by a divine passion's alchemy,
Pain's self compelled transformed to potent joy
Curing the antithesis between heaven and hell.
All life's high visions are embodied there,
Her wandering hopes achieved, her aureate combs
Caught by the honey-eater's darting tongue,
Her burning guesses changed to ecstasied truths,
Her mighty pantings stilled in deathless calm
And liberated her immense desires.
In that Paradise of perfect heart and sense
No lower note could break the endless charm
Of her sweetness ardent and immaculate;
Her steps are sure of their intuitive fall.
After the anguish of the soul's long strife
At length were found calm and celestial rest
And, lapped in a magic flood of sorrowless hours,
Healed were his warrior nature's wounded limbs
In the encircling arms of Energies
That brooked no stain and feared not their own bliss.
In scenes forbidden to our pallid sense
Amid miraculous scents and wonder-hues
He met the forms that divinise the sight,
To music that can immortalise the mind
And make the heart wide as infinity
Listened, and captured the inaudible
Cadences that awake the occult ear:
Out of the ineffable hush it hears them come
Trembling with the beauty of a wordless speech,
And thoughts too great and deep to find a voice,
Thoughts whose desire new-makes the universe.
A scale of sense that climbed with fiery feet
To heights of unimagined happiness,

Recast his being's aura in joy-glow,
His body glimmered like a skyey shell;
His gates to the world were swept with seas of light.
His earth, dowered with celestial competence,
Harboured a power that needed now no more
To cross the closed customs-line of mind and flesh
And smuggle godhead into humanity.
It shrank no more from the supreme demand
Of an untired capacity for bliss,
A might that could explore its own infinite
And beauty and passion and the depth's reply
Nor feared the swoon of glad identity
Where spirit and flesh in inner ecstasy join
Annulling the quarrel between self and shape.
It drew from sight and sound spiritual power,
Made sense a road to reach the intangible:
It thrilled with the supernal influences
That build the substance of life's deeper soul.
Earth-nature stood reborn, comrade of heaven.
A fit companion of the timeless Kings,
Equalled with the godheads of the living Suns,
He mixed in the radiant pastimes of the Unborn,
Heard whispers of the Player never seen
And listened to his voice that steals the heart
And draws it to the breast of God's desire,
And felt its honey of felicity
Flow through his veins like the rivers of Paradise,
Made body a nectar-cup of the Absolute.
In sudden moments of revealing flame,
In passionate responses half-unveiled
He reached the rim of ecstasies unknown;
A touch supreme surprised his hurrying heart,
The clasp was remembered of the Wonderful,
And hints leaped down of white beatitudes.
Eternity drew close disguised as Love
And laid its hand upon the body of Time.
A little gift comes from the Immensitudes,
But measureless to life its gain of joy;
All the untold Beyond is mirrored there.
A giant drop of the Bliss unknowable

Overwhelmed his limbs and round his soul became
A fiery ocean of felicity:
He foundered drowned in sweet and burning vasts:
The dire delight that could shatter mortal flesh,
The rapture that the gods sustain he bore.
Immortal pleasure cleansed him in its waves
And turned his strength into undying power.
Immortality captured Time and carried Life.

END OF CANTO NINE

CANTO TEN

THE KINGDOMS AND GODHEADS OF THE
LITTLE MIND

THIS too must now be overpassed and left,
    As all must be until the Highest is gained
In whom the world and self grow true and one:
Till that is reached our journeying cannot cease.
Always a nameless goal beckons beyond,
Always ascends the zigzag of the gods
And upward points the spirit's climbing Fire.
This breath of hundred-hued felicity
And its pure heightened figure of Time's joy,
Tossed upon waves of flawless happiness,
Hammered into single beats of ecstasy,
This fraction of the spirit's integer
Caught into a passionate greatness of extremes,
This limited being lifted to zenith bliss,
Happy to enjoy one touch of things supreme,
Packed into its sealed small infinity,
Its endless time-made world outfacing Time,
A little output of God's vast delight.
The moments stretched towards the eternal Now,
The hours discovered immortality,
But, satisfied with their sublime contents,
On peaks they ceased whose tops half-way to heaven
Pointed to an apex they could never mount,
To a grandeur in whose air they could not live.
Inviting to their high and exquisite sphere,
To their secure and fine extremities
This creature who hugs his limits to feel safe,
These heights declined a greater adventure's call.
A glory and sweetness of satisfied desire

[handwritten margin note, left: nature is zig-zag]

[handwritten margin note, right: Each plane has its joy]

217

Tied up the spirit to golden posts of bliss.
It could not house the wideness of a soul
Which needed all infinity for its home.
A memory soft as grass and faint as sleep,
The beauty and call receding sank behind
Like a sweet song heard fading far away
Upon the long high road to Timelessness.
Above was an ardent white tranquillity.
A musing spirit looked out on the worlds
And like a brilliant clambering of skies
Passing through clarity to an unseen Light
Large lucent realms of Mind from stillness shone.
But first he met a silver-grey expanse
Where Day and Night had wedded and were one:
It was a tract of dim and shifting rays
Parting Life's sentient flow from Thought's self-poise.
A coalition of uncertainties
There exercised uneasy government
On a ground reserved for doubt and reasoned guess,
A rendezvous of Knowledge with Ignorance.
At its low extremity held difficult sway
A mind that hardly saw and slowly found;
Its nature to our earthly nature close
And kin to our precarious mortal thought
That looks from soil to sky and sky to soil
But knows not the below nor the beyond,
It only sensed itself and outward things.
This was the first means of our slow ascent
From the half-conscience of the animal soul
Living in a crowded press of shape-events
In a realm it cannot understand nor change:
Only it sees and acts in a given scene
And feels and joys and sorrows for a while.
The ideas that drive the obscure embodied spirit
Along the roads of suffering and desire
In a world that struggles to discover Truth,
Found here their power to be and Nature-Force.
Here are devised the forms of an ignorant life
That sees the empiric fact as settled law,
Labours for the hour and not for eternity

218

And trades its gains to meet the moment's call:
The slow process of a material mind
Which serves the body it should rule and use
And needs to lean upon an erring sense,
Was born in that luminous obscurity.
Advancing tardily from a limping start,
Crutching hypothesis upon argument,
Throning its theories as certitudes,
It reasons from the half-known to the unknown,
Ever constructing its frail house of thought,
Ever undoing the web that it has spun.
A twilight sage whose shadow seems to him Self,
Moving from minute to brief minute lives;
A king dependent on his satellites
Signs the decrees of ignorant ministers,
A judge in half-possession of his proofs,
A voice clamant of uncertainty's postulates,
An architect of knowledge, not its source.
This powerful bondslave of his instruments
Thinks his low station Nature's highest top,
Oblivious of his share in all things made
And haughtily humble in his own conceit
Believes himself a spawn of Matter's mud
And takes his own creations for his cause.
To eternal light and knowledge meant to rise,
Up from man's bare beginning is our climb;
Out of earth's heavy smallness we must break,
We must search our nature with spiritual fire:
An insect crawl preludes our glorious flight;
Our human state cradles the future god,
Our mortal frailty an immortal force.

At the glow-worm top of these pale glimmer-realms
Where dawn-sheen gambolled with the native dusk
And helped the Day to grow and Night to fail,
Escaping over a wide and shimmering bridge,
He came into a realm of early Light
And the regency of a half-risen sun.
Out of its rays our mind's full orb was born.
Appointed by the Spirit of the Worlds
To mediate with the unknowing depths,

A prototypal deft Intelligence
Half-poised on equal wings of thought and doubt
Toiled ceaselessly twixt being's hidden ends.
A Secrecy breathed in life's moving act;
A covert nurse of Nature's miracles,
It shaped life's wonders out of Matter's mud:
It cut the pattern of the shapes of things,
It pitched mind's tent in the vague ignorant Vast.
A master Magician of measure and device
Has made an eternity from recurring forms
And to the wandering spectator thought
Assigned a seat on the inconscient stage.
On earth by the will of this Arch-Intelligence
A bodiless energy put on Matter's robe;
Proton and photon served the imager Eye
To change things subtle into a physical world
And the invisible appeared as shape
And the impalpable was felt as mass:
Magic of percept joined with concept's art
And lent to each object an interpreting name:
Idea was disguised in a body's artistry,
And by a strange atomic law's mystique
A frame was made in which the sense would put
Its symbol picture of the universe.
Even a greater miracle was done.
The mediating light linked body's power,
The sleep and dreaming of the tree and plant,
The animal's vibrant sense, the thought in man,
To the effulgence of a Ray above.
Its skill endorsing Matter's right to think
Cut sentient passages for the mind of flesh
And found a means for Nescience to know.
Offering its little squares and cubes of word
As figured substitutes for reality,
A mummified mnemonic alphabet,
It helped the unseeing force to read her works.
A buried consciousness arose in her
And now she dreams herself human and awake.
But all was still a mobile Ignorance;
Still Knowledge could not come and firmly grasp

This huge invention seen as a universe.
A specialist of logic's hard machine
Imposed its rigid artifice on the soul;
An aide of the inventor intellect,
It cut Truth into manageable bits
That each might have his ration of thought-food,
Then new-built Truth's slain body by its art:
A robot exact and serviceable and false
Displaced the spirit's finer view of things:
A polished engine did the work of a god.
None the true body found, its soul seemed dead:
None had the inner look which sees Truth's whole;
All glorified the glittering substitute.
Then from the secret heights a wave swept down,
A brilliant chaos of rebel light arose;
It looked above and saw the dazzling peaks,
It looked within and woke the sleeping god.
Imagination called her shining squads
That venture into undiscovered scenes
Where all the marvels lurk none yet has known:
Lifting her beautiful and miraculous head,
She conspired with inspiration's sister brood
To fill thought's skies with glimmering nebulae.
A bright Error fringed the mystery-altar's frieze;
Darkness grew nurse to wisdom's occult sun,
Myth suckled knowledge with her lustrous milk;
The infant passed from dim to radiant breasts.
Thus worked the Power upon the growing world;
Its subtle craft withheld the full-orbed blaze,
Cherished the soul's childhood and on fictions fed
Far richer in their sweet and nectarous sap
Nourishing its immature divinity
Than the staple or dry straw of Reason's tilth,
Its heaped fodder of innumerable facts,
Plebian fare on which today we thrive.
Thus streamed down from the realm of early Light,
Ethereal thinkings into Matter's world;
Its gold-horned herds trooped into earth's cave-heart.
Its morning rays illume our twilight's eyes,
Its young formations move the mind of earth

To labour and to dream and new-create,
To feel beauty's touch and know the world and self:
The Golden Child began to think and see.

soul—

* In those bright realms are Mind's first forward steps.
Ignorant of all but eager to know all,
Its curious slow enquiry there begins;
Ever searching it grasps at shapes around,
Ever it hopes to find out greater things.
Ardent and golden gleamed with sunrise fires,
Alert it lives upon invention's verge.
Yet all it does is on an infant's scale,
As if the cosmos were a nursery game,
Mind, life the playthings of a Titan's babe.
As one it works who builds a mimic fort
Miraculously stable for a while,
Made of the sands upon a bank of Time
Mid an occult eternity's shoreless sea.
A small keen instrument the great Puissance chose,
An arduous pastime passionately pursues;
To teach the Ignorance is her difficult charge,
Her thought starts from an original nescient Void
And what she teaches she herself must learn
Arousing knowledge from its sleepy lair.
For knowledge comes not to us as a guest

*To go on + on
in the
mental not
spiritual*

Called into our chamber from the outer world;
A friend and inmate of our secret self,
It hid behind our minds and fell asleep
And slowly wakes beneath the glows of life;
The mighty daemon lies unshaked within,
To evoke, to give it form is Nature's task.
All was a chaos of the true and false,
Mind sought amid deep mists of Nescience;
It looked within itself but saw not God.
A material interim diplomacy
Denied the truth that transient truths might live
And hid the deity in creed and guess
That the World-Ignorance might grow slowly wise.
This was the imbroglio made by sovereign Mind
Looking from a gleam-ridge into the Night

In its first tamperings with Inconscience:
Its alien dusk baffles her luminous eyes;
Her rapid hands must learn a cautious zeal;
Only a slow advance the earth can bear.
Yet was her strength unlike the unseeing earth's
Compelled to handle makeshift instruments
Invented by the life-force and the flesh.
Earth all perceives through doubtful images,
All she conceives in hazardous jets of sight,
Small lights kindled by touches of groping thought.
Incapable of the soul's direct inlook
She sees by spasms and solders knowledge-scrap,
Makes Truth the slave-girl of her indigence,
Expelling Nature's mystic unity
Cuts into quantum and mass the moving All;
She takes for measuring-rod her ignorance.
In her own domain a pontiff and a seer,
That greater Power with her half-risen sun
Wrought within limits but possessed her field;
She knew by a privilege of thinking force
And claimed an infant sovereignty of sight.
In her eyes however darkly fringed was lit
The Archangel's gaze who knows inspired his acts
And shapes a world in its far-seeing flame.
In her own realm she stumbles not nor fails,
But moves in boundaries of subtle power
Across which mind can step towards the sun.
A candidate for a higher suzerainty,
A passage she cut through from Night to Light,
And searched for an ungrasped Omniscience.

 A dwarf three-bodied trinity was her serf.
First, smallest of the three, but strong of limb,
A low-brow with a square and heavy jowl,
A pigmy Thought needing to live in bounds
For ever stooped to hammer fact and form.
Absorbed and cabined in external sight,
It takes its stand on Nature's solid base.
A technician admirable, a thinker crude,
A riveter of Life to habit's grooves,

Obedient to gross Matter's tyranny,
A prisoner of the moulds in which it works,
It binds itself by what itself creates.
A slave of a fixed mass of absolute rules,
It sees as Law the habits of the world,
It sees as Truth the habits of the mind.
In its realm of concrete images and events
Turning in a worn circle of ideas
And ever repeating old familiar acts,
It lives content with the common and the known.
It loves the old ground that was its dwelling-place:
Abhorring change as an audacious sin,
Distrustful of each new discovery
Only it advances step by careful step
And fears as if a deadly abyss the unknown.
A prudent treasurer of its ignorance,
It shrinks from adventure, blinks at glorious hope,
Preferring a safe foothold upon things
To the dangerous joy of wideness and of height.
The world's slow impressions on its labouring mind,
Tardy imprints almost indelible,
Increase their value by their poverty;
The old sure memories are its capital stock:
Only what sense can grasp seems absolute:
External fact it figures as sole truth,
Wisdom identifies with the earthward look,
And things long known and actions always done
Are to its clinging hold a balustrade
Of safety on the perilous stair of Time.
Heaven's trust to it are the established ancient ways,
Immutable laws man has no right to change,
A sacred legacy from the great dead past
Or the one road that God has made for life,
A firm shape of Nature never to be changed,
Part of the huge routine of the universe.
A smile from the Preserver of the Worlds
Sent down of old this guardian Mind to earth
That all might stand in their fixed changeless type
And from their secular posture never move.
One sees it circling faithful to its task,

Tireless in an assigned tradition's round;
In decayed and crumbling offices of Time
It keeps close guard in front of custom's wall,
Or in an ancient Night's dim environs
It dozes on a little courtyard's stones
And barks at every unfamiliar light
As at a foe who would break up its home,
A watch-dog of the spirit's sense-railed house
Against intruders from the Invisible,
Nourished on scraps of life and Matter's bones
In its kennel of objective certitude.
And yet behind it stands a cosmic might:
A measured Greatness keeps its vaster plan,
A fathomless sameness rhythms the tread of life;
The stars' changeless orbits furrow inert Space,
A million species follow one mute Law.
A huge inertness is the world's defence,
Even in change is treasured changelessness;
Into inertia revolution sinks,
In a new dress the old resumes its role;
The Energy acts, the stable is its seal:
On Shiva's breast is stayed the enormous dance.

A fiery spirit came, next of the three.
A hunchback rider of the red Wild-Ass,
A rash Intelligence leaped down lion-maned
From the great mystic Flame that rings the worlds
And with its dire edge eats at being's heart.
Thence sprang the burning vision of Desire.
A thousand shapes it wore, took numberless names:
A need of multitude and uncertainty
Pricks it for ever to pursue the One
On countless roads across the vasts of Time
Through circuits of unending difference.
It burns all breasts with an ambiguous fire.
A radiance gleaming on a murky stream,
It flamed towards heaven, then sank, engulfed towards hell;
It climbed to drag down Truth into the mire
And used for muddy ends its brilliant Force.
A huge chameleon gold and blue and red
Turning to black and grey and lurid brown,

Hungry it stared from a mottled bough of life
To snap up insect joys, its favourite food,
The dingy sustenance of a sumptuous frame
Nursing the splendid passion of its hues.
A snake of flame with a dark cloud for tail,
Followed by a dream-brood of glittering thoughts,
A lifted head with many-tinged flickering crests,
It licked at knowledge with a smoky tongue.
A whirlpool sucking in an empty air,
It based on vacancy stupendous claims,
In Nothingness born to Nothingness returned,
Yet all the time unwittingly it drove
Towards the hidden Something that is All.
Ardent to find, incapable to retain,
A brilliant instability was its mark,
To err its inborn trend, its native cue.
At once to an unreflecting credence prone,
It thought all true that flattered its own hopes;
It cherished golden nothings born of wish,
It snatched at the unreal for provender.
In darkness it discovered luminous shapes;
Peering into a shadow-hung half-light
It saw hued images scrawled on Fancy's cave;
Or it swept in circles through conjecture's night
And caught in imagination's camera
Bright scenes of promise held by transient flares,
Fixed in life's air the feet of hurrying dreams,
Kept prints of passing Forms and hooded Powers
And flash-images of half-seen verities.
An eager spring to seize and to possess
Unguided by reason or the seeing soul
Was its first natural motion and its last,
It squandered life's force to achieve the impossible:
It scorned the straight road and ran on wandering curves
And left what it had won for untried things;
It saw unrealised aims as instant fate
And chose the precipice for its leap to heaven.
Adventure its system in the gamble of life,
It took fortuitous gains as safe results;
Error discouraged not its confident view

Ignorant of the deep law of being's ways
And failure could not slow its fiery clutch;
One chance made true warranted all the rest.
Attempt, not victory, was the charm of life.
An uncertain winner of uncertain stakes,
Instinct its dam and the life-mind its sire,
It ran its race and came in first or last.
Yet were its works nor small and vain nor null;
It nursed a portion of infinity's strength
And could create the high things its fancy willed;
Its passion caught what calm intelligence missed.
Insight of impulse laid its leaping grasp
On heavens high Thought had hidden in dazzling mist,
Caught glimmers that revealed a lurking sun:
It probed the void and found a treasure there.
A half-intuition purpled in its sense;
It threw the lightning's fork and hit the unseen.
It saw in the dark and vaguely blinked in the light,
Ignorance was its field, the unknown its prize.
    Of all these Powers the greatest was the last.
Arriving late from a far plane of thought
Into a packed irrational world of Chance
Where all was grossly felt and blindly done,
Yet the haphazard seemed the inevitable,
Came Reason, the squat godhead artisan,
To her narrow house upon a ridge in Time.
Adept of clear contrivance and design,
A pensive face and close and peering eyes,
She took her firm and irremovable seat,
The strongest, wisest of the troll-like Three.
Armed with her lens and measuring-rod and probe,
She looked upon an object universe
And the multitudes that in it live and die
And the body of Space and the fleeing soul of Time,
And took the earth and stars into her hands
To try what she could make of these strange things.
In her strong purposeful laborious mind,
Inventing her scheme-lines of reality
And the geometric curves of her time-plan,
She multiplied her slow half-cuts at Truth:

227

Impatient of enigma and the unknown,
Intolerant of the lawless and unique,
Imposing reflection on the march of Force,
Imposing clarity on the unfathomable,
She strove to reduce to rules the mystic world.
Nothing she knew but all things hoped to know.
In dark inconscient realms once void of thought,
Missioned by a supreme Intelligence
To throw its ray upon the obscure Vast,
An imperfect light leading an erring mass
By the power of sense and the idea and word,
She ferrets out Nature's process, substance, cause.
All life to harmonise by thought's control
She with the huge imbroglio struggles still;
Ignorant of all but her own seeking mind
To save the world from Ignorance she came.
A sovereign worker through the centuries,
Observing and re-moulding all that is,
Confident she took up her stupendous charge.
There the low bent and mighty figure sits
Bowed under the arc-lamps of her factory-home
Amid the clatter and ringing of her tools.
A rigorous stare in her creative eyes
Coercing the plastic stuff of cosmic Mind,
She sets the hard inventions of her brain
In a pattern of eternal fixity:
Indifferent to the cosmic dumb demand,
Unconscious of too close realities,
Of the unspoken thought, the voiceless heart,
She leans to forge her credos and iron codes
And metal structures to imprison life
And mechanic models of all things that are.
For the world seen she weaves a world conceived:
She spins in stiff but unsubstantial lines
Her gossamer word-webs of abstract thought,
Her segment systems of the Infinite,
Her theodicies and cosmogonic charts
And myths by which she explains the inexplicable.
At will she spaces in thin air of mind
Like maps in the school-house of intellect hung,

Forcing wide Truth into a narrow scheme,
Her numberless warring strict philosophies;
Out of Nature's body of phenomenon
She carves with Thought's keen edge in rigid lines
Like rails for the World-Magician's power to run,
Her sciences precise and absolute.
On the huge bare walls of human nescience
Written round Nature's deep dumb hieroglyphs
She pens in clear demotic characters
The vast encyclopaedia of her thoughts;
An algebra of her mathematics' signs,
Her numbers and unerring formulas
She builds to clinch her summary of things.
On all sides runs as if in a cosmic mosque
Tracing the scriptural verses of her laws
The daedal of her patterned arabesques,
Art of her wisdom, artifice of her lore.
This art, this artifice are her only stock.
In her high works of pure intelligence,
In her withdrawal from the senses' trap,
There comes no breaking of the walls of mind,
There leaps no rending flash of absolute power,
There dawns no light of heavenly certitude.
A million faces wears her knowledge here
And every face is turbaned with a doubt.
All now is questioned, all reduced to nought.
Once monumental in their massive craft
Her old great mythic writings disappear
And into their place start strict ephemeral signs;
This constant change spells progress to her eyes:
Her thought is an endless march without a goal.
There is no summit on which she can stand
And see in a single glance the Infinite's whole.
  An inconclusive play is Reason's toil.
Each strong idea can use her as its tool;
Accepting every brief she pleads her case.
Open to every thought, she cannot know.
The eternal Advocate seated as judge
Armours in logic's invulnerable mail
A thousand combatants for Truth's veiled throne

And sets on a high horseback of argument
To tilt for ever with a wordy lance
In a mock tournament where none can win.
Assaying thought's values with her rigid tests
Balanced she sits on wide and empty air,
Aloof and pure in her impartial poise.
Absolute her judgments seem but none is sure;
Time cancels all her verdicts in appeal.
Although like sunbeams to our glow-worm mind
Her knowledge feigns to fall from a clear heaven,
Its rays are a lantern's lustres in the Night;
She throws a glittering robe on Ignorance.
But now is lost her ancient sovereign claim
To rule mind's high realm in her absolute right,
Bind thought with logic's forged infallible chain
Or see truth nude in a bright abstract haze.
A master and slave of stark phenomenon,
She travels on the roads of erring sight
Or looks upon a set mechanical world
Constructed for her by her instruments.
A bullock yoked in the cart of proven fact,
She drags huge knowledge-bales through Matter's dust
To reach utility's immense bazaar.
Apprentice she has grown to her old drudge;
An aided sense is her seeking's arbiter.
This now she uses as the assayer's stone.
As if she knew not facts are husks of truth,
The husks she keeps, the kernel throws aside.
An ancient wisdom fades into the past,
The ages' faith becomes an idle tale,
God passes out of the awakened thought,
An old discarded dream needed no more:
Only she seeks mechanic nature's keys.
Interpreting stone-laws inevitable
She digs into Matter's hard concealing soil,
To unearth the processes of all things done.
A loaded huge self-worked machine appears
To her eye's eager and admiring stare,
An intricate and meaningless enginery
Of ordered fateful and unfailing chance:

Ingenious and meticulous and minute,
Its brute unconscious accurate device
Unrolls an unerring march, maps a sure road;
It plans without thinking, acts without a will,
A million purposes serves with purpose none
And builds a rational world without a mind.
It has no mover, no maker, no idea:
Its vast self-action toils without a cause;
A lifeless Energy irresistibly driven,
Death's head on the body of Necessity,
Engenders life and fathers consciousness,
Then wonders why all was and whence it came.
Our thoughts are parts of the immense machine,
Our ponderings but a freak of Matter's law,
The mystic's lore was a fancy or a blind;
Of soul or spirit we have now no need:
Matter is the admirable Reality,
The patent unescapable miracle,
The hard truth of things, simple, eternal, sole.
A suicidal rash expenditure
Creating the world by a mystery of self-loss
Has poured its scattered works on empty space;
Late shall the self-disintegrating Force
Contract the immense expansion it has made:
Then ends this mighty and unmeaning toil,
The Void is left bare, vacant as before.
Thus vindicated, crowned, the grand new Thought
Explained the world and mastered all its laws,
Touched the dumb roots, woke veiled tremendous powers;
It bound to service the unconscious djinns
That sleep unused in Matter's ignorant trance.
All was precise, rigid, indubitable.
But when on Matter's rock of ages based
A whole stood up firm and clear-cut and safe,
All staggered back into a sea of doubt;
This solid scheme melted in endless flux:
She had met the formless Power inventor of forms;
Suddenly she stumbled upon things unseen:
A lightning from the undiscovered Truth
Startled her eyes with its perplexing glare

231

And dug a gulf between the Real and Known
Till all her knowledge seemed an ignorance.
Once more the world was made a wonder-web,
A magic's process in a magical space,
An unintelligible miracle's depths
Whose source is lost in the Ineffable.
Once more we face the blank Unknowable.
In a crash of values, in a huge doom-crack,
In the sputter and scatter of her breaking work
She lost her clear conserved constructed world.
A quantum dance remained, a sprawl of chance
In Energy's stupendous tripping whirl:
A ceaseless motion in the unbounded Void
Invented forms without a thought or aim:
Necessity and Cause were shapeless ghosts;
Matter was an incident in being's flow,
Law but a clock-work habit of blind force.
Ideals, ethics, systems had no base
And soon collapsed or without sanction lived;
All grew a chaos, a heave and clash and strife.
Ideas warring and fierce leaped upon life;
A hard compression held down anarchy
And liberty was only a phantom's name:
Creation and destruction waltzed inarmed
On the bosom of a torn and quaking earth;
All reeled into a world of Kali's dance.
Thus tumbled, sinking, sprawling in the Void,
Clutching for props, a soil on which to stand,
She only saw a thin atomic Vast,
The rare-point sparse substratum Universe
On which floats a solid world's phenomenal face.
Alone a process of events was there
And Nature's plastic and protean change
And, strong by death to slay, or to create
The riven invisible atom's omnipotent force.
One chance remained that here might be a power
To liberate man from the old inadequate means
And leave him sovereign of the earthly scene.
For Reason then might grasp the original Force
To drive her car upon the roads of Time.

All then might serve the need of the thinking race,
An absolute State found order's absolute,
To a standardised perfection cut all things,
In society build a just exact machine.
Then science and reason careless of the soul
Could iron out a tranquil uniform world,
Aeonic seekings glut with outward truths
And a single patterned thinking force on mind,
Inflicting Matter's logic on Spirit's dreams
A reasonable animal make of man
And a symmetrical fabric of his life.
This would be Nature's peak on an obscure globe,
The grand result of the long ages' toil,
Earth's evolution crowned, her mission done.
So might it be if the spirit fell asleep;
Man then might rest content and live in peace,
Master of Nature who wants her bondslave worked,
The world's disorder hardening into Law,—
If Life's dire heart arose not in revolt,
If God within could find no greater plan.
But many-visaged is the cosmic Soul;
A touch can alter the fixed front of Fate.
A sudden turn can come, a road appear,
A greater Mind may see a greater Truth,
Or we may find when all the rest has failed
Hid in ourselves the key of perfect change.
Ascending from the soil where creep our days,
Earth's consciousness may marry with the Sun,
Our mortal life ride on the spirit's wing,
Our finite thoughts commune with the Infinite.

In the bright kingdoms of the rising Sun
All is a birth into a power of light:
All here deformed guards there its happy shape,
Here all is mixed and marred, there pure and whole;
Yet each is a passing step, a moment's phase.
Awake to a greater Truth beyond her acts,
The mediatrix sat and saw her works
And felt the marvel in them and the force
But knew the power behind the face of Time:
She did the task, obeyed the knowledge given,

233

Her deep heart yearned towards great ideal things
And from the light looked out to wider light:
A brilliant hedge drawn round her narrowed her power;
Faithful to her limited sphere she toiled, but knew
Its highest, widest seeing was a half-search,
Its mightiest acts a passage or a stage.
For not by Reason was creation made
And not by Reason can the Truth be seen
Which through the veils of thought, the screens of sense
Hardly the spirit's vision can descry
Dimmed by the imperfection of its means:
The little Mind is tied to little things:
Its sense is but the spirit's outward touch
Half-waked in a world of dark Inconscience;
It feels out for its beings and its forms
Like one left fumbling in the ignorant Night.
In this small mould of infant mind and sense
Desire is a child-heart's cry crying for bliss,
Our reason only a toys' artificer,
A rule-maker in a strange stumbling game.
But she her dwarf aids knew whose confident sight
A bounded prospect took for the far goal.
The world she has made is an interim report
Of a traveller towards the half-found truth in things
Moving twixt nescience and nescience.
For nothing is known while aught remains concealed;
The Truth is known only when all is seen.
Attracted by the All that is the One,
She yearns towards a higher light than hers;
Hid by her cults and creeds she has glimpsed God's face:
She knows she has but found a form, a robe,
But ever she hopes to see him in her heart
And feel the body of his reality.
As yet a mask is there and not a brow,
Although sometimes two hidden eyes appear:
Reason cannot tear off that glimmering mask,
Her efforts only make it glimmer more;
In packets she ties up the Indivisible;
Finding her hands too small to hold vast Truth
She breaks up knowledge into alien parts

234

Or peers through cloud-rack for a vanished sun:
She sees, not understanding what she has seen,
Through the locked visages of finite things
The myriad aspects of infinity.
One day the Face must burn out through the mask.
Our ignorance is Wisdom's chrysalis,
Our error weds new knowledge on its way,
Its darkness is a blackened knot of light;
Thought dances hand in hand with Nescience
On the grey road that winds towards the Sun.
Even while her fingers fumble at the knots
Which bind them to their strange companionship,
Into the moments of their married strife
Sometimes break flashes of the enlightening Fire.
Even now great thoughts are here that walk alone:
Armed they have come with the infallible word
In an investiture of intuitive light
That is a sanction from the eyes of God;
Announcers of a distant Truth they flame
Arriving from the rim of eternity.
A fire shall come out of the infinitudes,
A greater Gnosis shall regard the world
Crossing out of some far omniscience
On lustrous seas from the still rapt Alone
To illumine the deep heart of self and things.
A timeless knowledge it shall bring to Mind,
Its aim to life, to Ignorance its close.

      Above in a high breathless stratosphere,
Overshadowing the dwarfish trinity,
Lived, aspirants to a limitless Beyond,
Captives of Space, walled by the limiting heavens,
In the unceasing circuit of the hours,
Yearning for the straight paths of eternity,
And from their high station looked down on this world
Two sun-gaze Daemons witnessing all that is.
A power to uplift the laggard world,
Imperious rode a huge high-winged Life-Thought
Unwont to tread the firm unchanging soil:
Accustomed to a blue infinity,

It planed in sunlit sky and starlit air;
It saw afar the unreached Immortal's home
And heard afar the voices of the gods.
Iconoclast and shatterer of Time's forts,
Overleaping limit and exceeding norm,
It lit the thoughts that glow through the centuries
And moved to acts of superhuman force.
As far as its self-winged airplanes could fly,
Visiting the future in great brilliant raids
It reconnoitred vistas of dream-fate.
Apt to conceive, unable to attain,
It drew its concept-maps and vision-plans
Too large for the architecture of mortal Space.
Beyond in wideness where no footing is,
An imagist of bodiless Ideas,
Impassive to the cry of life and sense,
A pure Thought-Mind surveyed the cosmic act.
Archangel of a white transcending realm,
It saw the world from solitary heights
Luminous in a remote and empty air.

END OF CANTO TEN

CANTO ELEVEN

THE KINGDOMS AND GODHEADS OF THE GREATER MIND

THERE ceased the limits of the labouring Power.
　　But being and creation cease not there.
For Thought transcends the circles of mortal mind,
It is greater than its earthly instrument:
The godhead crammed into mind's narrow space
Escapes on every side into some vast
That is a passage to infinity.
It moves eternal in the spirit's field,
A runner towards the far spiritual light,
A child and servant of the spirit's force.
But mind too falls back from a nameless peak.
His being stretched beyond the sight of Thought.
For the spirit is eternal and unmade
And not by thinking was its greatness born,
And not by thinking can its knowledge come.
It knows itself and in itself it lives,
It moves where no thought is nor any form.
Its feet are steadied upon finite things,
Its wings can dare to cross the Infinite.
Arriving into his ken a wonder space
Of great and marvellous meetings called his steps,
Where Thought leaned on a Vision beyond thought
And shaped a world from the Unthinkable.
On peaks imagination cannot tread,
In the horizons of a tireless sight,
Under a blue veil of eternity
The splendours of ideal Mind were seen
Outstretched across the boundaries of things known.
Origin of the little that we are,

Instinct with the endless more that we must be,
A prop of all that human strength enacts,
Creator of hopes by earth unrealised,
It spreads beyond the expanding universe;
It wings beyond the boundaries of Dream,
It overtops the ceiling of life's soar.
Awake in a luminous sphere unbound by Thought,
Exposed to omniscient immensities,
It casts on our world its great crowned influences,
Its speed that outstrips the ambling of the hours,
Its force that strides invincibly through Time,
Its mights that bridge the gulf twixt man and God,
Its lights that combat Ignorance and Death.
In its vast ambit of ideal Space
Where beauty and mightiness walk hand in hand,
The Spirit's truths take form as living Gods
And each can build a world in its own right.
In an air which doubt and error cannot mark
With the stigmata of their deformity,
In communion with the musing privacy
Of a truth that sees in an unerring light
Where the sight falters not nor wanders thought,
Exempt from our world's exorbitant tax of tears,
Dreaming its luminous creations gaze
On the Ideas that people eternity.
In a sun-blaze of joy and absolute power
Above the Masters of the Ideal throne
In sessions of secure felicity,
In regions of illumined certitude.
Far are those realms from our labour and yearning and call,
Perfection's reign and hallowed sanctuary
Closed to the uncertain thoughts of human mind,
Remote from the turbid tread of mortal life.
But since our secret selves are next of kin,
A breath of unattained divinity
Visits the imperfect earth on which we toil;
Across a gleaming ether's golden laugh
A light falls on our vexed unsatisfied lives,
A thought comes down from the ideal worlds
And moves us to new-model even here

Some image of their greatness and appeal
And wonder beyond the ken of mortal hope.
Amid the heavy sameness of the days
And contradicted by the human law,
A faith in things that are not and must be
Lives comrade of this world's delight and pain,
The child of the secret soul's forbidden desire
Born of its amour with eternity.
Our spirits break free from their environment;
The future brings its face of miracle near,
Its godhead looks at us with present eyes;
Acts deemed impossible grow natural;
We feel the hero's immortality,
The courage and the strength death cannot touch
Awake in limbs that are mortal, hearts that fail;
We move by the rapid impulse of a will
That scorns the tardy trudge of mortal Time.
These promptings come not from an alien sphere:
Ourselves are citizens of that mother State,
Adventurers, we have colonised Matter's night.
But now our rights are barred, our passports void;
We live self-exiled from our heavenlier home.
An errant ray from the immortal Mind
Accepted the earth's blindness and became
Our human thought, servant of Ignorance.
An exile, labourer on this unsure globe
Captured and driven in Life's nescient grasp,
Hampered by obscure cell and treacherous nerve,
It dreams of happier states and nobler powers,
The natural privilege of unfallen gods
Recalling still its old lost sovereignty.
Amidst earth's mist and fog and mud and stone
It still remembers its exalted sphere
And the high city of its splendid birth.
A memory steals from a lost heaven of Truth,
A wide release comes near, a Glory calls,
A might looks out, an estranged felicity.
In glamorous passages of half-veiled light
Wandering, a brilliant shadow of itself,
This quick uncertain leader of blind gods,

This tender of small lamps, this minister serf
Hired by a mind and body for earth-use
Forgets its work mid crude realities;
It recovers its renounced imperial right,
It wears once more its purple robe of thought
And knows itself the Ideal's seer and king,
Communicant and prophet of the Unborn,
Heir to delight and immortality.
All things are real that here are only dreams,
In our unknown depths sleeps their reserve of truth,
On our unreached heights they reign and come to us
In thought and muse trailing their robes of light.
But our dwarf will and cold pragmatic sense
Admit not the celestial visitants:
Awaiting us on the Ideal's peaks
Or guarded in our secret self unseen
Yet flashed sometimes across the awakened soul,
Hide from our lives their greatness, beauty, power.
Our present feels sometimes their regal touch,
Our future strives towards their luminous thrones:
Out of spiritual secrecy they gaze,
Immortal footfalls in mind's corridors sound:
Our souls can climb into the shining planes,
The breadths from which they came can be our home.
His privilege regained of shadowless sight
The Thinker entered the immortals' air
And drank again his pure and mighty source.
Immutable in rhythmic calm and joy
He saw, sovereignly free in limitless light,
The unfallen planes, the thought-created worlds
Where Knowledge is the leader of the act
And Matter is of thinking substance made,
Feeling, a heaven-bird poised on dreaming wings,
Answers Truth's call as to a parent's voice,
Form luminous leaps from the all-shaping beam
And Will is a conscious chariot of the Gods,
And Life, a splendour-stream of musing Force,
Carries the voices of the mystic Suns.
A happiness it brings of whispered truth;
There runs in its flow honeying the bosom of Space

A laughter from the immortal heart of Bliss,
And the unfathomed Joy of timelessness,
The sound of Wisdom's murmur in the Unknown
And the breath of an unseen Infinity.
In gleaming clarities of amethyst air
The chainless and omnipotent Spirit of Mind
Brooded on the blue lotus of the Idea.
A gold supernal sun of timeless Truth
Poured down the mystery of the eternal Ray
Through a silence quivering with the word of Light
On an endless ocean of discovery.
Far-off he saw the joining hemispheres.
On meditation's mounting edge of trance
Great stairs of thought climbed up to unborn heights
Where Time's last ridges touch eternity's skies
And Nature speaks to the spirit's absolute.

A triple realm of ordered thought came first,
A small beginning of immense ascent:
Above were bright ethereal skies of mind,
A packed and endless soar as if sky pressed sky
Buttressed against the Void on bastioned light;
The highest strove to neighbour eternity,
The largest widened into the infinite.
But though immortal, mighty and divine,
The first realms were close and kin to human mind;
Their deities shape our greater thinking's roads,
A fragment of their puissance can be ours:
These breadths were not too broad for our souls to range,
These heights were not too high for human hope.
A triple flight led to this triple world.
Although abrupt for common strengths to tread,
Its upward slope looks down on our earth-poise:
On a slant not too precipitously steep
One could turn back travelling deep descending lines
To commune with the mortal's universe.
The mighty wardens of the ascending stair
Who intercede with the all-creating Word,
There waited for the pilgrim heaven-bound soul;
Holding the thousand keys of the Beyond

They proffered their knowledge to the climbing mind
And filled the life with Thought's immensities.
The prophet hierophants of the occult Law,
The flame-bright hierarchs of the divine Truth,
Interpreters between man's mind and God's,
They bring the immortal fire to mortal men.
Iridescent, bodying the invisible,
The guardians of the Eternal's bright degrees
Fronted the sun in radiant phalanxes.
Afar they seemed a symbol imagery,
Illumined originals of the shadowy script
In which our sight transcribes the ideal Ray,
Or icons figuring a mystic Truth,
But, nearer, Gods and living Presences.
A march of friezes marked the lowest steps;
Fantastically ornate and richly small,
They had room for the whole meaning of a world,
Symbols minute of its perfection's joy,
Strange beasts that were Nature's forces made alive
And, wakened to the wonder of his role,
Man grown an image undefaced of God
And objects the fine coin of Beauty's reign;
But wide the terrains were those levels serve.
In front of the ascending epiphany
World-Time's enjoyers, favourites of World-Bliss,
The Masters of things actual, lords of the hours,
Playmates of youthful Nature and child God,
Creators of Matter by hid stress of Mind
Whose subtle thoughts support unconscious Life
And guide the fantasy of brute events,
Stood there, a race of young keen-visioned Gods,
King-children born on Wisdom's early plane,
Taught in her school world-making's mystic play.
Arch-masons of the eternal Thaumaturge,
Moulders and measurers of fragmented space,
They have made their plan of the concealed and known
A dwelling-house for the invisible King.
Obeying the Eternal's deep command
They have built in the material front of things
This wide world-kindergarten of young souls

Where the infant spirit learns through mind and sense
To read the letters of the cosmic script
And study the body of the cosmic self
And search for the secret meaning of the whole.
To all that Spirit conceives they give a mould;
Persuading Nature into visible moods
They lend a finite shape to infinite things.
Each power that leaps from the Unmanifest
Leaving the largeness of the Eternal's peace
They seized and held by their precisian eye
And made a figurante in the cosmic dance:
Its free caprice they bound by rhythmic laws
And compelled to accept its posture and its line
In the wizardry of an ordered universe.
The All-containing was contained in form,
Oneness was carved into units measurable,
The limitless built into a cosmic sum:
Unending Space was beaten into a curve,
Indivisible Time into small minutes cut,
The infinitesimal massed to keep secure
The mystery of the Formless cast into form.
Invincibly their craft devised for use
The magic of sequent number and sign's spell,
Design's miraculous potency was caught
Laden with beauty and significance
And by the determining mandate of their gaze
Figure and quality equating joined
In an inextricable identity.
On each event they stamped its curves of law
And its trust and charge of burdened circumstance;
A free and divine incident no more
At each moment willed or adventure of the soul,
A line foreseen of an immutable plan,
It lengthened a fate-bound mysterious chain,
One step more in Necessity's long march.
A term was set for every eager Power
Restraining its will to monopolise the world,
A groove of bronze prescribed for force and act
And shown to each moment its appointed place
Forewilled inalterably in the spiral

Huge Time-loop fugitive from eternity.
Inevitable their thoughts like links of Fate
Imposed on the leap and lightning race of mind
And on the frail fortuitous flux of life
And on the liberty of atomic things
Immutable cause and adamant consequence.
Idea gave up the plastic infinity
To which it was born and now traced out instead
Small separate steps of chain-work in a plot:
Immortal once, now tied to birth and end,
Torn from its immediacy of errorless sight,
Knowledge was rebuilt from cells of inference
Into a fixed body flasque and perishable;
Thus bound it grew, but could not last and broke
And to a new thinking's body left its place.
A cage for the Infinite's great-eyed seraphim Thoughts
Was closed with a criss-cross of world-laws for bars
And hedged into a curt horizon's arc
The irised vision of the Ineffable.
A timeless Spirit was made the slave of the hours;
The Unbound was cast into a prison of birth
To make a world that Mind could grasp and rule.
On an earth which looked towards a thousand suns,
That the created might grow Nature's lord
And Matter's depths be illumined with a soul
They tied to date and norm and finite scope
The million-mysteried movement of the One.

  Above stood ranked a subtle archangel race
With larger lids and looks that searched the unseen.
A light of liberating Knowledge shone
Across the gulfs of silence in their eyes;
They lived in the mind and knew truth from within;
A sight withdrawn in the concentrated heart
Could pierce behind the screen of Time's results
And the rigid cast and shape of visible things.
All that escaped conception's narrow noose
Vision descried and gripped; their seeing thoughts
Filled in the blanks left by the seeking sense.
High architects of possibility
And engineers of the impossible,

Mathematicians of the infinitudes
And theoricians of unknowable truths,
They formulate enigma's postulates
And join the unknown to the apparent worlds.
Acolytes they wait upon the timeless Power,
The cycle of her works investigate;
Passing her fence of wordless privacy
Their mind could penetrate her occult mind
And draw the diagram of her secret thoughts;
They read the codes and ciphers she had sealed,
Copies they made of all her guarded plans,
For every turn of her mysterious course
Assigned a reason and unchanging rule.
The Unseen grew visible to student eyes,
Explained was the immense Inconscient's scheme,
Audacious lines were traced upon the Void;
The Infinite was reduced to square and cube.
Arranging symbol and significance,
Tracing the curve of a transcendent Power,
They framed the cabbala of the cosmic Law,
The balancing line discovered of Life's technique
And structured her magic and her mystery.
Imposing schemes of knowledge on the Vast
They clamped to syllogisms of finite thought
The free logic of an infinite consciousness,
Grammared the hidden rhythms of Nature's dance,
Critiqued the plot of the drama of the worlds,
Made figure and number a key to all that is:
The psycho-analysis of cosmic Self
Was traced, its secrets hunted down, and read
The unknown pathology of the Unique.
Assessed was the system of the probable,
The hazard of fleeing possibilities,
To account for the Actual's unaccountable sum,
Necessity's logarithmic tables drawn,
Cast into a scheme the triple act of the One.
Unveiled, the abrupt invisible multitude
Of forces whirling from the hands of Chance
Seemed to obey some vast imperative:
Their tangled motives worked out unity.

A wisdom read their mind to themselves unknown,
Their anarchy rammed into a formula
And from their giant randomness of Force,
Following the habit of their million paths,
Distinguishing each faintest line and stroke
Of a concealed unalterable design,
Out of the chaos of the Invisible's moods
Derived the calculus of Destiny.
In its bright pride of universal lore
Mind's knowledge overtopped the Omniscient's power:
The Eternal's winging eagle puissances
Surprised in their untracked empyrean
Stooped from their gyres to obey the beck of Thought:
Each mysteried God forced to revealing form,
Assigned his settled moves in Nature's game,
Zigzagged at the gesture of a chess-player Will
Across the chequer-board of cosmic Fate.
In the wide sequence of Necessity's steps
Predicted, every act and thought of God,
Its values weighed by the accountant Mind,
Checked in his mathematised omnipotence,
Lost its divine aspect of miracle
And was a figure in a cosmic sum.
The mighty Mother's whims and lightning moods
Arisen from her all-wise unruled delight
In the freedom of her sweet and passionate breast,
Robbed of their wonder were chained to a cause and aim;
An idol of bronze replaced her mystic shape
That captures the movements of the cosmic vasts,
In the sketch precise of an ideal face
Forgotten was her eyelashes' dream-print
Carrying on their curve infinity's dreams,
Lost the alluring marvel of her eyes;
The surging wave-throbs of her vast sea-heart
They bound to a theorem of ordered beats:
Her deep designs which from herself she had veiled
Bowed self-revealed in their confessional.
For the birth and death of the worlds they fixed a date,
The diameter of Infinity was drawn,
Measured the distant arc of the unseen heights

And visualised the plumbless viewless depths
Till all seemed known that in all time could be.
All was coerced by number, name and form;
Nothing was left untold, incalculable.
Yet was their wisdom circled with a nought:
Truths they could find and hold but not the one Truth:
The Highest was to them unknowable.
By knowing too much they missed the Whole to be known:
The fathomless heart of the world was left unguessed
And the Transcendent kept its secrecy.
   In a sublimer and more daring soar
To the wide summit of the triple stairs
Bare steps climbed up like glowing rocks of gold
Burning their way to a pure absolute sky.
August and few the sovereign Kings of Thought
Have made of Space their wide all-seeing gaze
Surveying the enormous work of Time:
A breadth of all-containing consciousness
Supported Being in a still embrace.
Intercessors with a luminous Unseen,
They capt in the long passage to the world
The imperatives of the creator Self
Obeyed by unknowing earth, by conscious heaven;
Their thoughts are partners in its vast control.
A great all-ruling consciousness is there
And Mind unwitting serves a higher Power;
It is a channel, not the source of all.
The cosmos is no accident in Time;
There is a meaning in each play of Chance,
There is a freedom in each face of Fate.
A Wisdom knows and guides the mysteried world;
A Truth-gaze shapes its beings and events;
A Word self-born upon creation's heights,
Voice of the Eternal in the temporal spheres,
Prophet of the seeings of the Absolute,
Sows the Idea's significance in Form
And from that seed the growths of Time arise.
On peaks beyond our ken the All-Wisdom sits:
A single and infallible look comes down,
A silent touch from the supernal's air

Awakes to ignorant knowledge in its acts
The secret power in the inconscient depths,
Compelling the blinded Godhead to emerge,
Determining Necessity's rude dance
As she passes through the circuit of the hours
And vanishes from the chase of finite eyes
Down circling vistas of aeonic Time.
The unseizable forces of the cosmic whirl
Bear in their bacchant limbs the fixity
Of an original foresight that is Fate.
Even Nature's ignorance is Truth's instrument;
Our struggling ego cannot change her course:
Yet is it a conscious power that moves in us
And destiny the unrecognised child of Will.
Infallibly by Truth's directing gaze
All creatures here their secret self disclose,
Forced to become what in themselves they hide.
For He who is grows manifest in the years
And the slow Godhead shut within the cell
Climbs from the plasm to immortality.
But hidden, but denied to mortal grasp,
Mystic, ineffable is the Spirit's truth,
Unspoken, caught only by the spirit's eye.
When naked of ego and mind it hears the Voice;
It looks through light to ever greater light
And sees Eternity ensphering Life.
This greater Truth is foreign to our thoughts;
Where a free Wisdom works, they seek for a rule;
Or we only see a tripping game of Chance
Or a labour in chains forced by bound Nature's law,
An absolutism of dumb unthinking Power.
Audacious in their sense of God-born strength
These dared to grasp with their thought Truth's absolute;
By an abstract purity of godless sight,
By a percept nude, intolerant of forms,
They brought to Mind what Mind could never reach
And hope to conquer Truth's supernal base.
A stripped imperative of conceptual phrase
Architectonic and inevitable
Translated the Unthinkable into thought:

A silver-winged fire of naked subtle sense,
An ear of mind withdrawn from the outward's rhymes
Discovered the seed-sounds of the eternal Word,
The rhythm and music heard that built the worlds,
And seized in things the bodiless Will to be.
The Illimitable they measured with number's rods
And traced the last formula of limited things,
In transparent systems bodied termless truths,
The Timeless made accountable to Time
And valued the incommensurable Supreme.
To park and hedge the ungrasped infinitudes
They erected absolute walls of thought and speech
And made a vacuum to hold the One.
In their sight they drove towards an empty peak,
A mighty space of cold and sunlit air.
To unify their task, excluding life
Which cannot bear the nakedness of the Vast,
They made a cipher of a multitude,
In negation found the meaning of the All
And in nothingness the absolute positive.
A single law simplessed the cosmic theme,
Compressing Nature into a formula;
Their titan labour made all knowledge one,
A mental algebra of the Spirit's ways,
An abstract of the living Divinity.
Here the mind's wisdom stopped; it felt complete;
For nothing more was left to think or know;
In a spiritual zero it sat throned
And took its vast silence for the Ineffable.

This was the play of the bright gods of Thought.
Attracting into time the timeless Light,
Imprisoning eternity in the hours,
This they have planned, to snare the feet of Truth
In an aureate net of concept and of phrase
And keep her captive for the thinker's joy
In his little world built of immortal dreams:
There must she dwell mured in the human mind,
An empress prisoner in her subject's house,
Adored and pure and still on his heart's throne,

His splendid property cherished and apart
In the wall of silence of his secret muse,
Immaculate in white virginity,
The same for ever and for ever one,
His worshipped changeless Goddess through all time.
Or else, a faithful consort of his mind
Assenting to his nature and his will,
She sanctions and inspires his words and acts
Prolonging their resonance through the listening ears,
Companion and recorder of his march
Crossing a brilliant tract of thought and life
Carved out of the eternity of Time.
A witness of his high triumphant star,
Her godhead servitor to a crowned Idea,
He shall dominate by her a prostrate world;
A warrant for his deeds and his beliefs,
She attests his right divine to lead and rule.
Or as her lover clasps his one beloved,
Godhead of his life's worship and desire,
Icon of his heart's sole idolatry,
She now is his and must live for him alone:
She has invaded him with her sudden bliss,
An exhaustless marvel in his happy grasp,
An allurement, a caught ravishing miracle.
Her now he claims after long rapt pursuit,
The one joy of his body and his soul:
Inescapable is her divine appeal,
Her immense possession an undying thrill,
An intoxication and an ecstasy:
The passion of her self-revealing moods,
A heavenly glory and variety,
Makes ever new her body to his eyes,
Or else repeats the first enchantment's touch,
The luminous rapture of her mystic breasts
And beautiful vibrant limbs a living field
Of throbbing new discovery without end.
A new beginning flowers in word and laugh,
A new charm brings back the old extreme delight:
He is lost in her, she is his heaven here.
Truth smiled upon the gracious golden game.

Out of her hushed eternal spaces leaned
The great and boundless Goddess feigned to yield
The sunlit sweetness of her secrecies.
Incarnating her beauty in his clasp
She gave for a brief kiss her immortal lips
And drew to her bosom one glorified mortal head:
She made earth her home, for whom heaven was too small.
In a human breast her occult presence lived;
He carved from his own self his figure of her:
She shaped her body to a mind's embrace.
Into thought's narrow limits she has come;
Her greatness she has suffered to be pressed
Into the little cabin of the Idea,
The closed room of a lonely thinker's grasp:
She has lowered her heights to the stature of our souls
And dazzled our lids with her celestial gaze.
Thus each is satisfied with his high gain
And thinks himself beyond mortality blest,
A king of truth upon his separate throne.
To her possessor in the field of Time
A single splendour caught from her glory seems
The one true light, her beauty's glowing whole.
But thought nor word can seize eternal Truth:
The whole world lives in a lonely ray of her sun.
In our thinking's close and narrow lamp-lit house
The vanity of our shut mortal mind
Dreams that the chains of thought have made her ours;
But only we play with our own brilliant bonds;
Tying her down, it is ourselves we tie.
In our hypnosis by one luminous point
We see not what small figure of her we hold;
We feel not her inspiring boundlessness,
We share not her immortal liberty.
Thus is it even with the seer and sage;
For still the human limits the divine:
Out of our thoughts we must leap up to sight,
Breathe her divine illimitable air,
Her simple vast supremacy confess,
Dare to surrender to her absolute.
Then the Unmanifest reflects his form

In the still mind as in a living glass;
The timeless Ray descends into our hearts
And we are rapt into eternity.
For Truth is wider, greater than her forms.
A thousand icons they have made of her
And find her in the idols they adore;
But she remains herself and infinite.

END OF CANTO ELEVEN

CANTO TWELVE

THE HEAVENS OF THE IDEAL

ALWAYS the Ideal beckoned from afar.
        Awakened by the touch of the Unseen,
Deserting the boundary of things achieved,
Aspired the strong discoverer, tireless Thought,
Revealing at each step a luminous world.
It left known summits for the unknown peaks:
Impassioned, it sought the lone unrealised Truth,
It longed for the Light that knows not death and birth.
Each stage of the soul's remote ascent was built
Into a constant heaven felt always here.
At each pace of the journey marvellous
A new degree of wonder and of bliss,
A new rung formed in Being's mighty stair,
A great wide step trembling with jewelled fire
As if a burning spirit quivered there
Upholding with his flame the immortal hope,
As if a radiant God had given his soul
That he might feel the tread of pilgrim feet
Mounting in haste to the Eternal's house.
At either end of each effulgent stair
The heavens of the ideal Mind were seen
In a blue lucency of dreaming space
Like strips of brilliant sky clinging to the moon.
On one side glimmered hue on floating hue,
In a glory and surprise of the seized soul
And a tremulous rapture of the heart's insight
And the spontaneous bliss that beauty gives,
The lovely kingdoms of the deathless Rose.
Above the spirit cased in mortal sense
Are superconscious realms of heavenly peace,
Below, the Inconscient's sullen dim abyss,

Between, behind our life, the deathless Rose.
Across the covert air the spirit breathes,
A body of the cosmic beauty and joy
Unseen, unguessed by the blind suffering world,
Climbing from Nature's deep surrendered heart
It blooms for ever at the feet of God,
Fed by life's sacrificial mysteries.
Here too its bud is born in human breasts;
Then by a touch, a presence or a voice
The world is turned into a temple ground
And all discloses the unknown Beloved.
In an outburst of heavenly joy and ease
Life yields to the divinity within
And gives the rapture-offering of its all,
And the soul opens to felicity.
A bliss is felt that never can wholly cease,
A sudden mystery of secret Grace
Flowers goldening our earth of red desire.
All the high gods who hid their visages
From the soiled passionate ritual of our hopes,
Reveal their names and their undying powers.
A fiery stillness wakes the slumbering cells,
A passion of the flesh becoming spirit,
And marvellously is fulfilled at last
The miracle for which our life was made.
A flame in a white voiceless cupola
Is seen and faces of immortal light,
The radiant limbs that know not birth and death,
The breasts that suckle the first-born of the Sun,
The wings that crowd Thought's ardent silences,
The eyes that look into spiritual Space.
Our hidden centres of celestial force
Open like flowers to a heavenly atmosphere;
Mind pauses thrilled with the supernal Ray,
And even the transient body then can feel
Ideal love and flawless happiness
And laughter of the heart's sweetness and delight
Freed from the rude and tragic hold of Time,
And beauty and the rhythmic feet of the hours.
This in high realms touches immortal kind;

What here is in the bud has blossomed there.
There is the secrecy of the House of Flame,
The blaze of Godlike thought and golden bliss,
The rapt idealism of heavenly sense;
There are the wonderful voices, the sun-laugh,
A gurgling eddy in rivers of God's joy,
And the mysteried vineyards of the gold moon-wine,
All the fire and sweetness of which hardly here
A brilliant shadow visits mortal life.
Although are witnessed there the joys of Time,
Pressed on the bosom the Immortal's touch is felt,
Heard are the flutings of the Infinite.
Here upon earth are early awakenings,
Moments that tremble in an air divine,
And grown upon the yearning of her soil
Time's sun-flowers' gaze at gold Eternity:
There are the imperishable beatitudes.
A million lotuses swaying on one stem,
World after coloured and ecstatic world
Climbs towards some far unseen epiphany.
    On the other side of the eternal stairs
The mighty kingdoms of the deathless Flame
Aspired to reach the Being's absolutes.
Out of the sorrow and darkness of the world,
Out of the depths where life and thought are tombed,
Lonely mounts up to heaven the deathless Flame.
In a veiled Nature's hallowed secrecies
It burns for ever on the altar Mind,
Its priests the souls of dedicated gods,
Humanity its house of sacrifice.
Once kindled never can its flamings cease.
A fire along the mystic paths of earth
It rises through the mortal's hemisphere,
Till borne by runners of the Day and Dusk
It enters the occult eternal Light
And clambers whitening to the invisible Throne.
Its worlds are steps of an ascending Force:
A dream of giant contours, titan lines,
Homes of unfallen and illumined Might,
Heavens of unchanging Good pure and unborn,

Heights of the grandeur of Truth's ageless ray,
As in a symbol sky they start to view
And call our souls into a vaster air.
On their summits they bear up the sleepless Flame;
Dreaming of a mysterious Beyond,
Transcendent of the paths of Fate and Time,
They point above themselves with index peaks
Through a pale-sapphire ether of God-mind
Towards some gold Infinite's apocalypse.
A thunder rolling mid the hills of God,
Tireless, severe is their tremendous Voice:
Exceeding us, to exceed ourselves they call
And bid us rise incessantly above.
Far from our eager reach those summits live,
Too lofty for our mortal strength and height,
Hardly in a dire ecstasy of toil
Climbed by the spirit's naked athlete will.
Austere, intolerant they claim from us
Efforts too lasting for our mortal nerve
Our hearts cannot cleave to nor our flesh support;
Only the Eternal's strength in us can dare
To attempt the immense adventure of that climb
And the sacrifice of all we cherish here.
Our human knowledge is a candle burnt
On a dim altar to a sun-vast Truth;
Man's virtue, a coarse-spun ill-fitting dress,
Apparels wooden images of Good;
Passionate and blinded, bleeding, stained with mire
His energy stumbles towards a deathless Force.
An imperfection dogs our highest strength;
Portions and pale reflections are our share.
Happy the worlds that have not felt our fall,
Where Will is one with Truth and Good with Power;
Impoverished not by earth-mind's indigence,
They keep God's natural breath of mightiness,
His bare spontaneous swift intensities;
There is his great transparent mirror, Self,
And there his sovereign autarchy of bliss
In which immortal natures have their part,
Heirs and co-sharers of divinity.

He through the Ideal's kingdoms moved at will,
Accepted their beauty and their greatness bore,
Partook of the glories of their wonder fields,
But passed nor stayed beneath their splendour's rule.
All there was an intense but partial light.
In each a seraph-winged high-browed Idea
United all knowledge by one master thought,
Persuaded all action to one golden sense,
All powers subjected to a single power
And made a world where it could reign alone,
An absolute ideal's perfect home.
Insignia of their victory and their faith,
They offered to the Traveller at their gates
A quenchless flame or an unfading flower,
Emblem of a high kingdom's privilege.
A glorious shining Angel of the Way
Presented to the seeking of the soul
The sweetness and the might of an idea,
Each deemed Truth's intimate fount and summit force,
The heart of the meaning of the universe,
Perfection's key, passport to Paradise.
Yet were there regions where these absolutes met
And made a circle of bliss with married hands;
Light stood embraced by light, fire wedded fire,
But none in the other would his body lose
To find his soul in the world's single Soul,
A multiplied rapture of infinity.
Onward he passed to a diviner sphere:
There, joined in a common greatness, light and bliss,
All high and beautiful and desirable powers
Forgetting their difference and their separate reign
Become a single multitudinous whole.
Above the parting of the roads of Time,
Above the Silence and its thousandfold Word,
In the immutable and inviolate Truth
For ever united and inseparable,
The radiant children of Eternity dwell
On the wide spirit height where all are one.

END OF CANTO TWELVE

IN THE SELF OF MIND

A T last there came a bare indifferent sky
Where Silence listened to the cosmic Voice,
But answered nothing to a million calls;
The soul's endless question met with no response.
An abrupt conclusion ended eager hopes,
A deep cessation in a mighty calm,
A finis-line on the last page of thought
And a margin and a blank of wordless peace.
There paused the climbing hierarchy of worlds.
He stood on a wide arc of summit Space
Alone with an enormous Self of Mind
Which held all life in a corner of its vasts.
Omnipotent, immobile and aloof,
In the world which sprang from it, it took no part:
It gave no heed to the paeans of victory,
It was indifferent to its own defeats,
It heard the cry of grief and made no sign,
Impartial fell its gaze on evil and good,
It saw destruction come and did not move.
An equal Cause of things, a lonely Seer
And Master of its multitude of forms,
It acted not but bore all thoughts and deeds,
The witness Lord of Nature's myriad acts
Consenting to the movements of her Force.
His mind reflected this vast quietism.
This witness hush is the Thinker's secret base:
Hidden in silent depths the word is formed,
From hidden silences the act is born
Into the voiceful mind, the labouring world;
In secrecy wraps the seed the Eternal sows

Silence, the mystic birthplace of the soul.
In God's supreme withdrawn and timeless hush
A seeing Self and potent Energy met;
The Silence knew itself and thought took form:
Self-made from the dual power creation rose.
In the still self he lived and it in him;
Its mute immemorable listening depths,
Its vastness and its stillness were his own;
One being with it he grew wide, powerful, free.
As one who builds his own imagined scenes
And loses not himself in what he sees,
Spectator of a drama self-conceived,
He looked on the world and watched its motive thoughts
With the burden of luminous prophecy in their eyes,
Its forces with their feet of wind and fire
Arisen from the dumbness in his soul.
All now he seemed to understand and know;
Desire came not nor any gust of will,
The great perturbed inquirer lost his task;
Nothing was asked nor wanted any more.
There he could stay, the Self, the Silence won:
His soul had peace, it knew the cosmic Whole.
Then suddenly a luminous finger fell
On all things seen or touched or heard or felt
And showed his mind that nothing could be known;
That must be reached from which all knowledge comes.
The sceptic Ray disrupted all that seems
And smote at the very roots of thought and sense.
In a universe of Nescience they have grown,
Aspiring towards a superconscient Sun,
Playing in shine and rain from heavenlier skies
They never can win however high their reach
Or overpass however keen their probe.
A doubt corroded even the means to think,
Distrust was thrown upon Mind's instruments;
All that it takes for reality's shining coin,
Proved fact, fixed inference, deduction clear,
Firm theory, assured significance,
Appeared as frauds upon Time's credit bank
Or assets valueless in Truth's treasury.

An Ignorance on an uneasy throne
Travestied with a fortuitous sovereignty
A figure of knowledge garbed in dubious words
And tinsel thought-forms brightly inadequate.
A labourer in the dark dazzled by half-light,
What it knew was an image in a broken glass,
What it saw was real but its sight untrue.
All the ideas in its vast repertory
Were like the mutterings of a transient cloud
That spent itself in sound and left no trace.
A frail house hanging in uncertain air,
The thin ingenious web round which it moves,
Put out awhile on the tree of the universe,
And gathered up into itself again,
Was only a trap to catch life's insect food,
Winged thoughts that flutter fragile in brief light
But dead, once captured in fixed forms of mind,
Aims puny but looming large in man's small scale,
Flickers, of imagination's brilliant gauze
And cobweb-wrapped beliefs alive no more.
The magic hut of built-up certitudes
Made out of glittering dust and bright moonshine
In which it shrines its image of the Real,
Collapsed into the Nescience whence it rose.
Only a gleam was there of symbol facts
That shroud the mystery lurking in their glow,
And falsehoods based on hidden realities
By which they live until they fall from Time.
Our mind is a house haunted by the slain past,
Ideas soon mummified, ghosts of old truths,
God's spontaneities tied with formal strings
And packed into drawers of reason's trim bureau,
A grave of great lost opportunities,
Or an office for misuse of soul and life
And all the waste man makes of heaven's gifts
And all his squanderings of Nature's store,
A stage for the comedy of Ignorance.
The world seemed a long aeonic failure's scene:
All sterile grew, no base was left secure.
Assailed by the edge of the convicting beam

The builder Reason lost her confidence
In the successful sleight and turn of thought
That makes the soul the prisoner of a phrase.
Its highest wisdom was a brilliant guess,
Its mighty structured science of the worlds
A passing light on being's surfaces.
There was nothing there but a schema drawn by sense,
A substitute for eternal mysteries,
A scrawl figure of reality, a plan
And elevation by the architect Word
Imposed upon the semblances of Time.
Existence' self was shadowed by a doubt;
Almost it seemed a lotus-leaf afloat
On a nude pool of cosmic Nothingness.
This great spectator and creator Mind
Was only some half-seeing's delegate,
A veil that hung between the soul and Light,
An idol, not the living body of God.
Even the still spirit that looks upon its works
Was some pale front of the Unknowable;
A shadow seemed the wide and witness Self,
Its liberation and immobile calm
A void recoil of being from Time-made things,
Not the self-vision of Eternity.
Deep peace was there, but not the nameless Force:
Our sweet and mighty Mother was not there
Who gathers to her bosom her children's lives,
Her clasp that takes the world into her arms
In the fathomless rapture of the Infinite,
The Bliss that is creation's splendid grain
Or the white passion of God-ecstasy
That laughs in the blaze of the boundless heart of Love.
A greater Spirit than the Self of Mind
Must answer to the questioning of his soul.
For here was no firm clue and no sure road;
High-climbing pathways closed in the unknown;
An artist sight constructed the Beyond
In contrary patterns and conflicting hues;
A part-experience fragmented the Whole.
He looked above, but all was blank and still;

A sapphire firmament of abstract Thought
Escaped into a formless Vacancy.
He looked below, but all was dark and mute.
A noise was heard, between, of thought and prayer,
A strife, a labour without end or pause;
A vain and ignorant seeking raised its voice.
A rumour and a movement and a call,
A foaming mass, a cry innumerable
Rolled ever upon the ocean surge of Life
Along the coasts of mortal Ignorance.
On its unstable and enormous breast
Beings and forces, forms, ideas like waves
Jostled for figure and supremacy,
And rose and sank and rose again in Time,
And at the bottom of the sleepless stir,
A Nothingness parent of the struggling worlds,
A huge creator Death, a mystic Void,
For ever sustaining the irrational cry,
For ever excluding the supernal Word,
Motionless, refusing question and response,
Reposed beneath the voices and the march
The dim Inconscient's dumb incertitude.
Two firmaments of darkness and of light
Opposed their limits to the spirit's walk;
It moved veiled in from Self's infinity
In a world of beings and momentary events
Where all must die to live and live to die.
Immortal by renewed mortality,
It wandered in the spiral of its acts
Or ran around the cycles of its thought,
Yet was no more than its original self
And knew no more than when it first began.
To be was a prison, extinction the escape.

END OF CANTO THIRTEEN

CANTO FOURTEEN

THE WORLD-SOUL

A COVERT answer to his seeking came.
     In a far-shimmering background of Mind-Space
A glowing mouth was seen, a luminous shaft;
A recluse-gate it seemed, musing on joy,
A veiled retreat and escape to mystery.
Away from the unsatisfied surface world
It fled into the bosom of the unknown,
A well, a tunnel of the depths of God.
It plunged as if a mystic groove of hope
Through many layers of formless voiceless self
To reach the last profound of the world's heart,
And from that heart there surged a wordless call
Pleading with some still impenetrable Mind,
Voicing some passionate unseen desire.
As if a beckoning finger of secrecy
Outstretched into a crystal mood of air,
Pointing at him from some near hidden depth,
As if a message from the world's deep soul,
An intimation of a lurking joy
That flowed out from a cup of brooding bliss,
There shimmered stealing out into the Mind
A mute and quivering ecstasy of light,
A passion and delicacy of roseate fire.
As one drawn to his lost spiritual home
Feels now the closeness of a waiting love,
Into a passage dim and tremulous
That clasped him in from day and night's pursuit,
He travelled led by a mysterious sound.
A murmur, multitudinous and lone,
All sounds it was in turn, yet still the same.

A hidden call to unforeseen delight
In the summoning voice of one long-known and loved,
But nameless to the unremembering mind,
It led to rapture back the truant heart.
The immortal cry ravished the captive ear,
Then, lowering its imperious mystery,
It sank to a whisper circling round the soul.
It seemed the yearning of a lonely flute
That roamed along the shores of memory
And filled the eyes with tears of longing joy.
A cricket's rash and fiery single note,
It marked with shrill melody night's moonless hush
And beat upon a nerve of mystic sleep
Its high insistent magical reveille.
A jingling silver laugh of anklet bells
Travelled the roads of a solitary heart;
Its dance solaced an eternal loneliness:
An old forgotten sweetness sobbing came.
Or from a far harmonious distance heard
The tinkling pace of a long caravan
It seemed at times, or a vast forest's hymn,
The solemn reminder of a temple gong,
A bee-croon honey-drunk in summer isles
Ardent with ecstasy in a slumberous noon,
Or the far anthem of a pilgrim sea.
An incense floated in the quivering air,
A mystic happiness trembled in the breast
As if the invisible Beloved had come
Assuming the sudden loveliness of a face
And close glad hands could seize his fugitive feet
And the world change with the beauty of a smile.
Into a wonderful bodiless realm he came,
The home of a passion without name or voice,
A depth he felt answering to every height,
A nook was found that could embrace all worlds,
A point that was the conscious knot of space,
An hour eternal in the heart of Time.
The silent soul of all the world was there:
A Being lived, a Presence and a Power,
A single Person who was himself and all

And cherished Nature's sweet and dangerous throbs
Transfigured into beats divine and pure.
One who could love without return for love,
Meeting and turning to the best the worst,
It healed the bitter cruelties of earth
Transforming all experience to delight;
Intervening in the sorrowful paths of birth
It rocked the cradle of the cosmic Child
And stilled all weeping with its hand of joy;
It led things evil towards their secret good,
It turned racked falsehood into happy truth;
Its power was to reveal divinity.
Infinite, coeval with the mind of God,
It bore within itself a seed, a flame,
A seed from which the Eternal is new-born,
A flame that cancels death in mortal things.
All grew to all kindred and self and near,
The intimacy of God was everywhere,
No veil was felt, no brute barrier inert,
Distance could not divide, Time could not change.
A fire of passion burned in spirit-depths,
A constant touch of sweetness linked all hearts,
The throb of one adoration's single bliss
In a rapt ether of undying love.
An inner happiness abode in all,
A sense of universal harmonies,
A measureless secure eternity
Of truth and beauty and good and joy made one.
There was the welling core of finite life;
A formless spirit became the soul of form.

All there was soul or made of sheer soul-stuff:
A sky of soul covered a deep soul-ground.
All here was known by a spiritual sense:
Thought was not there but a knowledge near and one
Seized on all things by a moved identity,
A sympathy of self with other selves,
The touch of consciousness on consciousness
And being's look on being with inmost gaze
And heart laid bare to heart without walls of speech

And the unanimity of seeing minds
In myriad forms luminous with the one God.
Life was not there, but an impassioned force,
Finer than fineness, deeper than the deeps
Felt as a subtle and spiritual power,
A quivering out from soul to answering soul,
A mystic movement, a close influence,
A free and happy and intense approach
Of being to being with no screen or check,
Without which life and love could never have been.
Body was not there, for bodies were needed not,
The soul itself was its own deathless form
And met at once the touch of other souls
Close, blissful, concrete, wonderfully true.
As when one walks in sleep through luminous dreams
And, conscious, knows the truth their figures mean,
There where reality was its own dream,
He knew things by their soul and not their shape:
As those who have lived long made one in love
Need word nor sign for heart's reply to heart,
He met and communed without bar of speech
With beings unveiled by a material frame.
There was a strange spiritual scenery,
A loveliness of lakes and streams and hills,
A flow, a fixity in a soul-space,
And plains and valleys, stretches of soul-joy,
And gardens that were flower-tracts of the spirit,
Its meditations of tinged reverie.
Air was the breath of a pure infinite.
A fragrance wandered in a coloured haze
As if the scent and hue of all sweet flowers
Had mingled to copy heaven's atmosphere.
Appealing to the soul and not the eye
Beauty lived there at home in her own house,
There all was beautiful by its own right
And needed not the splendour of a robe.
All objects were like bodies of the Gods,
A spirit symbol environing a soul,
For world and self were one reality.

Immersed in voiceless internatal trance
The beings that once wore forms on earth sat there
In shining chambers of spiritual sleep.
Passed were the pillar-posts of birth and death,
Passed was their little scene of symbol deeds,
Passed were the heavens and hells of their long road;
They had returned into the world's deep soul.
All now was gathered into pregnant rest:
Person and nature suffered a slumber change.
In trance they gathered back their bygone selves,
In a background memory's foreseeing muse
Prophetic of new personality
Arranged the map of their coming destiny's course:
Heirs of their past, their future's discoverers,
Electors of their own self-chosen lot,
They waited for the adventure of new life.
A Person persistent through the lapse of worlds,
Although the same for ever in many shapes
By the outward mind unrecognisable
Assuming names unknown in unknown climes
Imprints through Time upon the earth's worn page
A growing figure of its secret self,
And learns by experience what the spirit knew,
Till it can see its truth alive and God.
Once more they must face the problem-game of birth,
The soul's experiment of joy and grief
And thought and impulse lighting the blind act,
And venture on the roads of circumstance
Through inner movements and external scenes
Travelling to self across the forms of things.
Into creation's centre he had come.
The spirit wandering from state to state
Finds here the silence of its starting-point
In the formless force and the still fixity
And brooding passion of the world of Soul.
All that is made and once again unmade,
The calm persistent vision of the One
Inevitably re-makes, it lives anew:
Forces and lives and beings and ideas
Are taken into the stillness for a while;

There they remould their purpose and their drift,
Recast their nature and re-form their shape.
Ever they change and changing ever grow,
And passing through a fruitful stage of death
And after long reconstituting sleep
Resume their place in the process of the Gods
Until their work in cosmic Time is done.
    Here was the fashioning chamber of the worlds.
An interval was left twixt act and act,
Twixt birth and birth, twixt dream and waking dream,
A pause that gave new strength to do and be.
Beyond were regions of delight and peace,
Mute birth-places of light and hope and love,
And cradles of heavenly rapture and repose.
In a slumber of the voices of the world
He of the eternal moment grew aware;
His knowledge stripped bare of the garbs of sense
Knew by identity without thought or word,
His being saw itself without its veils,
Life's line fell from the spirit's infinity.
Along a road of pure interior light,
Alone between tremendous Presences,
Under the watching eye of nameless Gods,
His soul passed on, a single conscious power
Towards the end which ever begins again,
Approaching through a stillness dumb and calm
To the source of all things human and divine.
There he beheld in their mighty union's poise
The figure of the deathless Two-in-One,
A single being in two bodies clasped,
A diarchy of two united souls,
Seated absorbed in deep creative joy;
Their trance of bliss sustained the mobile world.
Behind them in a morning dusk One stood
Who brought them forth from the Unknowable.
Ever disguised she awaits the seeking spirit;
Watcher on the supreme unreachable peaks,
Guide of the traveller of the unseen paths,
She guards the austere approach to the Alone.
At the beginning of each far-spread plane

Pervading with her power the cosmic suns
She reigns, inspirer of its multiple works
And thinker of the symbol of its scene.
Above them all she stands supporting all,
The sole omnipotent Goddess ever-veiled
Of whom the world is the inscrutable mask;
The ages are the footfalls of her tread,
Their happenings the figure of her thoughts,
And all creation is her endless act.
His spirit was made a vessel of her force;
Mute in the fathomless passion of his will
He outstretched to her his folded hands of prayer.
Then in a sovereign answer to his heart
A gesture came as of worlds thrown away,
And from her raiment's lustrous mystery raised
One arm half-parted the eternal veil.
A light appeared still and imperishable.
Attracted to the large and luminous depths
Of the ravishing enigma of her eyes,
He saw the mystic outline of a face.
Overwhelmed by her implacable light and bliss,
An atom of her illimitable self
Mastered by the honey and lightning of her power,
Tossed towards the shores of her ocean ecstasy,
Drunk with a deep golden spiritual wine,
He cast from the rent stillness of his soul
A cry of adoration and desire
And the surrender of his boundless mind
And the self-giving of his silent heart.
He fell down at her feet unconscious, prone.

END OF CANTO FOURTEEN

THE KINGDOMS OF THE GREATER KNOWLEDGE

AFTER a measureless moment of the soul
    Again returning to these surface fields
Out of the timeless depths where he had sunk,
He heard once more the slow tread of the hours.
All once perceived and lived was far away;
Himself was to himself his only scene.
Above the Witness and his universe
He stood in a realm of boundless silences
Awaiting the Voice that spoke and built the worlds.
A light was round him wide and absolute,
A diamond purity of eternal sight;
A consciousness lay still, devoid of forms,
Free, wordless, uncoerced by sign or rule,
For ever content with only being and bliss;
A sheer existence lived in its own peace
On the single spirit's bare and infinite ground.
Out of the sphere of Mind he had arisen,
He had left the reign of Nature's hues and shades;
He dwelt in his self's colourless purity.
It was a plane of undetermined spirit
That could be a zero or round sum of things,
A state in which all ceased and all began.
All it became that figures the absolute,
A high vast peak whence spirit could see the worlds,
Calm's wide epiphany, wisdom's mute home,
A lonely station of Omniscience,
A diving-board of the Eternal's power,
A white floor in the house of All-Delight.
Here came the thought that passes beyond Thought,
Here the still Voice which our listening cannot hear,

The Knowledge by which the Knower is the Known,
The Love in which Beloved and Lover are one.
All stood in an original plenitude,
Hushed and fulfilled before they could create
The glorious dream of their universal acts;
Here was engendered the spiritual birth,
Here closed the finite's crawl to the Infinite.
A thousand roads leaped into Eternity
Or singing ran to meet God's veilless face.
The known released him from its limiting chain,
He knocked at the doors of the Unknowable.
Thence gazing with an immeasurable outlook
One with self's inlook into its own pure vasts,
He saw the splendour of the spirit's realms,
The greatness and wonder of its boundless works,
The power and passion leaping from its calm,
The rapture of its movement and its rest,
And its fire-sweet miracle of transcendent life,
The million-pointing undivided grasp
Of its vision of one same stupendous All,
Its inexhaustible acts in a timeless Time,   .
A space that is its own infinity.
A glorious multiple of one radiant Self,
Answering to joy with joy, to love with love,
All there were moving mansions of God-bliss;
Eternal and unique they lived the One.
There forces are great outbursts of God's truth
And objects are its pure spiritual shapes;
Spirit no more is hid from its own view,
All sentience is a sea of happiness
And all creation is an act of light.
Out of the neutral silence of his soul
He passed to its fields of puissance and of calm
And saw the Powers that stand above the world,
Traversed the realms of the supreme Idea
And sought the summit of created things
And the almighty source of cosmic change.
There knowledge called him to her mystic peaks
Where thought is held in a vast internal sense
And feeling swims across a sea of peace

And vision climbs beyond the reach of Time.
An equal of the first creator seers,
Accompanied by an all-revealing light
He moved through regions of transcendent Truth
Inward, immense, innumerably one.
There distance was his own huge spirit's extent;
Delivered from the fictions of the mind
Time's triple dividing step baffled no more;
Its inevitable and continuous stream,
The long flow of its manifesting course,
Was held in spirit's single wide regard.
A universal beauty showed its face;
The invisible deep-fraught significances,
Here sheltered behind form's insensible screen,
Uncovered to him their deathless harmony
And the key to the wonder-book of common things.
In their uniting law stood up revealed
The multiple measures of the uplifting force,
The lines of the World-Geometer's technique,
The enchantments that uphold the cosmic web
And the magic underlying simple shapes.
On peaks where Silence listens with still heart
To the rhythmic metres of the rolling worlds,
He served the sessions of the triple fire.
On the rim of two continents of slumber and trance
He heard the ever unspoken Reality's voice
Awaken revelation's mystic cry,
The birth-place found of the sudden infallible Word
And lived in the rays of an intuitive Sun.
Absolved from the ligaments of death and sleep
He rode the lightning seas of cosmic Mind
And crossed the ocean of original sound;
On the last step to the supernal birth
He trod along extinction's narrow edge
Near the high verges of eternity,
And mounted the gold ridge of the World-dream
Between the slayer and the saviour fires;
The belt he reached of the unchanging Truth,
Met borders of the inexpressible Light
And thrilled with the presence of the Ineffable.

Above him he saw the flaming Hierarchies,
The wings that fold around created space,
The sun-eyed Guardians and the golden Sphinx
And the tiered planes and the immutable Lords.
A wisdom waiting on Omniscience
Sat voiceless in a vast passivity;
It judged not, measured not, nor strove to know,
But listened for the all-seeing Thought
And the burden of a calm transcendent Voice.
He had reached the top of all that can be known:
His sight surpassed creation's head and base;
Ablaze the triple heavens revealed their suns,
The obscure Abyss exposed its monstrous rule.
All but the ultimate Mystery was his field,
Almost the Unknowable disclosed its rim.
His self's infinities began to emerge,
The hidden universes cried to him;
Eternities called to eternities
Sending their speechless message still remote.
Arisen from the marvel of the depths
And burning from the superconscious heights
And sweeping in great horizontal gyres
A million energies joined and were the One.
All flowed immeasurably to one sea:
All living forms became its atom homes.
A Panergy that harmonised all life
Held now existence in its vast control;
A portion of that majesty he was made.
At will he lived in the unoblivious Ray.

In that high realm where no untruth can come,
Where all are different and all is one,
In the Impersonal's ocean without shore
The Person in the World-Spirit anchored rode;
It thrilled with the mighty marchings of World-Force,
Its acts were the comrades of God's infinite peace.
An adjunct glory and a symbol self,
The body was delivered to the soul,—
An immortal point of power, a block of poise
In a cosmicity's wide formless surge,
A conscious edge of the Transcendent's might

18

Carving perfection from a bright world-stuff,
It figured in it a universe's sense.
There consciousness was a close and single weft;
The far and near were one in spirit-space,
The moments there were pregnant with all time.
The superconscient's screen was ripped by thought,
Idea rotated symphonies of sight,
Sight was a flame-throw from identity;
Life was a marvellous journey of the spirit,
Feeling a wave from the universal Bliss.
In the kingdom of the Spirit's power and light,
As if one who arrived out of infinity's womb
He came new-born, infant and limitless
And grew in the wisdom of the timeless Child;
He was a vast that soon became a Sun.
A great luminous silence whispered to his heart;
His knowledge an inview caught unfathomable,
An outview by no brief horizons cut:
He thought and felt in all, his gaze had power.
He communed with the Incommunicable;
Beings of a wider consciousness were his friends,
Forms of a larger subtler make drew near;
The Gods conversed with him behind Life's veil.
Neighbour his being grew to Nature's crests.
The primal Energy took him in its arms;
His brain was wrapped in overwhelming Light,
An all-embracing knowledge seized his heart:
Thoughts rose in him no earthly mind can hold,
Mights played that never coursed through mortal nerves:
He scanned the secrets of the Overmind,
He bore the rapture of the Oversoul.
A borderer of the empire of the Sun,
Attuned to the supernal harmonies,
He linked creation to the Eternal's sphere,
His finite parts approached their absolutes,
His actions framed the movements of the Gods,
His will took up the reins of cosmic Force.

END OF CANTO FIFTEEN

END OF BOOK TWO

BOOK THREE
The Book of the Divine Mother

CANTO ONE

THE PURSUIT OF THE UNKNOWABLE

ALL is too little that the world can give:
    Its power and knowledge are the gifts of Time
And cannot fill the spirit's sacred thirst.
Although of One these forms of greatness are
And by its breath of grace our lives abide,
Although more near to us than nearness' self,
It is some utter truth of what we are;
Hidden by its own works it seemed far off,
Impenetrable, occult, voiceless, obscure.
The Presence was lost by which all things have charm,
The Glory lacked of which they are dim signs.
The world lived on made empty of its Cause,
Like Love when the Beloved's face is gone.
The labour to know seemed a vain strife of Mind;
All knowledge ended in the Unknowable:
The effort to rule seemed a vain pride of Will;
A trivial achievement scorned by Time,
All power retired into the Omnipotent.
A cave of darkness guards the eternal Light.
A silence settled on his striving heart;
Absolved from the voices of the world's desire,
He turned to the Ineffable's timeless call.
A Being intimate and unnameable,
A wide compelling ecstasy and peace
Felt in himself and all and yet ungrasped,
Approached and faded from his soul's pursuit
As if for ever luring him beyond.
Near, it retreated; far, it called him still.
Nothing could satisfy but its delight:
Its absence left the greatest actions dull,

Its presence made the smallest seem divine.
When it was there, the heart's abyss was filled;
But when the uplifting Deity withdrew,
Existence lost its aim in the Inane.
The order of the immemorial planes,
The godlike fullness of the instruments
Were turned to props for an impermanent scene.
But who that mightiness was he knew not yet.
Impalpable, yet filling all that is,
It made and blotted out a million worlds
And took and lost a thousand shapes and names.
It wore the guise of an indiscernible Vast,
Or was a subtle kernel in the soul:
A distant greatness left it huge and dim,
A mystic closeness shut it sweetly in:
It seemed sometimes a figment or a robe
And seemed sometimes his own colossal shade.
A giant doubt overshadowed his advance.
Across a neutral all-supporting Void
Whose blankness nursed his lone immortal spirit,
Allured towards some recondite Supreme,
Aided, coerced by enigmatic Powers,
Aspiring and half-sinking and upborne,
Invincibly he ascended without pause.
Always a signless vague Immensity
Brooded, without approach, beyond response,
Condemning finite things to nothingness,
Fronting him with the incommensurable.
Then to the ascent there came a mighty term:
A height was reached where nothing made could live,
A line where every hope and search must cease
Neared some intolerant bare Reality,
A zero formed pregnant with boundless change.
On a dizzy verge where all disguises fail
And human mind must abdicate in Light
Or die like a moth in the naked blaze of Truth,
He stood compelled to a tremendous choice.
All he had been and all towards which he grew
Must now be left behind or else transform
Into a self of That which has no name.

Alone and fronting an intangible Force
Which offered nothing to the grasp of Thought,
His spirit faced the adventure of the Inane.
Abandoned by the worlds of form he strove.
A fruitful world-wide Ignorance foundered there;
Thought's long far-circling journey touched its close
And ineffective paused the actor Will.
The symbol modes of being helped no more,
The structures Nescience builds collapsing failed,
And even the spirit that holds the universe
Fainted in luminous insufficiency.
In an abysmal lapse of all things built
Transcending every perishable support
And joining at last its mighty origin,
The separate self must melt or be reborn
Into a Truth beyond the mind's appeal.
All glory of outline, sweetness of harmony,
Rejected like a grace of trivial notes,
Expunged from Being's silence nude, austere,
Died into a fine and blissful Nothingness.
The Demiurges lost their names and forms,
The great schemed worlds that they had planned and wrought
Passed, taken and abolished one by one.
The universe removed its coloured veil,
And at the unimaginable end
Of the huge riddle of created things
Appeared the far-seen Godhead of the whole,
His feet firm-based on Life's stupendous wings,
Omnipotent or lonely seer of Time,
Inward, inscrutable, with diamond gaze.
Attracted by the unfathomable regard
The unsolved slow cycles to their fount returned
To rise again from that invisible sea.
All from his puissance born was now undone;
Nothing remained the cosmic Mind conceives.
Eternity prepared to fade and seemed
A hue and imposition on the Void,
Space was the fluttering of a dream that sank
Before its ending into Nothing's deeps.
The spirit that dies not and the Godhead's self

Seemed myths projected from the Unknowable;
From It all sprang, in It is called to cease.
But what That was, no thought or sight could tell.
Only a formless Form of self was left,
A tenuous ghost of something that had been,
The last experience of a lapsing wave
Before it sinks into a bourneless sea,—
As if it kept even on the brink of Nought
Its bare feeling of the ocean whence it came.
A Vastness brooded free from sense of Space,
An Everlastingness cut off from Time;
A strange sublime unalterable Peace
Silent rejected from it world and soul.
A stark companionless Reality
Answered at last to his soul's passionate search:
Passionless, wordless, absorbed in fathomless peace,
Keeping the mystery none would ever pierce,
It brooded inscrutable and intangible
Facing him with its dumb tremendous calm.
It had no kinship with the universe:
There was no act, no movement in its Vast:
Life's question met by its silence died on her lips,
The world's effort ceased convicted of ignorance
Finding no sanction of supernal Light:
There was no mind there with its need to know,
There was no heart there with its need to love.
All person perished in its namelessness.
There was no second, it had no partner or peer;
Only itself was real to itself.
A pure existence safe from thought and mood,
A consciousness of unshared immortal bliss,
It dwelt aloof in its bare infinite,
One and unique, unutterably sole.
A Being formless, featureless and mute
That knew itself by its own timeless self,
Aware for ever in its motionless depths,
Uncreating, uncreated and unborn,
The One by whom all live, who lives by none,
An immeasurable luminous secrecy
Guarded by the veils of the Unmanifest,

Above the changing cosmic interlude
Abode supreme, immutably the same,
A silent Cause occult, impenetrable,—
Infinite, eternal, unthinkable, alone.

END OF CANTO ONE

CANTO TWO

THE ADORATION OF THE DIVINE MOTHER

A STILLNESS absolute, incommunicable,
　　Meets the sheer self-discovery of the soul;
A wall of stillness shuts it from the world,
A gulf of stillness swallows up the sense
And makes unreal all that mind has known,
All that the labouring senses still would weave
Prolonging an imaged unreality.
Self's vast spiritual silence occupies space;
Only the Inconceivable is left,
Only the Nameless without space and time:
Abolished is the burdening need of life:
Thought falls from us, we cease from joy and grief;
The ego is dead; we are free from being and care,
We have done with birth and death and work and fate.
O soul, it is too early to rejoice!
Thou hast reached the boundless silence of the Self,
Thou hast leaped into a glad divine abyss;
But where hast thou thrown self's mission and self's power?
On what dead bank on the Eternal's road?
One was within thee who was self and world,
What hast thou done for his purpose in the stars?
Escape brings not the victory and the crown!
Something thou cam'st to do from the Unknown,
But nothing is finished and the world goes on,
Because only half God's cosmic work is done.
Only the everlasting No has neared
And stared into thy eyes and killed thy heart:
But where is the Lover's everlasting Yes,
And immortality in the secret heart,
The voice that chants to the creator Fire,

The symboled OM, the great assenting Word,
The bridge between the rapture and the calm,
The passion and the beauty of the Bride,
The chamber where the glorious enemies kiss,
The smile that saves, the golden peak of things?
This too is Truth at the mystic fount of Life.
A black veil has been lifted; we have seen
The mighty shadow of the omniscient Lord;
But who has lifted up the veil of light
And who has seen the body of the King?
The mystery of God's birth and acts remains
Leaving unbroken the last chapter's seal,
Unsolved the riddle of the unfinished Play;
The cosmic Player laughs within his mask,
And still the last inviolate secret hides
Behind the human glory of a Form,
Behind the gold eidolon of a Name.
A large white line has figured as a goal,
But far beyond the ineffable suntracks blaze.
What seemed the source and end was a wide gate,
A last bare step into eternity.
An eye has opened upon timelessness,
Infinity takes back the forms it gave,
And through God's darkness or his naked light
His million rays return into the Sun.
There is a zero sign of the Supreme;
Nature left nude and still uncovers God.
But in her grandiose nothingness all is there:
When her strong garbs are torn away from us,
The soul's ignorance is slain but not the soul.
The zero covers an immortal face.
A high and black negation is not all,
A huge extinction is not God's last word,
Life's ultimate sense, the close of being's course,
The meaning of this great mysterious world.
In absolute silence sleeps an absolute Power.
Awaking, it can wake the trance-bound soul
And in the ray reveal the parent sun:
It can make the world a vessel of Spirit's force,
It can fashion in the clay God's perfect shape.

To free the self is but one radiant pace;
Here to fulfil himself was God's desire.

    Even while he stood on being's naked edge
And all the passion and seeking of his soul
Faced their extinction in some featureless Vast,
The Presence he yearned for suddenly drew close.
Across the silence of the ultimate Calm,
Out of a marvellous Transcendence' core,
A body of wonder and translucency
As if a sweet mystic summary of her self,
Escaping into the original Bliss
Had come enlarged out of eternity,
Someone came infinite and absolute.
A being of wisdom, power and delight,
Even as a mother draws her child to her arms,
Took to her breast Nature and world and soul.
Abolishing the signless emptiness,
Breaking the vacancy and voiceless hush,
Piercing the limitless Unknowable,
Into the liberty of the motionless depths
A beautiful and felicitous lustre stole,
Imaged itself in a surprising beam
And built a golden passage to his heart
Touching through him all longing sentient things.
A moment's sweetness of the All-Beautiful
Cancelled the vanity of the cosmic whirl.
A Nature throbbing with a Heart divine
Was felt in the unconscious universe;
It made the breath a happy mystery
And brought a love sustaining pain with joy;
A love that bore the cross of pain with joy,
Eudaemonised the sorrow of the world,
Made happy the weight of long unending Time,
The secret caught of God's felicity.
Affirming in life a hidden ecstasy
It held the spirit to its miraculous course;
Carrying immortal values to the hours
It justified the labour of the suns.
For one was there supreme behind the God.

A Mother Might brooded upon the world;
A Consciousness revealed its marvellous front
Transcending all that is, denying none:
Imperishable above our fallen heads
He felt a rapturous and unstumbling Force.
The undying Truth appeared, the enduring Power
Of all that here is made and then destroyed,
The Mother of all godheads and all strengths
Who, mediatrix, binds earth to the Supreme.
The Enigma ceased that rules our nature's night,
The covering Nescience was unmasked and slain;
Its mind of error was stripped off from things
And the dull moods of its perverting will.
Illumined by her all-seeing identity
Knowledge and Ignorance could strive no more;
No longer could the titan Opposites,
Antagonist poles of the world's artifice,
Impose the illusion of their twofold screen
Throwing their figures between us and her.
The Wisdom was near, disguised by its own works,
Of which the darkened universe is the robe.
No more existence seemed an aimless fall,
Extinction was no more the sole release.
The hidden Word was found, the long-sought clue,
Revealed was the meaning of our spirit's birth,
Condemned to an imperfect body and mind,
In the inconscience of material things
And the indignity of mortal life.
A Heart was felt in the spaces wide and bare,
A burning Love from white spiritual founts
Annulled the sorrow of the ignorant depths;
Suffering was lost in her immortal smile.
A Life from beyond grew conqueror here of Death;
To err no more was natural to mind;
Wrong could not come where all was light and love.
The Formless and the Formed were joined in her.
Immensity was exceeded by a look,
A Face revealed the crowded Infinite.
Incarnating inexpressibly in her limbs
The boundless joy the blind world-forces seek,

Her body of beauty mooned the seas of bliss.
At the head she stands of birth and toil and fate,
In their slow round the cycles turn to her call;
Alone her hands can change Time's dragon base.
Hers is the mystery the Night conceals;
The spirit's alchemist energy is hers;
She is the golden bridge, the wonderful fire.
The luminous heart of the Unknown is she,
A power of silence in the depths of God;
She is the Force, the inevitable Word,
The magnet of our difficult ascent,
The Sun from which we kindle all our suns,
The Light that leans from the unrealised Vasts,
The joy that beckons from the impossible,
The Might of all that never yet came down.
All Nature dumbly calls to her alone
To heal with her feet the aching throb of life
And break the seals on the dim soul of man
And kindle her fire in the closed heart of things.
All here shall be one day her sweetness's home,
All contraries prepare her harmony;
Towards her our knowledge climbs, our passion gropes,
In her miraculous rapture we shall dwell,
Her clasp will turn to ecstasy our pain.
Our self shall be one self with all through her.
In her confirmed because transformed in her,
Our life shall find in its fulfilled response
Above, the boundless hushed beatitudes,
Below, the wonder of the embrace divine.
This known as in a thunder-flash of God,
The rapture of things eternal filled his limbs;
Amazement fell upon his ravished sense;
His spirit was caught in her intolerant flame.
Once seen, his heart acknowledged only her.
Only a hunger of infinite bliss was left.
All aims in her were lost, then found in her;
His base was gathered into one pointing spire.

Thus was a seed cast into endless Time.
A Word is spoken or a Light is shown,

A moment sees, the ages toil to express.
So flashing out of the Timeless leaped the worlds;
An eternal instant is the cause of the years.
All he had done was to prepare a field;
His small beginnings asked for a mighty end:
For all that he had been must now new-shape
In him her joy to embody, to enshrine
Her beauty and greatness in his house of life.
But now his being was too wide for self;
His heart's demand had grown immeasurable:
His single freedom could not satisfy,
Her light, her bliss he asked for earth and men.
But vain are human power and human love
To break earth's seal of ignorance and death;
His nature's might seemed now an infant's grasp;
Heaven is too high for outstretched hands to seize.
This Light comes not by struggle or by thought;
In the mind's silence the Transcendent acts
And the hushed heart hears the unuttered Word.
A vast surrender was his only strength.
A Power that lives upon the heights must act,
Bring into life's closed room the Immortal's air
And fill the finite with the Infinite.
All that denies must be torn out and slain
And crushed the many longings for whose sake
We lose the One for whom our lives were made.
Now other claims had hushed in him their cry:
Only he longed to draw her presence and power
Into his heart and mind and breathing frame;
Only he yearned to call for ever down
Her healing touch of love and truth and joy
Into the darkness of the suffering world.
His soul was freed and given to her alone.

 END OF CANTO TWO

287

CANTO THREE

THE HOUSE OF THE SPIRIT AND THE NEW CREATION

A MIGHTIER task remained than all he had done.
  To that he turned from which all being comes,
A sign attending from the Secrecy
Which knows the Truth ungrasped behind our thoughts
And guards the world with its all-seeing gaze.
In the unapproachable stillness of his soul,
Intense, one-pointed, monumental, lone
Patient he sat like an incarnate hope
Motionless on a pedestal of prayer.
A Strength he sought that was not yet on earth,
Help from a Power too great for mortal will,
The Light of a Truth now only seen afar,
A sanction from his high omnipotent Source.
But from the appalling heights there stooped no voice;
The timeless lids were closed; no opening came.
A neutral helpless void oppressed the years.
In the texture of our bound humanity
He felt the stark resistance huge and dumb
Of our inconscient and unseeing base,
The stubborn mute rejection in Life's depths,
The ignorant No in the origin of things.
A veiled collaboration with the Night
Even in himself survived and hid from his view:
Still something in his earthly being kept
Its kinship with the Inconscient whence it came.
A shadowy unity with a vanished past
Treasured in an old world-frame was lurking there,
Secret, unnoted by the illumined mind,
And in subconscious whispers and in dream

288

Still murmured at the mind's and spirit's choice.
Its treacherous elements spread like slippery grains
Hoping the incoming Truth might stumble and fall,
And old ideal voices wandering moaned
And pleaded for a heavenly leniency
To the gracious imperfections of our earth
And the sweet weaknesses of our mortal state.
This now he willed to discover and exile,
The element in him betraying God.
All Nature's recondite spaces were stripped bare,
All her dim crypts and corners searched with fire
Where refugee instincts and unshaped revolts
Could shelter find in darkness' sanctuary
Against the white purity of heaven's cleansing flame.
All seemed to have perished that was undivine:
Yet some minutest dissident might escape
And still a centre lurk of the blind force.
For the Inconscient too is infinite;
The more its abysses we insist to sound,
The more it stretches, stretches endlessly.
Then lest a human cry should spoil the Truth
He tore desire up from its bleeding roots
And offered to the gods the vacant place.
Thus could he bear the touch immaculate.
A last and mightiest transformation came.
His soul was all in front like a great sea
Flooding the mind and body with its waves;
His being, spread to embrace the universe,
United the within and the without
To make of life a cosmic harmony,
An empire of the immanent Divine.
In this tremendous universality
Not only his soul-nature and mind-sense
Included every soul and mind in his,
But even the life of flesh and nerve was changed
And grew one flesh and nerve with all that lives;
He felt the joy of others as his joy,
He bore the grief of others as his grief;
His universal sympathy upbore,
Immense like ocean, the creation's load

As earth upbears all beings' sacrifice,
Thrilled with the hidden Transcendent's joy and peace.
There was no more division's endless scroll;
One grew the Spirit's secret unity,
All nature felt again the single bliss;
There was no cleavage between soul and soul,
There was no barrier between world and God.
Overpowered were form and memory's limiting line;
The covering mind was seized and torn apart;
It was dissolved and now no more could be,
The one Consciousness that made the world was seen;
All now was luminosity and force.
Abolished in its last thin fainting trace
The circle of the little self was gone;
The separate being could no more be felt;
It disappeared and knew itself no more,
Lost in the Spirit's wide identity.
His nature grew a movement of the All,
Exploring itself to find that all was He,
His soul was a delegation of the All
That turned from itself to join the one Supreme.
Transcended was the human formula;
Man's heart that had obscured the Inviolable
Assumed the mighty beating of a god's;
His seeking mind ceased in the Truth that knows;
His life was a flow of the universal life.
He stood fulfilled on the world's highest line
Awaiting the ascent beyond the world,
Awaiting the Descent the world to save.
A Splendour and a Symbol wrapped the earth,
Serene epiphanies looked and hallowed vasts
Surrounded, wise infinitudes were close
And bright remotenesses leaned near and kin.
Sense failed in that tremendous lucency;
Ephemeral voices from his hearing fell
And Thought potent no more sank large and pale
Like a tired god into mysterious seas.
The robes of mortal thinking were cast down
Leaving his knowledge bare to absolute sight;
Fate's driving ceased and Nature's sleepless spur:

The athlete heavings of the will were stilled
In the Omnipotent's unmoving peace.
Life in his members lay down vast and mute;
Naked, unwalled, unterrified it bore
The immense regard of Immortality.
The last movement died and all at once grew still.
A weight that was the unseen Transcendent's hand
Laid on his limbs the spirit's measureless seal,
Infinity swallowed him into shoreless trance.

As one who sets his sail towards mysteried shores
Driven through huge oceans by the breath of God,
The fathomless below, the unknown around,
His soul abandoned the blind star-field, Space.
Afar from all that makes the measured world,
Plunging to hidden eternities it withdrew
Back from mind's foaming surface to the Vasts
Voiceless within us in omniscient sleep.
Above the imperfect reach of word and thought,
Beyond the sight, the last support of form,
Lost in deep tracts of superconscient Light,
Or voyaging in blank featureless Nothingness,
Sole in the trackless Incommensurable,
Or past not-self and self and selflessness,
Transgressing the dream-shores of conscious mind
He reached at last his sempiternal base.
On sorrowless heights no winging cry disturbs,
Pure and untouched above the mortal play
Is spread the spirit's hushed immobile air.
There no beginning is and there no end;
There is the stable force of all that moves;
There the aeonic labourer is at rest.
There turns no keyed creation in the void,
No giant mechanism watched by a soul;
There creaks no fate-turned huge machinery;
The marriage of evil with good within one breast,
The clash of strife in the very clasp of love,
The dangerous pain of life's experiment
In the values of Inconsequence and Chance,
The peril of mind's gamble, throwing our lives

As stake in a wager of indifferent gods
And the shifting lights and shadows of the idea
Falling upon the surface consciousness,
And in the dream of a mute witness soul
Creating the error of a half-seen world
Where knowledge is a seeking ignorance,
Life's steps a stumbling series without suit,
Its aspect of fortuitous design,
Its equal measure of the true and false
In that immobile and immutable realm
Find no access, no cause, no right to live:
There only reigns the Spirit's motionless power
Poised in itself through still eternity
And its omniscient and omnipotent peace.
Thought clashes not with thought and truth with truth,
There is no war of right with rival right;
There are no stumbling and half-seeing lives
Passing from chance to unexpected chance,
No suffering of hearts compelled to beat
In bodies of the inert Inconscient's make.
Armed with the immune occult unsinking Fire
The guardians of Eternity keep its law
For ever fixed upon Truth's giant base
In her magnificent and termless home.
There Nature on her dumb spiritual couch
Immutably transcendent knows her source
And to the stir of multitudinous worlds
Assents unmoved in a perpetual calm.
All-causing, all-sustaining and aloof,
The Witness looks from his unshaken poise,
An Eye immense regarding all things done.
Apart, at peace above creation's stir,
Immersed in the eternal altitudes,
He abode defended in his shoreless self,
Companioned only by the all-seeing One.
A Mind too mighty to be bound by Thought,
A Life too boundless for the play in space,
A Soul without borders unconvinced of Time,
He felt the extinction of the world's long pain,
He became the unborn Self that never dies,

He joined the sessions of Infinity.
On the cosmic murmur primal loneliness fell,
Annulled was the contact formed with time-born things,
Empty grew Nature's wide community.
All things were brought back to their formless seed,
The world was silent for a cyclic hour.
Although the afflicted Nature he has left
Maintained beneath him her broad numberless fields,
Her enormous act, receding, failed remote
As if a soulless dream at last had ceased.
No voice came down from the high silences,
None answered from her desolate solitudes.
A stillness of cessation reigned, the wide
Immortal hush before the gods were born;
A universal Force awaited, mute,
The veiled Transcendent's ultimate decree.

Then suddenly there came a downward look
As if a sea exploring its own depths;
A living Oneness widened at its core
And joined him to unnumbered multitudes.
A Bliss, a Light, a Power, a flame-white Love
Caught all into a sole immense embrace;
Existence found its truth on Oneness' breast
And each became the self and space of all.
The great world-rhythms were heart-beats of one Soul,
To feel was a flame-discovery of God,
All mind was a single harp of many strings,
All life a song of many meeting lives;
For worlds were many, but the Self was one.
This knowledge was now made a cosmos' seed:
This seed was cased in the safety of the Light,
It needed not a sheath of Ignorance.
Then from the trance of that tremendous clasp
And from the throbbings of that single Heart
And from the naked Spirit's victory
A new and marvellous creation rose.
Incalculable outflowing infinitudes
Laughing out an unmeasured happiness
Lived their innumerable unity;

Worlds where the being is unbound and wide
Bodied unthinkably the egoless Self,
Rapture of beatific energies
Joined Time to the Timeless, poles of a single joy;
White vasts were seen where all is wrapped in all.
There were no contraries, no sundered parts,
All by spiritual links were joined to all
And bound indissolubly to the One:
Each was unique but took all lives as its own,
And, following out these tones of the Infinite,
Recognised in himself the universe.
A splendid centre of infinity's whirl
Pushed to its zenith's height, its last expanse,
Felt the divinity of its own self-bliss
Repeated in its numberless other selves.
It took up tirelessly into its scope
Persons and figures of the Impersonal,
As if prolonging in a celestial count,
In a rapturous multiplication's sum,
The recurring decimals of eternity.
None was apart, none lived for himself alone,
Each lived for God in him and God in all,
Each soleness inexpressibly held the whole.
There Oneness was not tied to monotone;
It showed a thousand aspects of itself,
Its luminous immutable stability
Upbore on a changeless ground for ever safe,
Compelled to a spontaneous servitude,
The ever-changing incalculable steps,
The seeming-reckless dance's subtle plan
Of immense world-forces in their perfect play.
Appearance looked back to its hidden truth
And made of difference oneness' smiling play;
It made all persons fractions of the Unique,
Yet all were being's secret integers.
All struggle was turned to a sweet strife of love
In the harmonised circle of a sure embrace.
Identity's reconciling happiness gave
A rich security to difference.
On a meeting line of hazardous extremes

The Game of games was played to its breaking point,
Where through self-finding by divine self-loss
There leaps out unity's supreme delight
Whose blissful undivided sweetness feels
A commonalty of the Absolute.
There was no sob of suffering anywhere;
Experience ran from point to point of joy:
Bliss was the pure undying truth of things.
All Nature was a conscious front of God:
A wisdom worked in all, self-moved, self-sure,
A plenitude of illimitable Light,
An authenticity of intuitive Truth,
A glory and passion of creative Force.
Infallible, leaping from eternity,
The moment's thought inspired the passing act,
A word, a laughter sprang from Silence' breast,
A rhythm of Beauty in the calm of Space,
A Knowledge in the fathomless heart of Time.
All turned to all without reserve's recoil:
A single ecstasy without a break,
Love was a close and thrilled identity
In the throbbing heart of all that luminous life.
A universal vision that unites,
A sympathy of nerve replying to nerve,
Hearing that listens to thought's inner sound
And follows the rhythmic meanings of the heart,
A touch that needs not hands to feel, to clasp,
Were there the native means of consciousness
And heightened the intimacy of soul with soul.
A grand orchestra of spiritual powers,
A diapason of soul interchange
Harmonised a oneness deep, immeasurable.
In these new worlds projected he became
A portion of the universal gaze,
A station of the all-inhabiting light,
A ripple on a single sea of peace.
His mind answered to countless communing minds,
His words were syllables of the cosmos' speech,
His life a field of the vast cosmic stir.
He felt the footsteps of a million wills

Moving in unison to a single goal.
A stream ever new-born that never dies,
Caught in its thousandfold current's ravishing flow,
With its eddies of immortal sweetness thrilled,
He bore coiling through his members as they passed
Calm movements of interminable delight,
The bliss of a myriad myriads who are one.

In this vast outbreak of perfection's law
Imposing its fixity on the flux of things
He saw a hierarchy of lucent planes
Enfeoffed to this highest kingdom of God-state.
Attuning to one Truth their own right rule
Each housed the gladness of a bright degree,
Alone in beauty, perfect in self-kind,
An image cast by one deep truth's absolute,
Married to all in happy difference.
Each gave its powers to help its neighbours' parts,
But suffered no diminution by the gift;
Profiteers of a mystic interchange,
They grew by what they took and what they gave,
All others they felt as their own complements,
One in the might and joy of multitude.
Even in the poise where Oneness draws apart
To feel the rapture of its separate selves,
The Sole in its solitude yearned towards the All
And the Many turned to look back at the One.
An all-revealing all-creating Bliss,
Seeking for forms to manifest truths divine,
Aligned in their significant mystery
The gleams of the symbols of the Ineffable
Blazoned like hues upon a colourless air
On the white purity of the Witness Soul.
These hues were the very prism of the Supreme,
His beauty, power, delight creation's cause.
A vast Truth-Consciousness took up these signs
To pass them on to some divine child Heart
That looked on them with laughter and delight
And joyed in these transcendent images
Living and real as the truths they house.

The Spirit's white neutrality became
A playground of miracles, a rendezvous
For the secret powers of a mystic Timelessness:
It made of space a marvel house of God,
It poured through Time its works of ageless might,
Unveiled seen as a luring rapturous face
The wonder and beauty of its Love and Force.
The eternal Goddess moved in her cosmic house
Sporting with God as a Mother with her child:
To him the universe was her bosom of love,
His toys were the immortal verities.
All here self-lost had there its divine place.
The Powers that here betray our hearts and err,
Were there sovereign in truth, perfect in joy,
Masters in a creation without flaw,
Possessors of their own infinitude.
There Mind, a splendid sun of vision's rays,
Shaped substance by the glory of its thoughts
And moved amidst the grandeur of its dreams.
Imagination's great ensorcelling rod
Summoned the unknown and gave to it a home,
Outspread luxuriantly in golden air
Truth's iris-coloured wings of fantasy,
Or sang to the intuitive heart of joy
Wonder's dream-notes that bring the Real close.
Its Power that makes the unknowable near and true,
In the temple of the ideal shrined the One:
It peopled thought and mind and happy sense
Filled with bright aspects of the might of God
And living persons of the one Supreme,
The speech that voices the ineffable,
The ray revealing unseen Presences,
The virgin forms through which the Formless shines,
The Word that ushers divine experience
And the Ideas that crowd the Infinite.
There was no gulf between the thought and fact;
Ever they replied like bird to calling bird;
The will obeyed the thought, the act the will,
There was a harmony woven twixt soul and soul.
A marriage with eternity divinised Time.

There Life pursued unwearied of her sport,
Joy in her heart and laughter on her lips,
The bright adventure of God's game of chance.
In her ingenious ardour of caprice,
In her transfiguring mirth she mapped on Time
A fascinating puzzle of events,
Lured at each turn by new vicissitudes
To self-discovery that could never cease.
Ever she framed stark bonds for the will to break,
Brought new creations for the thought's surprise
And passionate ventures for the heart to dare,
Where Truth recurred with an unexpected face
Or else repeated old familiar joy
Like the return of a delightful rhyme.
At hide and seek on a Mother-Wisdom's breast,
An artist teeming with her world-idea,
She never could exhaust its numberless thoughts
And vast adventure into thinking shapes
And trial and lure of a new living's dreams.
Untired of sameness and untired of change,
Endlessly she unrolled her moving act,
A mystery drama of divine delight,
A living poem of world ecstasy,
A kakemono of significant forms,
A coiled perspective of developing scenes,
A brilliant chase of self-revealing shapes,
An ardent hunt of soul looking for soul,
A seeking and a finding as of gods.
There Matter is the Spirit's firm density,
An artistry of glad outwardness of self,
A treasure-house of lasting images
Where sense can build a world of pure delight:
The home of a perpetual happiness,
It lodged the hours as in a pleasant inn.
The senses there were outlets of the soul;
Even the youngest child-thought of the mind
Incarnated some touch of highest things.
There substance was a resonant harp of self,
A net for the constant lightnings of the Spirit,
A magnet power of love's intensity

Whose yearning throb and adoration's cry
Drew God's approaches close, sweet, wonderful.
Its solidity was a mass of heavenly make;
Its fixity and sweet permanence of charm
Made a bright pedestal for felicity.
Its bodies woven by a divine sense
Prolonged the nearness of soul's clasp with soul;
Its warm play of external sight and touch
Reflected the glow and thrill of the heart's joy,
Mind's climbing brilliant thoughts, the spirit's bliss;
Life's rapture kept for ever its flame and cry.
All that now passes lived immortal there
In the proud beauty and fine harmony
Of Matter plastic to spiritual light.
Its ordered hours proclaimed the eternal Law;
Vision reposed on a safety of deathless forms;
Time was Eternity's transparent robe.
An architect hewing out self's living rock,
Phenomenon built Reality's summer-house
On the beaches of the sea of Infinity.

Against this glory of spiritual states,
Their parallels and yet their opposites
Floated and swayed, eclipsed and shadow-like
As if a doubt made substance, flickering, pale,
This other scheme two vast negations found.
A world that knows not its inhabiting Self,
Labours to find its cause and need to be;
A spirit ignorant of the world it made,
Obscured by Matter, travestied by Life,
Struggles to emerge, to be free, to know and reign;
These were close-tied in one disharmony,
Yet the divergent lines met not at all.
Three Powers governed its irrational course,
In the beginning an unknowing Force,
In the middle an embodied striving soul,
In its end a silent spirit denying life.
A dull and infelicitous interlude
Unrolls its dubious truth to a questioning Mind
Compelled by the ignorant Power to play its part

And to record her inconclusive tale,
The mystery of her inconscient plan
And the riddle of a being born from Night
By a marriage of Necessity with Chance.
This darkness hides our nobler destiny.
A chrysalis of a great and glorious truth,
It stifles the winged marvel in its sheath
Lest from the prison of Matter it escape
And, wasting its beauty on the formless Vast,
Merged into the Unknowable's mystery,
Leave unfulfilled the world's miraculous fate.
As yet thought only some high spirit's dream
Or a vexed illusion in man's toiling mind,
A new creation from the old shall rise,
A Knowledge inarticulate find speech,
Beauty suppressed burst into paradise bloom,
Pleasure and pain dive into absolute bliss.
A tongueless oracle shall speak at last,
The Superconscient conscious grow on earth,
The Eternal's wonders join the dance of Time.
But now all seemed a vainly teeming vast
Upheld by a deluded Energy
To a spectator self-absorbed and mute,
Careless of the unmeaning show he watched,
Regarding the bizarre procession pass
Like one who waits for an expected end.
He saw a world that is from a world to be.
There he divined rather than saw or felt,
Far off upon the rim of consciousness,
Transient and frail this little whirling globe
And on it left like a lost dream's vain mould,
A fragile copy of the spirit's shell,
His body gathered into mystic sleep.
A foreign shape it seemed, a mythic shade.

Alien now seemed that dim far universe,
Self and eternity alone were true.
Then memory climbed to him from the striving planes
Bringing a cry from once-loved cherished things,
And to the cry as to its own lost call

A ray replied from the occult Supreme.
For even there the boundless Oneness dwells.
To its own sight unrecognisable,
It lived still sunk in its own tenebrous seas,
Upholding the world's inconscient unity
Hidden in Matter's insentient multitude.
This seed-self sown in the Indeterminate
Forfeits its glory of divinity,
Concealing the omnipotence of its Force,
Concealing the omniscience of its Soul;
An agent of its own transcendent Will,
It merges knowledge in the inconscient deep;
Accepting error, sorrow, death and pain,
It pays the ransom of the ignorant Night,
Redeeming by its substance Nature's fall.
Himself he knew and why his soul had gone
Into earth's passionate obscurity
To share the labour of an errant Power
Which by division hopes to find the One.
Two beings he was, one wide and free above,
One struggling, bound, intense, its portion here.
A tie between them still could bridge two worlds;
There was a dim response, a distant breath;
All had not ceased in the unbounded hush.
His heart lay somewhere conscious and alone
Far down below him like a lamp in night;
Abandoned it lay, alone, imperishable,
Immobile with excess of passionate will,
His living, sacrificed and offered heart
Absorbed in adoration mystical,
Turned to its far-off fount of light and love.
In the luminous stillness of its mute appeal
It looked up to the heights it could not see;
It yearned from the longing depths it could not leave.
In the centre of its vast and fateful trance
Half way between his free and fallen selves,
Interceding twixt God's day and the mortal's night,
Accepting worsihp as its single law,
Accepting bliss as the sole cause of things,
Refusing the austere joy which none can share,

Refusing the calm that lives for calm alone,
To her it turned for whom it willed to be.
In the passion of its solitary dream
It lay like a closed soundless oratory
Where sleeps a consecrated argent floor
Lit by a single and untrembling ray
And an invisible Presence kneels in prayer.
On some deep breast of liberating peace
All else was satisfied with quietude;
This only knew there was a truth beyond.
All other parts were dumb in centred sleep
Consenting to the slow deliberate Power
Which tolerates the world's error and its grief,
Consenting to the cosmic long delay,
Timelessly waiting through the patient years
Her coming they had asked for earth and men;
This was the fiery point that called her now.
Extinction could not quench that lonely fire;
Its seeing filled the blank of mind and will;
Thought dead, its changeless force abode and grew.
Armed with the intuition of a bliss
To which some moved tranquillity was the key,
It persevered through life's huge emptiness
Amid the blank denials of the world.
It sent its voiceless prayer to the Unknown;
It listened for the footsteps of its hopes
Returning through the void immensities,
It waited for the fiat of the Word
That comes through the still self from the Supreme.

END OF CANTO THREE

CANTO FOUR

THE VISION AND THE BOON

THEN suddenly there rose a sacred stir.
    Amid the lifeless silence of the Void
In a solitude and an immensity
A sound came quivering like a loved footfall
Heard in the listening spaces of the soul;
A touch perturbed his fibres with delight.
An influence had approached the mortal range,
A boundless Heart was near his longing heart,
A mystic Form enveloped his earthly shape.
All at her contact broke from silence' seal;
Spirit and body thrilled identified,
Linked in the grasp of an unspoken joy;
Mind, members, life were merged in ecstasy.
Intoxicated as with nectarous rain
His nature's passioning stretches flowed to her
Flashing with lightnings, mad with luminous wine.
All was a limitless sea that heaved to the moon.
A divinising stream possessed his veins,
His body's cells awoke to spirit sense,
Each nerve became a burning thread of joy:
Tissue and flesh partook beatitude.
Alight, the dun unplumbed subconscient caves
Thrilled with the prescience of her longed-for tread
And filled with flickering crests and praying tongues.
Even lost in slumber, mute, inanimate
His very body answered to her power.
The One he worshipped was within him now:
Flame-pure, ethereal-tressed a mighty Face
Appeared and lips moved by immortal words;
Lids, wisdom's leaves, drooped over rapture's orbs.

A marble monument of ponderings, shone
A forehead, sight's crypt, and large like ocean's gaze
Towards Heaven two tranquil eyes of boundless thought
Looked into man's and saw the god to come.
A shape was seen on threshold Mind, a Voice
Absolute and wise in the heart's chambers spoke:
"O Son of Strength who climbst creation's peaks,
No soul is thy companion in the light;
Alone thou standest at the eternal doors.
What thou hast won is thine, but ask no more.
O Spirit aspiring in an ignorant frame,
O Voice arisen from the Inconscient's world,
How shalt thou speak for men whose hearts are dumb,
Make purblind earth the soul's seer-vision's home
Or lighten the burden of the senseless globe?
I am the Mystery beyond reach of mind,
I am the goal of the travail of the suns;
My fire and sweetness are the cause of life.
But too immense my danger and my joy.
Awake not the immeasurable descent,
Speak not my secret name to hostile Time;
Man is too weak to bear the Infinite's weight.
Truth born too soon might break the imperfect earth.
Leave the all-seeing Power to hew its way:
In thy single vast achievement reign apart
Helping the world with thy great lonely days.
I ask thee not to merge thy heart of flame
In the Immobile's wide uncaring bliss,
Turned from the fruitless motion of the years,
Deserting the fierce labour of the worlds,
Aloof from beings, lost in the Alone.
How shall thy mighty spirit brook repose
While Death is still unconquered on the earth
And Time a field of suffering and pain?
Thy soul was born to share the laden Force;
Obey thy nature and fulfil thy fate:
Accept the difficulty and godlike toil,
For the slow-paced omniscient purpose live.
The Enigma's knot is tied in human kind.
A lightning from the heights that think and plan,

Ploughing the air of life with vanishing trails,
Man, sole awake in an unconscious world,
Aspires in vain to change the cosmic dream.
Arrived from some half-luminous Beyond
He is a stranger in the mindless vasts;
A traveller in his oft-shifting home
Amid the tread of many infinitudes,
He has pitched a tent of life in desert Space.
Heaven's fixed regard beholds him from above,
In the house of Nature a perturbing guest,
A voyager twixt Thought's inconstant shores,
A hunter of unknown and beautiful Powers,
A nomad of the far mysterious Light,
In the wide ways a little spark of God.
Against his spirit all is in dire league,
A Titan influence stops his Godward gaze.
Around him hungers the unpitying Void,
The eternal Darkness seeks him with her hands,
Inscrutable Energies drive him and deceive,
Immense implacable deities oppose.
An inert Soul and a somnambulist Force
Have made a world estranged from life and thought;
The Dragon of the dark foundations keeps
Unalterable the law of Chance and Death;
On his long way through Time and Circumstance
The grey-hued riddling nether shadow-Sphinx,
Her dreadful paws upon the swallowing sands,
Awaits him armed with the soul-slaying word:
Across his path sits the dim camp of Night.
His day is a moment in perpetual Time;
He is the prey of the minutes and the hours.
Assailed on earth and unassured of heaven,
Descended here unhappy and sublime,
A link between the demigod and the beast,
He knows not his own greatness nor his aim;
He has forgotten why he has come and whence;
His spirit and his members are at war;
His heights break off too low to reach the skies,
His mass is buried in the animal mire.
A strange antinomy is his nature's rule.

A riddle of opposites is made his field:
Freedom he asks but needs to live in bonds,
He has need of darkness to perceive some light
And need of grief to feel a little bliss;
He has need of death to find a greater life.
All sides he sees and turns to every call;
He has no certain light by which to walk;
His life is a blind-man's-buff, a hide and seek;
He seeks himself and from himself he runs;
Meeting himself, he thinks it other than he.
Always he builds, but finds no constant ground,
Always he journeys, but nowhere arrives;
He would guide the world, himself he cannot guide;
He would save his soul, his life he cannot save.
The light his soul has brought his mind has lost;
All he has learned is soon again in doubt;
A sun to him seems the shadow of his thoughts,
Then all is shadow again and nothing is true:
Unknowing what he does or whither he tends
He fabricates signs of the Real in Ignorance.
He has hitched his mortal error to Truth's star.
Wisdom attracts him with her luminous masks,
But never has he seen the face behind:
A giant Ignorance surrounds his lore.
Assigned to meet the cosmic mystery
In the dumb figure of a material world,
His passport of entry false and his personage,
He is compelled to be what he is not;
He obeys the Inconscience he has come to rule
And sinks in Matter to fulfil his soul.
Awakened from her lower driven forms
The Earth-Mother gave her forces to his hands
And painfully he guards the heavy trust;
His mind is a lost torch-bearer on her roads.
Illumining breath to think and plasm to feel,
He labours with his slow and sceptic brain
Helped by the reason's vacillating fires,
To make his thought and will a magic door
For knowledge to enter the darkness of the world
And love to rule a realm of strife and hate.

A mind impotent to reconcile heaven and earth
And tied to Matter with a thousand bonds,
He lifts himself to be a conscious god.
Even when a glory of wisdom crowns his brow,
When mind and spirit shed a grandiose ray
To exalt this product of the sperm and gene,
This alchemist's miracle from plasm and gas,
And he who shared the animal's run and crawl,
Lifts his thought-stature to the Immortal's heights,
His life still keeps the human middle way;
His body he resigns to death and pain,
Abandoning Matter, his too heavy charge.
A thaumaturge sceptic of miracles,
A spirit left sterile of its occult power
By an unbelieving brain and credulous heart
He leaves the world to end where it began:
His work unfinished he claims a heavenly prize.
Thus has he missed creation's absolute.
Halfway he stops his star of destiny:
A vast and vain long-tried experiment,
An ill-served high conception doubtfully done,
The world's life falters on not seeing its goal,—
A zigzag towards unknown dangerous ground
Ever repeating its habitual walk,
Ever retreating after marches long
And hardiest victories without sure result,
Drawn endlessly an inconclusive game.
In an ill-fitting and voluminous robe
A radiant purpose still conceals its face,
A mighty blindness stumbles hoping on
Feeding its strength on gifts of luminous Chance.
Because the human instrument has failed,
The Godhead frustrate sleeps within its seed,
A spirit entangled in the forms it made.
His failure is not failure whom God leads;
Through all the slow mysterious march goes on:
An immutable Power has made this mutable world;
A self-fulfilling transcendence treads man's road;
The driver of the soul upon its path,
It knows its steps, its way is inevitable

And how shall the end be vain when God is guide?
However man's mind may tire or fail his flesh,
A will prevails cancelling his conscious choice:
The goal recedes, a bourneless vastness calls
Retreating into an immense Unknown;
There is no end to the world's stupendous march,
There is no rest for the embodied soul.
It must live on, describe all Time's huge curve.
An Influx presses from the closed Beyond
Forbidding to him rest and earthly ease,
Till he has found himself he cannot pause.
A Light there is that leads, a Power that aids;
Unmarked, unfelt it sees in him and acts:
Ignorant, he forms the All-conscient in his depths,
Human, looks up to superhuman peaks:
A borrower of Supernature's gold,
He paves his road to Immortality.
The high gods look on man and watch and choose
Today's impossibles for the future's base.
His transience trembles with the Eternal's touch,
His barriers cede beneath the Infinite's tread;
The Immortals have their entries in his life:
The Ambassadors of the Unseen draw near;
A Splendour sullied by the mortal air,
Love passes through his heart, a wandering guest,
Beauty surrounds him for a magic hour,
He has visits of a large revealing joy,
Brief widenesses release him from himself,
Enticing towards a glory ever in front
Hopes of a deathless sweetness lure and leave.
His mind is crossed by strange discovering fires,
Rare intimations lift his stumbling speech
To a moment's kinship with the eternal Word;
A masque of wisdom circles through his brain
Perturbing him with glimpses half-divine.
He lays his hands sometimes on the Unknown;
He communes sometimes with Eternity.
A strange and grandiose symbol was his birth
And immortality and spirit-room
And pure perfection and a shadowless bliss

Are this afflicted creature's mighty fate.
In him the Earth-Mother sees draw near the change
Foreshadowed in her dumb and fiery depths,
A godhead drawn from her transmuted limbs,
An alchemy of Heaven on Nature's base.
Adept of the self-born unfailing line,
Leave not the light to die the ages bore,
Help still humanity's blind and suffering life:
Obey thy spirit's wide omnipotent urge.
A witness to God's parley with the Night
It leaned compassionate from immortal calm
And housed desire, the troubled seed of things.
Assent to thy high self, create, endure.
Cease not from knowledge, let thy toil be vast,
No more in earthly limits pen thy force;
Equal thy work with long unending Time's.
Traveller upon the bare eternal heights,
Tread still the difficult and dateless path
Joining the cycles with its austere curve
Measured for man by the initiate Gods.
My light shall be in thee, my strength thy force.
Let not the impatient Titan drive thy heart,
Ask not the imperfect fruit, the partial prize.
Only one boon, to greaten thy spirit, demand;
Only one joy, to raise thy kind, desire.
Above blind fate and the antagonist powers
Moveless there stands a high unchanging Will;
To its omnipotence leave thy work's result.
All things shall change in God's transfiguring hour."

August and sweet sank hushed that mighty Voice.
Nothing now moved in the vast brooding space:
A stillness came upon the listening world,
A mute immensity of the Eternal's peace.
But Aswapathy's heart replied to her,
A cry amid the silence of the Vasts:
"How shall I rest content with mortal days
And the dull measure of terrestrial things,
I who have seen behind the cosmic mask
The glory and the beauty of thy face?

Hard is the doom to which thou bindst thy sons!
How long shall our spirits battle with the Night
And bear defeat and the brute yoke of Death,
We who are vessels of a deathless Force
And builders of the godhead of the race?
Or if it is thy work I do below
Amid the error and waste of human life
In the vague light of man's half-conscious mind,
Why breaks not in some distant gleam of thee?
Ever the centuries and millenniums pass.
Where in the greyness is thy coming's ray?
Where is the thunder of thy victory's wings?
Only we hear the feet of passing gods.
A plan in the occult eternal Mind
Mapped out to backward and prophetic sight,
The aeons ever repeat their changeless round,
The cycles all rebuild and ever aspire.
All we have done is ever still to do.
All breaks and all renews and is the same.
Huge revolutions of life's fruitless gyre,
The new-born ages perish like the old,
As if the sad Enigma kept its right
Till all is done for which this scene was made.
Too little the strength that now with us is born,
Too faint the light that steals through Nature's lids,
Too scant the joy with which she buys our pain.
In a brute world that knows not its own sense,
Thought-racked upon the wheel of birth we live,
The instruments of an impulse not our own
Moved to achieve with our heart's blood for price
Half-knowledge, half-creations that soon tire.
A foiled immortal soul in perishing limbs,
Baffled and beaten back we labour still;
Annulled, frustrated, spent, we still survive.
In anguish we labour that from us may rise
A larger-seeing man with nobler heart,
A golden vessel of the incarnate Truth,
The executor of the divine attempt
Equipped to wear the earthly body of God,
Communicant and prophet and lover and king.

I know that thy creation cannot fail.
For even through the mists of mortal thought
Infallible are thy mysterious steps,
And, though Necessity dons the garb of Chance,
Hidden in the blind shifts of Fate she keeps
The slow calm logic of Infinity's pace
And the inviolate sequence of its will.
All life is fixed in an ascending scale
And adamantine is the evolving Law;
In the beginning is prepared the close.
This strange irrational product of the mire,
This compromise between the beast and God,
Is not the crown of thy miraculous world.
I know there shall inform the inconscient cells,
At one with Nature and at height with heaven,
A spirit vast as the containing sky
And swept with ecstasy from invisible founts,
A god come down and greater by the fall.
A power arose out of my slumber's cell.
Abandoning the tardy limp of the hours
And the inconstant blink of mortal sight,
There where the Thinker sleeps in too much light
And intolerant flames the lone all-witnessing Eye
Hearing the word of Fate from Silence' heart
In the endless moment of Eternity,
It saw from timelessness the works of Time.
Overpassed were the leaden formulas of the Mind,
Overpowered the obstacle of mortal Space:
The unfolding Image showed the things to come.
A giant dance of Shiva tore the past,
There was a thunder as of worlds that fall;
Earth was o'errun with fire and the roar of Death
Clamouring to slay a world his hunger had made;
There was a clangour of Destruction's wings:
The Titan's battle-cry was in my ears,
Alarm and rumour shook the armoured Night.
I saw the Omnipotent's flaming pioneers
Over the heavenly verge which turns towards life
Come crowding down the amber stairs of birth;
Forerunners of a divine multitude

Out of the paths of the morning star they came
Into the little room of mortal life.
I saw them cross the twilight of an age,
The sun-eyed children of a marvellous dawn,
The great creators with wide brows of calm,
The massive barrier-breakers of the world
And wrestlers with destiny in her lists of will,
The labourers in the quarries of the gods,
The messengers of the Incommunicable,
The architects of immortality.
Into the fallen human sphere they came,
Faces that wore the Immortal's glory still,
Voices that communed still with the thoughts of God,
Bodies made beautiful by the Spirit's light,
Carrying the magic word, the mystic fire,
Carrying the Dionysian cup of joy,
Approaching eyes of a diviner man,
Lips chanting an unknown anthem of the soul,
Feet echoing in the corridors of Time.
High priests of wisdom, sweetness, might and bliss,
Discoverers of beauty's sunlit ways
And swimmers of Love's laughing fiery floods
And dancers within rapture's golden doors,
Their tread one day shall change the suffering earth
And justify the light on Nature's face.
Although Fate lingers in the high Beyond
And the work seems vain on which our heart's force was spent,
All shall be done for which our pain was borne.
Even as of old man came behind the beast
This high divine successor surely shall come
Behind man's inefficient mortal pace,
Behind his vain labour, sweat and blood and tears:
He shall know what mortal mind barely durst think,
He shall do what the heart of the mortal could not dare.
Inheritor of the toil of human time
He shall take on him the burden of the gods;
All heavenly light shall visit the earth's thoughts,
The might of heaven shall fortify earthly hearts;
Earth's deeds shall touch the superhuman's height,
Earth's seeing widened into the infinite.

Heavy unchanged weighs still the imperfect world;
The splendid youth of Time has passed and failed;
Heavy and long are the years our labour counts
And still the seals are firm upon man's soul
And weary is the ancient Mother's heart.
O Truth defended in thy secret sun,
Voice of her mighty musings in shut heavens
On things withdrawn within her luminous depths,
O Wisdom-Splendour, Mother of the universe,
Creatrix, the Eternal's artist Bride,
Linger not long with thy transmuting hand
Pressed vainly on one golden bar of Time,
As if Time dare not open its heart to God.
O radiant fountain of the world's delight
World-free and unattainable above,
O Bliss who ever dwellst deep hid within
While men seek thee outside and never find,
Mystery and Muse with hieratic tongue,
Incarnate the white passion of thy force,
Mission to earth some living form of thee.
One moment fill with thy eternity,
Let thy infinity in one body live,
All-Knowledge wrap one mind in seas of light,
All-Love throb single in one human heart.
Immortal, treading the earth with mortal feet
All heaven's beauty crowd in earthly limbs!
Omnipotence, girdle with the power of God
Movements and moments of a mortal will,
Pack with the eternal might one human hour
And with one gesture change all future time.
Let a great word be spoken from the heights
And one great act unlock the doors of Fate."

His prayer sank down in the resisting Night
Oppressed by the thousand forces that deny,
As if too weak to climb to the Supreme.
But there arose a wide consenting Voice;
The spirit of beauty was revealed in sound:
Light floated round the marvellous Vision's brow
And on her lips the Immortal's joy took shape.

"O strong forerunner, I have heard thy cry.
One shall descend and break the iron Law,
Change Nature's doom by the lone Spirit's power.
A limitless Mind that can contain the world,
A sweet and violent heart of ardent calms
Moved by the passions of the gods shall come.
All mights and greatnesses shall join in her;
Beauty shall walk celestial on the earth,
Delight shall sleep in the cloud-net of her hair
And in her body as on his homing tree
Immortal Love shall beat his glorious wings.
A music of griefless things shall weave her charm;
The harps of the Perfect shall attune her voice,
The streams of Heaven shall murmur in her laugh,
Her lips shall be the honeycombs of God,
Her limbs his golden jars of ecstasy,
Her breasts the rapture-flowers of Paradise.
She shall bear Wisdom in her voiceless bosom,
Strength shall be with her like a conqueror's sword
And from her eyes the Eternal's bliss shall gaze.
A seed shall be sown in Death's tremendous hour,
A branch of heaven transplant to human soil;
Nature shall overleap her mortal step;
Fate shall be changed by an unchanging will."

As a flame disappears in endless Light
Immortally extinguished in its source,
Vanished the splendour and was stilled the word.
An echo of delight that once was close,
The harmony journeyed towards some distant hush,
A music failing in the ear of trance,
A cadence called by distant cadences,
A voice that trembled into strains withdrawn.
Her form retreated from the longing earth
Forsaking nearness to the abandoned sense,
Ascending to her unattainable home.
Lone, brilliant, vacant lay the inner fields;
All was unfilled inordinate spirit space,
Indifferent, waste, a desert of bright peace.
Then a line moved on the far edge of calm:

The warm-lipped sentient soft terrestrial wave,
A quick and many-murmured moan and laugh,
Came gliding in upon white feet of sound.
Unlocked was the deep glory of Silence' heart;
The absolute unmoving stillnesses
Surrendered to the breath of mortal air,
Dissolving boundlessly the heavens of trance
Collapsed to waking mind. Eternity
Cast down its incommunicable lids
Over its solitudes remote from ken
Behind the voiceless mystery of sleep.
The grandiose respite failed, the wide release.
Across the light of fast-receding planes
That fled from him as from a falling star
Compelled to fill his human house in Time
His soul drew back into the speed and noise
Of the vast business of created things.
A chariot of the marvels of the heavens
Broad-based to bear the gods on fiery wheels,
Flaming he swept through the spiritual gates.
The mortal stir received him in its midst.
Once more he moved amid material scenes,
Lifted by intimations from the heights
And twixt the pauses of the building brain
Touched by the thoughts that skim the fathomless surge
Of Nature and wing back to hidden shores.
The eternal seeker in the aeonic field
Besieged by the intolerant press of hours
Again was strong for great swift-footed deeds.
Awake beneath the ignorant vault of Night,
He saw the unnumbered people of the stars
And heard the questioning of the unsatisfied flood
And toiled with the form-maker, measuring Mind.
A wanderer from the occult invisible suns
Accomplishing the fate of transient things,
A god in the figure of the arisen beast,
He raised his brow of conquest to the heavens
Establishing the empire of the soul
On Matter and its bounded universe
As on a solid rock in infinite seas.

The Lord of Life resumed his mighty rounds
In the scant field of the ambiguous globe.

END OF PART ONE